Sharing Economies in Times of Crisis

The 'new sharing economy' is a growing phenomenon across the Global North. It claims to transform relationships of production and consumption in a way that can improve our lives, reduce environmental impacts, and reduce the cost of living. Amidst various economic, environmental, and other crises, this message has strong resonance. Yet, it is not without controversy, and there have been heated debates over negative dimensions for workers and consumers alike. This book stretches far beyond the sharing economy as it is popularly defined, and explores the complex intersections of 'sharing' and 'the economy', and how a better understanding of these relationships might help us address the multiple crises that confront contemporary societies.

The contributors to this book explore a wide diversity of sharing systems and practices from various empirical case studies, ranging from hospitality to seed-swapping, and from indigenous land rights to alcohol consumption. In each chapter, a different crisis or vulnerability frames and shapes the study, allowing contributors to unpick the ways in which crisis and sharing relate to each other in real life. The book is divided into three thematic sections. Following an extended introduction to the themes and ideas of the book by the editors, the first section foregrounds the shaping of sharing practices by already existing or anticipated crises. The second section focuses on the lived relations between sharing and economic practice. In the third section, authors conclude the book by exploring the possibilities and challenges for creating alternative economic forms grounded in practices of sharing.

This edited volume makes a major, original contribution towards academic understandings of sharing economies in the context of crises. It is suitable for both students and academics who are interested in political economy, economic geography and consumption.

Anthony Ince is Lecturer in Human Geography at Cardiff University, UK. His primary research interests concern the everyday spatialities of political agency in relation to wider-scale social and economic processes. Previous and current research includes radical social movements, local labour market change and non-financial economies.

Sarah Marie Hall is Lecturer in Human Geography at the University of Manchester, UK. Her research sits in the broad field of geographical feminist political economy: understanding how socio-economic processes are shaped by gender relations, lived experience and social difference.

Routledge Frontiers of Political Economy

Sharing Economies in Times of Crisis

Practices, Politics and Possibilities

Edited by Anthony Ince and Sarah Marie Hall

LONDON AND NEW YORK

First published 2018 by Routledge

2 Park Square, Milton Park, Abingdon, Oxfordshire OX14 4RN

52 Vanderbilt Avenue, New York, NY 10017

Routledge is an imprint of the Taylor & Francis Group, an informa business

First issued in paperback 2019

British Library Cataloguing-in-Publication Data
A catalogue record for this book is available from the British Library

Library of Congress Cataloging-in-Publication Data
Names: Ince, Anthony, editor. | Hall, Sarah Marie, editor.
Title: Sharing economies in times of crisis : practices, politics and possibilities / edited by Anthony Ince and Sarah Marie Hall.
Description: 1 Edition. | New York : Routledge, 2017. | Includes index.
Identifiers: LCCN 2017009586 | ISBN 9781138959415 (hardback) | ISBN 9781315660646 (ebook)
Subjects: LCSH: Sharing—Social aspects. | Economic geography. | Social interaction.
Classification: LCC HM1033 .S483 2017 | DDC 302—dc23
LC record available at https://lccn.loc.gov/2017009586

ISBN: 978-1-138-95941-5 (hbk)
ISBN: 978-0-367-87456-8 (pbk)

Typeset in Times New Roman
by diacriTech, Chennai

Contents

Figures

Tables

Contributors

Clive Barnett, Amory Building, University of Exeter, UK

Russell Belk, York University, Canada

Paula Bialski, Leuphana University, Germany

Erin Borger, University of Wollongong, Australia

Chris Gibson, University of Wollongong, Australia

Nicole Gombay, University of Montreal, Canada

Katharina Hellwig, Université de Lausanne, Switzerland

Sarah L. Holloway, Loughborough University, UK

Anthony Ince, Cardiff University, UK

Mark Jayne, Cardiff University, UK

Sophie-May Kerr, University of Wollongong, Australia

Natascha Klocker, University of Wollongong, Australia

Nicola Livingstone, University College London, UK

Juliana Mansvelt, Massey University, New Zealand

Sarah Marie Hall, University of Manchester, UK

Felicitas Morhart, Université de Lausanne, Switzerland

Laura Pottinger, University of Manchester, UK

Lucy Sargisson, University of Nottingham, UK

Gill Valentine, University of Sheffield, UK

Emma Waight, University of Southampton, UK

Richard White, Sheffield Hallam University, UK

Colin Williams, The University of Sheffield, UK

Foreword

Clive Barnett

'We're all in this together'

The idea of the sharing economy brings to mind the whiz-bang excitement of constant innovation, the libertarian promise of peer-to-peer collaboration, the instant pleasures of friction-free online transactions, the mould-breaking potential of crowdfunding. It might, too, bring to mind the downside associated with rental-based economies: Airbnb contributing to artificially inflated property markets; the de-regulation of services in the name of consumer convenience typified by the growth of Uber; the insecurities of the gig economy.

The essays collected here move beyond the hype of *the* sharing economy, in both its positive and negative forms. They do so by placing the more well-known versions of the sharing economy, which often emphasise the libertarian promise of technologically enhanced interaction, alongside various forms of everyday coping that have emerged in response to the insecurities associated with contemporary economic life. Here, sharing economies emerge not so much as the cutting edge of a bright and shiny future, and look instead like responses to precarious employment, reduced public spending, and shrivelled welfare provision. The exemplars of sharing practices turn out to be food bank experiments or alternative housing schemes; the prevalent norms at work have less to do with entrepreneurialism than with care, need, and vulnerability; its subjects are elderly people, the addicted, the poor. Sharing is, the contributors to this book remind us, a practice – it is something that people *do*. It turns out they do it out of all sorts of motivations, charitable ones and instrumental ones, self-regarding ones as well as selfless ones. And this raises some interesting questions about the values associated with sharing.

If we want to grasp what sharing is good for, then we might start by noticing the way in which public debates about the sharing economy tend to invoke two distinct but related meanings of 'sharing'. First, there is a vision of sharing as unmediated interaction, freed up from the intrusions of bureaucratic red tape, top-down planning, or corporate strategy. Sharing, in this vision, is a kind of spontaneous process that can be cultivated but not planned, directed or regulated. There is, though, a second, and more interesting, sense of sharing evident in such discussions, one in which what is shared is the infrastructure upon which apparently unmediated interactions depend – whether it is open source software or user-generated content or social media platforms, or the proliferation of creative co-working spaces in towns and cities. The second idea of sharing draws into view questions about the conditions upon which forms of social interaction depend. And thinking of the conditions of social life through the lens of sharing practices might well disrupt the established economy of value associated with the idea of sharing.

While sharing sounds like an unambiguously positive thing, it is in fact a rather complex concept. Sharing may bring to mind images of collective life and togetherness, of all sorts of pastimes people share in alongside one another. But the objects of sharing practices are often burdens of certain sorts – sharing the responsibilities of caring for elderly relatives, or sharing the risks of misfortune with one's fellow citizens. Sharing, in this sense, is a way of managing with the unavoidable ups and downs of life.

There is a strand of philosophical analysis, developed by thinkers including Jacques Derrida, Jacques Rancière, and above all Jean-Luc Nancy, that makes a great deal out of the apparent paradoxes that lie at the heart of the idea of sharing. All of these thinkers exploit the polysemy associated with the French the verb *partager*, which suggests sharing but also separating, participating, dividing, partitioning. *Partage*, it turns out, refers to an idea of sharing in and sharing out, to partaking in as well as partitioning out – so that we might best think in terms of practices of 'sharing (out)' (Derrida 2005). What this line of thought draws attention to is the double sense of sharing, as both form of collective action or making things common, alongside a sense of sharing as allocating, distributing or dividing.

In Jacques Rancière's work, the idea of *"le partage du sensible"* is used to refer to the idea that the opening up of a world of shared perception is constituted by the simultaneous restriction of what is made available to be seen and sensed. Rancière makes use of related senses of *partage* and *avoir-part* – of division and separation as well as taking part, of partaking and participation – to propose that the 'the partition of the sensible' involves an inaugural separation off and exclusion that opens up a common world of shared perception (Rancière 2004). In Rancière's vision, drawing on a longer train of modernist thought in which a shared world of perception and intelligibility is presented as being founded through exclusion, identifying the paradoxes of sharing means that settled patterns of life might always be disrupted and rearranged in new ways.

In Nancy's work, and in Derrida's engagement with it too, the polysemy of *partage* is given a somewhat different inflection. One finds there the same idea that a series of ideas usually associated with positive values – communication, participation, collective life – necessarily entrain forms of separation, splitting, partitioning, distancing or dissociation as their very conditions of possibility. But this is interpreted as indicating a form of spacing that is internal to community life, so that the varied connotations of sharing – as sharing in, sharing with, sharing out – are presented not as resources with which to

disrupt settled orders, but rather as the means of re-describing existing images
of collective life by drawing attention to aspects of them too easily overlooked. Nancy uses the theme of *partage* to insist that any and all experience
of commonality always takes the form of what he calls 'being-in-common', in
which the singularity of individuals is not subsumed by a higher form of unified identity (Nancy 1991). His elaboration of the theme of *partage* is meant
to underscore the problem of imagining co-existence between and amongst
singular beings.

Across their differences, Nancy, Derrida and Rancière all emphasise the
distributive aspects of practices of sharing, where sharing in and sharing with
presupposes some form of sharing out. They ask us, in short, to attend more
closely to the constitution of *what* it is possible to share 'in common' with
others.

We might also think a little more about *how* sharing practices are enacted.
The political theorist Patrick Chabal, in his discussion of the formations of
political life in contemporary Africa, suggests that normative models of participation, often sourced from idealised models of political practices in the
global North, do not actually capture the range of motivations shaping collective action. He proposes instead the idea of partaking, in order to signal
the degree to which collective life combines an aspect of taking part in activities with others with an aspect of making use of shared resources (Chabal
2009). The sense of partaking identified by Chabal, with its suggestions of
ritualised engagements in collective practices, also reminds us of the degree to
which sharing always involves an aspect of sacrifice, at least in the sense that
it involves the giving over of one's own self to others, to purposes other than
pure egoistical self-interest.

So, if we reflect a little about the meaning of sharing, with the help of
thinkers such as Nancy and Chabal, we begin to spot different aspects of
sharing practices: there is a sense in which sharing involves the appropriation
or making use of shared resources; a sense of sharing as a form of collective
action that depends upon not just division and distribution, but separation,
and therefore raises problems of coordination and co-existence; and there is
a sense that what is shared is, more often than not, burdens and risks and
sacrifices. In other words, sharing turns out to be a topic that foregrounds
problems of living together in ways that avoid simple moral contrasts between
(bad) individualism and (good) solidarity. And if we are to take the theme
of sharing seriously, then it requires us to give up the easy habits associated
with radical social theory, in which a grasp of the virtues of collective life are
assumed to be the preserve of those able to de-familiarise the ruses of rampant individualism.

Thinking of sharing as an heuristic for ongoing analysis might, even, help
dislodge some of the settled ways of thinking about 'neoliberalism' and its
associated ills. For example, Margaret Thatcher's famous remark to the effect
that "There is no such thing as society" has often been invoked as if it encapsulates all that is wrong with a form of political and economic project that

valorises selfish egoism over public life and citizenly virtue. But the force of Thatcher's remark lay in specifying where shared responsibility lies, not with dismissing it out of hand. Sharing the burdens of care and responsibility for life's travails, Thatcher asserted, was a matter for families and communities, not the welfare state. It is, it should be said, an emphatically conservative prejudice that she expressed, hardly a distinctively neoliberal one at all. Thatcher's remark did not embody a divide between collective values and individual ones, so much as a division between two very different visions of the type of social bond upon which sharing in the collective life of a community should be based. We might say that it is the *abstraction* implied by the idea of Society that most offended Thatcher. What is rejected is the idea that one should expect assistance from others or be expected to provide it to others who do not conform to the models of social bond epitomised by family, community, or nation. The rhetorical force of the remark lies in its rejection of the commitment to sharing equally in the fate of one's fellow *citizens* – a rejection, even, of the kind of justification that would allow the costs of unfettered financial speculation to be borne collectively by the most vulnerable of citizens on the grounds that 'we are all in this together'.

Inadvertently, Thatcher's remark helps us see that modern public life can be thought of as a family of practices of sharing with others, whether this is sharing goods and services, sharing risks, or sharing in political discourse and cultural life. It is a form of sharing that is necessarily mediated, anonymous, and abstracted in certain ways. The specifically public content of the values associated with ideas of publicness, across their variety, depends on a certain mode of partaking with others in which sharing always involves relations with strangers. Being-public is a form of sharing that necessarily involves making use of resources of different kinds, and is therefore also always likely to generate conflicts and disagreements (Barnett 2014).

The single most arresting conceptualisation of sharing as a principle of analysis in modern social thought is to be found in the resolutely liberal theory of justice developed by John Rawls (1971). Rawls's famous 'difference principle', according to which unequal distributions of primary goods can be justified only if they benefit those least advantaged by that inequality, is often interpreted as if it were either a thinly veiled justification of inequality or a weakly developed justification of a presumption against inequality. Either way, it is presumed to lack the appropriate radical insight into the real dynamics of injustice. But Rawls's distinctive contribution to social thought was to suggest that the diversity of talents and the contingent distribution of life-chances should be thought of not as reflections of individual merit or desert, but as a sort of collective asset, the benefits of which should be shared fairly amongst everyone. His concern was, accordingly, with thinking through how to share out the benefits that accrue from cooperative life in a way that respected individuals as having diverse needs, endowments and vulnerabilities, and treating them always as ends not means, that is, as equal and free fellow citizens. Rawls's theory of justice is, whatever else its faults might be, an exemplar of an attempt to think through problems of cooperation, co-existence, and interaction – that is, problems of sharing – without reducing these problems to either the utilitarian aggregation of the preferences of self-owning selves, or enveloping the pluralism of human life beneath higher-order categories of class, community, or nation.

If at first sight, sharing seems to be a model of reciprocity, mutuality, and commonality, then by following the thoughts of thinkers as different as Nancy, Chabal, and Rawls, we can see that making sense of practices of sharing requires us to think more deeply about the constitutive pluralism of human life, and also to address problems of co-operation, co-existence, togetherness and being-in-common. Taken as a whole, this collection outlines the promise of re-ordering social analysis around these problems precisely because it foregrounds the importance of thinking of sharing as a difficult practice.

References

Barnett, C. (2014) 'Theorising emergent public spheres: negotiating development, democracy and dissent' *Acta Academica* 46(1): 1–21.

Chabal, P. (2009) *Africa: The Politics of Suffering and Smiling*. London: Zed Books.

Derrida, J. (2005) *Rogues: Two Essays on Reason*. Stanford: Stanford University Press.

Nancy, J-L. (1991) *The Inoperative Community*. Minneapolis: University of Minnesota Press.

Rancière, J. (2004) *The Politics of Aesthetics: The Distribution of the Sensible*, trans. G. Rockhill. London: Continuum.

Rawls, J. (1971) *A Theory of Justice*. Oxford, Oxford University Press.

1 Introduction

Sharing economies in times of crisis

Sarah Marie Hall and Anthony Ince

'Sharing is caring'… 'a problem shared is a problem halved'… 'share and share alike'…

Sharing is used as a means of moral measurement – of people and society. It is positioned as so inherently beneficial that its innate goodness is rarely questioned. Yet, real-life manifestations of sharing, whether they be skills, stuff or stories, are far more complex and contested than we might think. This is, we posit, especially the case in those situations where sharing has become instituted as a driving factor of economic systems and a means of getting by in times of crisis – and is the inspiration for putting together this collection.

Sharing can be understood as a socio-economic practice and principle, although in recent years sharing has been increasingly described as a more formalised economic arrangement. These so-called sharing economies have emerged across a range of capitalist, alternative-capitalist and non-capitalist economic fields (Bradley 2014; Germann Molz 2012; Richardson 2016), partly as a response to the growing instabilities and vulnerabilities in the present political-economic fabric. Especially in the business world, these new sharing economies have been perceived by many as exciting new innovations promising to transform our economic and social lives (e.g. Gansky 2012).

This volume interrogates such optimism and definitional narrowness, and undertakes a constructive critique of sharing as practice, politic and possibility. We consider sharing as a mode of political-economic organisation, investigating political, social and ethical dimensions of a range of its diverse forms. In the midst of neoliberal capital's reinvention and reassertion post-2008 (Christophers 2014), we argue that it is important to consider the ways in which 'purely' economic processes – usually focused on capitalism – intersect with other forms of valuing, exchanging, producing and consuming. Sharing is one such form, though of course it is not entirely removed from circulations of capital – they can intersect, overlap and irritate.

Deconstructing and questioning sharing as practice and politic serves to reminds us that the political economy does not exist in a vacuum, hence this collection seeks to rethink both *sharing* and *economy*, in conversation with one another. The interdisciplinary collection of authors and their empirical topics are in many ways quite different from one another, but herein they coalesce around a unique and timely question: What is the role of sharing in a contemporary period characterised by crisis and turbulence?

Current scholarship within and beyond the field of political economy indicates how non-financial economies can produce counternarratives to the dominance of formalised capitalism, and generate spaces of economic alterity that sit within, against and beyond capitalist economies (Gibson-Graham 2008). In particular, getting by in times of crisis often requires connectedness and inter-relationality (Hall 2016a) – support that includes but commonly transcends purely financial transactions. However, what remains to be asked is how sharing and shared economic practices and relationships are altered, proliferated, co-opted or entrenched in times of crisis. What do sharing economies mean for these crisis-stricken times of ecological, political and economic uncertainty? In what ways are sharing economies resisting, evading, recuperated by, or entangled within spaces of dominant political-economic order? To what extent can sharing practices be seen as reshaping social, economic or moral values? And how might we take inspiration from these sharing economies to address the profound challenges that societies now face?

By raising and addressing these questions, this collection interrogates the complex and overlapping relationships between various coexisting forms of sharing within the economy, and the broader socio-political relations that intersect through them. Differing motivations such as need, convenience and ideology cut through dynamic classed, gendered and racialised relations in particular contexts, and at particular times. In this sense, constructions of superficially 'non-economic' relationships and institutions - such as kinship, authority and nation – also have a bearing on the way subjects and objects of economic life are understood, appreciated and replicated.

The sharing economy

With the unwavering dominance of neoliberal globalisation, the recent collapse of global financial markets, growing energy demand, pan-European humanitarian crises, and a growing cohort of so-called failed states, contemporary economic life for many is now characterised by multiple uncertainties and vulnerabilities. Amidst this instability, new or renewed forms of 'more-than-capitalist' economic practice have surfaced, variously challenging, deflecting or destabilising the underlying economic relationships that underpin contemporary crises. These variously named 'sharing' (Gold 2004), 'moral' (Wilson 2013) or 'gift' (Mauss 1954) economies are not only 'alternative capitalisms' – many of which circumvent or transgress capitalist relations of production altogether – but they may also offer hints of an alternative future to the crisis-prone present. Indeed, some of the most powerful examples of sharing economies are the everyday, informal practices of mutuality, solidarity and resourcefulness that all-too-easily go unnoticed (e.g. White 2009). In this collection we therefore seek to explore and expand these multiple ontologies of sharing economies, broadening the scope of current scholarship.

The growth of the so-called sharing economy in the context of crisis has produced significant shifts in the ways that resources, products and services are distributed and used. The sharing economy has been positioned by its supporters as a practical 'win-win' solution to various societal challenges, especially those related to community cohesion, ecological sustainability and economic resilience. To share in this context, we are told, is to address our individual needs while also generating positive externalities beyond the economic realm – forging meaningful connections with others and minimising wasteful overconsumption (Richardson 2015). Often drawing on recent developments in peer-to-peer and collaborative online technologies (Bradley 2014), businesses such as Uber, Lyft and Airbnb demonstrate that the sharing with others of intellectual and physical resources that would otherwise be privately used has become a viable mode not only of managing and distributing those resources but also extracting profit from them.

Within this new, formalised sharing economy, a range of economic forms coexist through a "semantic confusion" (Belk 2014). For instance, start-ups, entrepreneurs, multinational corporations, co-operatives, social enterprises, informal voluntary networks and not-for-profit models have found themselves awkwardly bundled together, occupying ostensibly the same economic and discursive spaces. Within this multiplicity of economic and organisational forms, the universally positive idea of sharing has, however, acted as a smokescreen for sharing-focused businesses to undertake various strategies of capital accumulation that impact negatively on their clients, workers and broader economic environments.

The meteoric rise of the spare room rental platform Airbnb is a prominent – and commonly cited – example. On the surface, the platform assists people renting out their spare rooms to guests, often at a cost lower than hotel prices. But it has simultaneously become a vehicle for undermining hospitality workers' pay and conditions (Kann 2015), facilitating aggressive entrepreneurial property speculation and forcing up rental prices (New York Communities for Change 2015), while also undermining free and non-profit alternatives such as Hospitality Club and CouchSurfing (Ince 2016).

Nevertheless, although prominent examples of sharing economy businesses are increasingly identified as problematic, other initiatives are beginning to use these technological innovations to develop modes of supporting, stabilising, and up-scaling socially progressive causes (Scholz 2016). Given that the technological innovations of the sharing economy in fact drew their narratives of 'democratising access' to resources from decentralised and grassroots peer-to-peer experiments among alternative programmers and hackers (e.g. Andersson 2011), it is unsurprising that these technologies have recently begun to feed back into new projects rooted in social justice, such as the emerging 'Platform Co-op' movement (Scholz 2016). Alongside technological change, then, the crisis in the Fordist mode of production and subsequent emergence of deregulated neoliberalism have paved the way for the growth of the capitalist sharing economy, yet they have also rendered the production and circulation of valued things open to alternative sharing economies outside, at the peripheries of, or even in opposition to, the capitalist commodity form.

As such, the formal sharing economy has been constitutive of diverse currents, making it difficult to define its borders with much accuracy. The technological model on which it is based merges as easily into open-source and wiki-based information sharing as it does into online platforms for vast corporations; its organisational model can produce both social integration and disintegration; its ecological outcomes can blend into circular and low-carbon futures as easily as resource-intensive ones; and its relationship to its growing workforce can be one of empowerment or exploitation. The chameleon-like character of *the* sharing economy thus belies its superficially unified and coherent identity.

Sharing and economies

Although *the* sharing economy might be considered a contemporary phenomenon – at least by current understandings as originating in technological innovations (see Benkler 2002) – it is not the only way that sharing and the economy intersect. There is an implicit political economy to the notion of sharing, defined in its most basic terms as the division and distribution of something – be it profits, goods or knowledge – amongst several people. And, while not our intended use of the term, 'shares' are also a form of company capital in financial markets, entitling shareholders to a proportion of business profits in exchange for their investment, which may in turn be exchanged for money. Economies are also built on trade and exchange with others, whether near or distant, and therefore also on inter-subjectivity and varying degrees of connectivity.

While inter-relationality and communicability form the basis for sharing-as-practice, familiarity is not necessarily a prerequisite to sharing, as the explosion of online sharing platforms have shown. Beyond kinship, friendship or community relations, there are various means of sharing that constitute economic practice but likewise do not entail personal or sustained interaction. While sharing certainly can be conducive to powerful encounters of difference (Ince 2015), it may equally include online interactions at a distance, as well as forms of face-to-face voluntarism, donation, and hand-me-downs that do not require emotional closeness or even meaningful interactions. The everyday geographies of sharing therefore do not necessarily revolve around inter-subjectivity but can assume affective and material forms.

Longer-standing, perhaps more subtle shades of sharing economies – or, rather, sharing-as-economic-practice – also exist beyond or at the edge of the commodified sphere. Here the ethic of sharing, as it were, places the exchange or contract on alternative forms of transaction, rather than a purely monetised exchange value. Instead, the inherent worth of the economic interaction is founded on the provision of conviviality, commensality, time, effort or labour. Examples of these more informal sharing economies include hitchhiking, time-banks, local currency schemes, community dinner clubs, or jumble sales (e.g. Ince 2016; Seyfang and Longhurst 2013). There are, of course, social dimensions that cut through these sharing practices, shaping how (and by whom) they are encountered and the types of economic relations that are produced. The geographically intimate and trust-bound means of sharing in the form of couch-surfing and hitchhiking are, for instance, also gendered encounters; for women, these activities can be associated with fear of physical and sexual violence, and can in fact *constrain* personal mobilities (Falconer 2009).

In a quotidian sense, sharing is also a likely component of most economies, as an endemic practice within and beyond the formal economic sphere. In their research on the 'second economy', Smith and Stenning (2006: 206) argue that the practices associated with informal economic transactions, such as sharing, are often 'seen to be useful only in times of crisis, when the market can no longer provide for well-being and sustenance, when there is simply no other choice, or they are associated with people "on the make", "grabbing" at informal and/or illegal economic opportunities'. Similarly, in a discussion of friendship, Bowlby (2011) points out that the sharing of activities and ideas can involve transactions and reciprocities that might not be considered typical of sharing economies, or economies in general. As she explains, 'reciprocation does not need to be immediate…, nor of the same form, nor involve a precisely calculated scale of obligation. I may "pay back" the friend who gave me a lift to the station by listening to their tales of trouble with their daughter. This "pay back" may be removed in both time and space from the incident of the lift and neither of us may think about the equivalence or otherwise of these two incidents' (Bowlby 2011: 612).

However, and as these contributions identify, while sharing can contribute to resistance and mutual aid, it should not be romanticised or assumed to be an always successful fix (e.g. Williams et al. 2016). For instance, in our own empirical work we have revealed the tensions encircling sharing within families, whether material, emotional or financial, as not always or necessarily reciprocal (Hall 2016a), and of the contested terms of shared identities through which communities are constituted (Ince 2011). We therefore must think of sharing as a pervasive and contested practice which can bring to light multiple, contradictory dimensions of contemporary economic life.

As should now be apparent, sharing economies are diverse – even contradictory – in their various manifestations. This plurality indicates that we cannot see sharing economies in isolation from one another, nor from the orthodox capitalist economy. In many cases, different economies of sharing overlap and intersect, especially those forms of sharing that are unarticulated or that operate under the radar of formal economic structures. For example, as Germann Molz (2012) and others (e.g. Ince 2016) have indicated in the context of tourism, our economic 'gaze' might register a formalised online system of hospitality exchange but overlook the multiplicity of informally shared spaces, intellectual and physical resources, and other solidarities that operate through and beyond formal initiatives. This volume embraces and interrogates the diversity of economic forms that fall under the broad umbrella of sharing, yet it also explores kinds of sharing that arguably operate outside, and in spite of, the economic realm altogether.

It is therefore important to sensitise our economic 'radar' to these pluralities and the dynamic interactions between different forms, spaces and scales of sharing. What they all have in common is their emphasis on unmediated forms of exchange and value circulation – or, what has been increasingly referred to as peer-to-peer systems. This autonomy and fluidity has generated intense debate regarding the fine line between democratisation of access and infringement of legal ownership rights. Thus, the plurality of sharing economies is underlined by a plurality of political and ethical questions that reach into the very core of economic (in)justice, the neoliberal state, and social reproduction. Our task, then, is to unravel some of these questions in relation to the contemporary period characterised by entanglements of the gradual decomposition of binary certainties (owner/user, producer/consumer, formal/informal) and the omnipresent threat of crisis.

The politics of crisis

Crisis is a multifaceted and ever-changing concept, and one that has become part of everyday lexicon. Despite its apparent singularity, much like *sharing*, the term has diverse meanings, is riddled with contradictions, and must be understood in terms of human agency (Featherstone et al. 2015). Crises can take different forms, and may coexist or overlap in time and space. They can be felt at multiple scales, within and between nations and societies, bodies and experiences – both localised and endemic (Hall 2016b).

The term itself derives from the Greek *krisis*, meaning 'decision', suggesting a meeting of particular circumstances, an accumulation of specific events that intersect around a common focal point. Crises might be typified by a critical mass of activity or anticipation, the crescendo of a situation that reaches a tipping point requiring urgent attention. Crises are in this sense always realised; the commotion caused by the momentum of a looming or unfolding crisis means that crises do not – indeed, cannot – go unnoticed. More often than not, crises are also *shared*; drawing people together through common experiences, material conditions and anxieties. Even in the case of personal crises, these are articulated into internal narratives about the world and one's place in it.

While there are no temporal parameters to what may constitute a crisis, the concept is somewhat defined by what is *not* crisis. Crises by definition ultimately pass, are resolved, or can merge and separate into new (or newly defined) crises. Moments and incidents during the 'lifecourse' of a crisis can accelerate, dissipate or change its trajectory and tempo. Despite the longevity of some crises, for a situation to be understood as a crisis, it must be somewhat *extraordinary*, since crises by their very definition are not constant or all-encompassing. Crises are nonetheless experienced in and as part of everyday life, and can also reverberate as memories, habits, policies, materialities and other legacies. Indeed, crisis is as much an embodied phenomenon as it is a systemic one. In this sense, lived experiences of crises are charged with ethical and political currents that relate to how they are experienced and negotiated by differentially situated groups, institutions and individuals. One's experience of a crisis is heavily shaped by class, gender, race and other dimensions of social difference. This also affects the nature and effectiveness of an individual or group's response to crises, since structural inequities can be amplified in such situations (e.g. Elliot and Pais 2006).

In terms of its recent uses, the notion of crisis has represented a wide range of often unconnected instabilities, be they economic, ecological, cultural, moral, political or personal. The diversity of crises shows how the notion can have wildly different spatial and temporal stories and trajectories, and it is worth briefly exploring some examples to unpack how crises emerge, develop and are manifested in many ways.

While multiple definitions of crisis proliferate, notions of economic and financial upheaval often dominate. Triggered by a crash in the US subprime mortgage market, the so-called credit crisis began when a large flow of credit in the virtual economy 'spilled over into real markets', resulting in 'a restriction to the amount of credit available to both industry and consumers' (Hinton and Goodman 2010: 256; Hall 2016a). Emmel and Hughes (2010: 178) explain that 'the collapse of Lehman Brothers on the 16 September 2008 is widely accepted as a marker of the start of the recession', leading to panic and the steady disintegration of confidence in the global economy. Anticipation and the build-up of momentum often associated with crises are evident in this example; in the UK as early as 2007, 'banks stopped lending to each other' and one bank, Northern Rock, was nationalised by the UK government to prevent its collapse (Edwards and Irwin 2010: 120; Thain 2009). The impacts of the Global Financial Crisis of 2008–2009 still resonate, particularly in the US and Europe. Indeed, as we write, a fresh round of austerity policies is being arranged for the Greek economy, and senior politicians and financial institutions in the UK are pronouncing stark warnings of the severe economic shocks that may hit the UK economy following its citizens' vote to leave the European Union. Thus, even threats of economic crises can 'regulate everyday life' (Pollard 2013: 413), and are 'simultaneously personal and provocative' experiences (Hall 2016b: 7).

An example which speaks to the urgency that is constitutive of both political and environmental crises, is the so-called energy crisis. In the last decade, energy generation and use have become increasingly politicised, with growing 'concerns over security of supply, rising prices and climate change' (Hall et al. 2013: 413). Energy thus represents an intersection of multiple crises – not only as finite fuel resources deplete, but also as a key indicator of social and environmental inequality, with many consumers now faced with the dilemma of whether to 'eat or heat'. Moreover, it is through the example of energy that the 'knottiness' of crises can be realised. For example, Ukraine's struggle over the sovereignty of Crimea following a Russian insurgence exposed instabilities in energy supply and security, with concerns that Russia may restrict gas supplies into Europe. Indeed, 'this crisis marked a fundamental shift from an era characterised by more orderly market functioning to a less organised scramble for resources' (Goldthau and Boersma 2014: 15). In amongst this complexity of crises a significant environmental crisis is argued to be afoot; the Russian economy is reportedly one of the most energy intensive, and yet there is a substantial lack of policies ensuring environmental protection or sustainable development (Crotty and Hall 2014).

Another of the foremost crises facing the Global North, especially Europe, is the mass movement of refugees and migrants, most notably from parts of Africa and the Middle East experiencing political instability, poverty and war. For example, between April 2011 and November 2015 there were an estimated 807,337 asylum applications in Europe from Syrians alone (UNHCR 2015), most of which were made in 2015. These growing human mobilities, combined with ongoing neoliberalisation, an ageing European population, high levels of internal mobility among Europeans, and continued economic uncertainty, have produced a sense of crisis through multiple vectors, including intensified labour market competition and segmentation (e.g. Ince et al. 2015) and increased pressures on rapidly dwindling welfare structures and social housing stocks (e.g. Hedin et al. 2012). Migration crises are also evident in the Global South, with displaced populations settling in formal camps or informal shanty towns in urban and rural areas of neighbouring states (Crisp et al. 2012), often experiencing significant levels of exclusion (e.g. Amisi 2006).

These political-economic dimensions of migration have co-articulated with parallel debates about perceived cultural vulnerabilities and a so-called crisis of multiculturalism in regions experiencing high rates of in-migration, especially Western Europe (Lentin and Titley 2012). According to media and government discourses across the Global North, state-led multicultural policies of the past two decades have produced a situation in which 'native' ethnocultural norms have been marginalised. Such cultural anxieties have often been manifested through a rightward shift in political discourse, promoting ever-stricter migration and labour controls and a return to an idealised cultural homogeneity that never really existed (e.g. Ince 2011; Koefoed and Simonsen 2007; Moore and Forkert 2014). In some states, such as the UK, these rather 'utopian' imaginaries of cultural unity have, ironically, found a home in new forms of far-right politics that present inclusiveness and respect for difference as inherently British (Copsey 2010). Against this is counterposed a menacing (and usually Islamic) Other which threatens this delicate fabric of 'native' culture with 'foreign' or 'imported' theocratic uniformity.

Amidst these diverse crises and crisis-tendencies cross-cutting contemporary societies, the state and other supra- and sub-national institutions of government are perceived as under increasing strain. The difficulties of balancing and managing competing demands, conflicts and crises have been compounded by increasingly complex landscapes of governance, with growing numbers of non-state actors intersecting with radically restructured and rescaled states (e.g. Anderson 2016; Stark and Taylor 2014). The result is a complex, "variegated" (Brenner et al. 2010) meshwork of governance relations within neoliberal political systems, highly vulnerable to changes and ruptures in the societies they seek to manage. So-called failed states represent the *sine qua non* of these anxieties about state stability (Hill 2005), perceived as but one crisis away from losing their monopoly of violence to (different factions of) their subjects. There is therefore a growing mistrust of government and its ability to cope with a crisis-prone world, including at macro-regional scales of governance (e.g. the European Union), where a sense of democratic deficit often compounds this mistrust further.

Additionally, there are many types of crises on the political landscape that we have not discussed here, not for lack of interest, rather for lack of space – moral crises, housing crises, food crises, care crises, personal crises – some of which are discussed by our contributors, some are not. However, this serves to illustrate our point that crises have become a normative expectation in contemporary societies. And while diverse and discriminating, what all these examples have in common is that crises can bring together both very real and imaginary geographies that can be personally, socially, nationally or even globally affective – at the same time and at different times. Therefore, to denote a situation as a 'crisis' is to acknowledge the spatio-temporal situatedness of a particular moment or event – a moment that will eventually pass but will inevitably leave traces and remnants that long outlive the crisis itself.

Seeing sharing and economies anew: practices, politics and possibilities

We are interested in what these varied and precarious social, political, economic and environmental conditions mean for sharing economies, and what it means to share in and through crisis. To unpack the complexities of sharing, economies and crises, we posit that a three-part focus – on practices, politics and possibilities – provides a useful conceptual foundation.

Viewing sharing as a practice can foreground the embedded, active and engaged nature of sharing, the economy, and indeed crisis. It is all too easy to think of such abstract concepts or processes as existing 'over the heads' of people, when in fact they are produced by individual and collective forms of everyday agency. Sharing is very much a lived practice; it is done for and with others, building direct connections between individuals and groups through common purpose and common use of resources. Sharing economies may also occupy shared spaces, in that they do not necessarily sit in isolation, but individuals and groups may participate and benefit from multiple sharing economies and at different scales. Indeed, pluralising understandings of sharing and the economy is a key aim of this collection. Furthermore, in the context of crisis, sharing practices might be understood to challenge, circumvent, and destabilise economic relationships underpinning current crises, as well as provide possible modes of mitigating risk or 'retrofitting' economic systems to adapt to changing circumstances.

Sharing can also be understood as a form of politics, whether as a result of sharing, or by considering sharing as a political stance. This can include sharing as a means of redistributing public goods and services, such as through taxation and public amenities, or in charitable acts such as sharing food or volunteering time or labour. And yet, many, if not most, of the examples of sharing economies in this collection are not political in an explicit sense. By this we mean they are not necessarily 'noisily' or 'disruptively' political, but instead bring to light a 'quiet politics': small acts and kind words (Horton and Kraftl 2009), 'everyday activities in quotidian spaces which are part of a broader continuum of movements for change' (Askins 2015: 475). They are, however, undoubtedly normative, mobilising ways of being and relating to things, nature and people in a globalised, crisis-prone world that do not conform to the confined visions of neoliberal elites. Instead, they may point towards a "politics of economic possibility" (Gibson-Graham 2006).

As a practice with political and normative dimensions, sharing also presents various possibilities: some likelier than others, some more radical, but all within the scope of the imagination. We consider sharing economies not as extraordinary, but as embedded in everyday politics, ethics and relationalities, and as open to change and contestation. The 'everydayness' of these economic practices foregrounds a tension between the ordinary and the extraordinary – a tension that brings to light how everyday productions of space are inflected with alternative political imaginations. This echoes notions of the *prefigurative* in contemporary political economic thought – of creating 'ordinary' spaces, relationships and structures in the here-and-now that make pathways to envisioned 'extraordinary' future worlds. Suffice to say, our own understandings of what might be considered sharing have expanded in the crafting of this collection. While already broad in temporal framing (whether sharing be historical, current, or futurist), expanding the remit to include personal or collective memories, other-worldly experiences, national imaginaries, ideals, and alternative futures, for instance, adds colour and texture to the possibilities of sharing.

The remainder of this collection critically yet constructively interrogates the practices, politics, possibilities and pitfalls of applying sharing economies to contemporary crises and crisis tendencies. In doing so, it offers a diverse yet focused, and politically engaged yet rigorous series of studies into these questions, developing new critical understandings of the politics, spatialities, temporalities, relationalities and practices that constitute sharing as a possible element of our responses to or prevention of crises.

The chapters that follow are richly illustrative of the ambiguous practices, politics and possibilities running through sharing economies, and the exclusions and inequities that sharing can engender and aggravate. But what connects them is an underpinning notion that the context(s) of crisis requires us to see sharing economies anew. This involves moving beyond, yet representing and extending formal and informal understandings of the sharing economy. It necessitates a reconsideration of what sharing economies are and what they can do, and of the implications of context in these reconceptualisations. We argue that it is, therefore, important not to be confined by established ideas of 'the sharing economy' but instead to retrace the intricate socio-economic relationships between sharing *and* the economy.

In doing so, we have been motivated by two key goals for this collection. Firstly, to mark a major theoretical, conceptual and empirical contribution to scholarly understandings of contemporary sharing economies; and, secondly, to open up innovative new research agendas and questions in the theoretical and empirical study of the intersections between everyday practices, alternative economies and crises. Towards these ends, the book is organised across three interlinked and overlapping themes, each of which encompasses the practices, politics and possibilities of sharing in different ways.

In our first theme, *Sharing In and Through Crisis*, we present four chapters that deal most explicitly with the intersections of sharing and crisis, and how the two interweave in deeply politicised ways. Laura Pottinger's ethnographic study of seed exchanges sheds light on how the threat of ecological crisis (in this case, biodiversity) may draw together diverse collectivities which not only have profound social and emotional impacts on participants but also generate material challenges to the underlying commodification of our relationships with food. Chris Gibson, Natascha Klocker, Erin Borger and Sophie-May Kerr's chapter on extended family life explores the ways in which family and personal crises are managed and addressed through families' relationships with materialities and micro-spatialities of the home, drawing out the complex role that shared domestic space plays in mediating social and economic relations. Juliana Mansvelt then investigates the obligations and limitations of sharing among older people in the context of rapid social and economic change in New Zealand, picking through the complex tensions embedded within the process of aging and its economies. In the final paper of this theme, Mark Jayne, Gill Valentine and Sarah Holloway foreground in their discussion an understanding of how the delicate, embodied negotiations and meanings of shared drinking experiences might be reframed as an antidote to perceptions of mass alcohol consumption as constitutive of an "urban crisis" of disorder and violence.

In the second theme of the book, the simmering tensions and compatibilities of sharing economies and the sharing economy, noted earlier in this introduction, are brought to the fore. Paula Bialski opens the section with a critical reflection on the renting of home-space as part of the sharing economy, and the commodification of the domestic, material and otherwise. Based on ethnographic accounts, she troubles common dualisms such as public/private, home/work, leisure/labour, whilst simultaneously offering new ways of thinking about home-space through the lens of sharing. In her chapter unpacking the phenomenon of sales of nearly new children's clothes and toys among middle-class mothers, Emma Waight explores the complex classed dynamics of consuming the second-hand objects that are shared and circulated among parenting networks, and the subtle meanings embedded within the objects themselves. Nicola Livingstone's chapter on UK food banks offers a powerful critique of the ways in which multiple scales of economic crisis (global, state-level, and domestic) can be weaponised by governing elites to construct punitive regimes that ultimately harm the most vulnerable. To round off this section, Katharina Hellwig, Russell Belk and Felicitas Morhart then compare and contrast the "shared moments" constituted through for-profit and free hospitality platforms. Their comparison of participants' experiences of Airbnb and CouchSurfing foregrounds the role of spontaneity and the unexpected in encounters, and calls for us to reconsider the role of money in sharing relations.

The third and final theme of the book contains chapters that engage more directly with how sharing economies might signal the possibility of alternative futures in the way we live, work, distribute resources, and relate to one another more generally. The growth of cohousing, in which residents form democratically and co-operatively controlled housing communities, is the subject of Lucy Sargisson's chapter; she argues that this growth indicates a promising and viable, if imperfect, solution to housing crises in the Global North rooted explicitly in shared ownership, control and responsibility. Nicole Gombay's contribution is an exploration of the interweaving of Indigenous and settler-colonial land claims in northern Canada, considering how Indigenous populations have sought to maintain and promote their collective, sharing-oriented understandings of land use in the face of intense pressure from the Canadian state to conform to commodified, Eurocentric models of property ownership. Lastly, Richard White and Colin Williams conclude the volume on a deeply hopeful and transformative note, using their analysis of non-commodified forms of sharing and mutual aid in households to argue that another society organised along non-hierarchical and co-operative lines is not only necessary to challenge capitalism's destructive crisis-tendencies but also already living amongst us today.

Taken together, the collection makes distinctive theoretical and empirical contributions to understanding the everyday practices, politics and possibilities of sharing economies in an uncertain and volatile world. How people and communities cope, survive, or even thrive in crises is a pivotal question of contemporary society. By critically engaging with sharing-based economies as an increasingly prominent and innovative field of everyday economic practice, this volume ultimately considers the possibilities and challenges to the development of equitable and just relationships among people and with the turbulent world around them.

References

Amisi, B.B. (2006) *An Exploration of the Livelihood Strategies of Durban Congolese Refugees*. Working Paper No. 123. Geneva: UNHCR.

Anderson, B. (2016) 'Governing emergencies: the politics of delay and the logic of response' *Transactions of the Institute of British Geographers* 41(1): 14–26.

Andersson, J. (2011) 'The origins and impacts of Swedish filesharing: a case study' *Journal of Peer Production* 1(1): 1–18.

Askins, K. (2015) 'Being together: everyday geographies and the quiet politics of belonging', *ACME: An International E-Journal for Critical Geographies*, 14(2): 470–478.

Belk, R. (2014) 'Sharing versus pseudo-sharing in Web 2.0' *Anthropologist* 18(1): 7–23.

Benkler, Y. (2002) 'Coase's penguin, or, Linux and "The nature of the firm"' *Yale Law Journal* 112(3): 369–446.

Bowlby, S. (2011) 'Friendship, co-presence and care: neglected spaces' *Social and Cultural Geography* 12(6): 605–622.

Bradley, K. (2014) 'Towards a peer economy: how open source and peer-to-peer architecture, hardware, and consumption are transforming the economy' in Bradley, K. and Hedrén, J. [eds.] *Green Utopianism: Perspectives, Politics and Micro-Practices*. London and New York: Routledge, 183–204.

Brenner, N., Peck, J. and Theodore, N. (2010) 'Variegated neoliberalisation: geographies, modalities, pathways' *Global Networks* 10(2): 182–222.

Christophers, B. (2014) 'Geographies of finance I: historical geographies of the crisis-ridden present' *Progress in Human Geography* 38(2): 285–293.

Copsey, N. (2010) *The English Defence League: Challenging Our Country and Our Values of Social Inclusion, Fairness and Equality*. London: Faith Matters.

Crisp, J., Morris, T. and Refstie, H. (2012) 'Displacement in urban areas: new challenges, new partnerships' *Disasters* 36(Supplement S1): 23–42.

Crotty, J. and Hall, S.M. (2014) 'Environmental awareness and sustainable development in the Russian Federation', *Sustainable Development*, 22(5): 311–320.

Edwards, R., and Irwin, S. (2010). 'Lived experience through economic downturn in Britain – perspectives across time and across the life-course' *Twenty-First Century Society* 5(2): 119–124.

Elliot, J.R. and Pais, J. (2006) 'Race, class and Hurricane Katrina: social differences in human responses to disaster' *Social Science Research* 35(2): 295–321.

Emmel, N. and Hughes, K. (2010) '"Recession, it's all the same to us son": the longitudinal experience (1999–2010) of deprivation' *Twenty-First Century Society* 5(2): 171–181.

Falconer, E. (2009) 'Telling tales: a feminist interpretation of women's travel narratives', *Enquire*, 2(1): 21–40.

Featherstone, D., Strauss, K. and MacKinnon, D. (2015) 'In, against and beyond neoliberalism: The "crisis" and alternative political futures' *Space and Polity* 19(1): 1–11.

Gansky, L. (2012) *The Mesh: Why the Future of Business Is Sharing*. New York: Portfolio Penguin.

Germann Molz, J. (2012) 'Solidarity on the move: technology, mobility and activism in a hospitality exchange network' in Vannini, P., Budd, L., Jensen, O.B., Fisker, P. and Jirón, P. [eds.] *Technologies of Mobility in the Americas*. New York: Peter Lang.

Gibson-Graham, J.K. (2006) *A Postcapitalist Politics*. Minneapolis: University of Minnesota Press.

Gibson-Graham, J.K. (2008) 'Diverse economies: performative practices for "other worlds"' *Progress in Human Geography* 32(5): 613–632.

Gold, L. (2004) *The Sharing Economy: Solidarity Networks Transforming Globalisation*. Aldershot: Ashgate.

Goldthau, A. and Boersma, T. (2014) 'The 2014 Ukraine-Russia crisis: implications for energy markets and scholarship', *Energy Research and Social Science*, 3: 13–15.

Hall, S.M. (2016a) 'Everyday family experiences of the financial crisis: getting by in the recent economic recession. *Journal of Economic Geography* 16(2): 305–330.

Hall, S.M. (2016b) Personal, relational and intimate geographies of austerity: ethical and empirical considerations. *Area*, DOI: 10.1111/area.12251.

Hall, S.M., Hards, S. and Bulkeley, H. (2013) 'New approaches to energy: equity, justice and vulnerability', *Local Environment*, 18(4): 413–421.

Hedin, K., Clark, E., Lundholm, E. and Malmberg, G. (2012) 'Neoliberalisation of housing in Sweden: gentrification, filtering, and social polarisation' *Annals of the Association of American Geographers* 102(2): 443–463.

Hill, J. (2005) 'Beyond the other? A postcolonial critique of the failed state thesis' *African Identities* 3(2): 139–154.

Hinton, E. and Goodman, M. (2010) 'Sustainable consumption: developments, considerations and new directions' in Redclift, M.R. and Woodgate, G. [eds.] *The international handbook of environmental sociology*. Edward Elgar: London, 245–261.

Horton, J. and Kraftl, P. (2009) 'Small acts, kind words and "not too much fuss": Implicit activisms', *Emotion, Space and Society*, 2(1): 14–23.

Ince, A. (2011) 'Contesting the "authentic" community: Far-right spatial strategy and everyday responses in an era of crisis' *Ephemera: Theory and Politics in Organisation* 11(1): 6–26.

Ince, A. (2015) 'From middle ground to common ground: self-management and spaces of encounter in organic farming networks' *Annals of the Association of American Geographers* 105(4): 824–840.

Ince, A. (2016) 'Autonomy, territory, mobility: everyday (geo)politics in voluntary exchange networks' *L'Espace Politique* 28(1): 2–16.

Ince, A., Featherstone, D., Cumbers, A., MacKinnon, D. and Strauss, K. (2015) 'British jobs for British workers? Negotiating work, nation and globalisation through the Lindsey Oil Refinery disputes' *Antipode* 47(1): 139–157.

Kann, J. (2015) 'AirBnB is making it harder for workers in the hospitality industry to make ends meet' *In These Times* [online]. Available: http://inthesetimes.com/working/entry/18026/subcontracting_in_the_digital_era_the_consequences_of_your_airbnb_reservati [Accessed 20 June 2016]

Koefoed, L. and Simonsen, K. (2007) 'The price of goodness: everyday nationalist discourses in Denmark' *Antipode* 39(2): 310–330.

Lentin, A. and Titley, G. (2012) 'The crisis of "multiculturalism" in Europe: mediated minarets, intolerable subjects' *European Journal of Cultural Studies* 15(2): 123–138.

Mauss, M. (1954). *The Gift: Forms and Functions of Exchange in Archaic Societies.* London: Cohen & West.

Moore, P. and Forkert, K. (2014) 'Class and panic in British immigration' *Capital and Class* 38(3): 497–505.

New York Communities for Change (2015) *AirBnB in NYC: A Housing Report.* New York.

Pollard, J.S. (2013) 'Gendering capital: financial crisis, financialisation and an agenda for economic geography' *Progress in Human Geography* 37: 403–23.

Richardson, L. (2015) 'Performing the sharing economy' *Geoforum* 67: 121–129.

Scholz, T. (2016) *Platform Cooperativism: Challenging the Corporate Sharing Economy.* New York: Rosa Luxemburg Foundation.

Seyfang, G. and Longhurst, N. (2013) 'Growing green money? Mapping community currencies for sustainable development' *Ecological Economics* 86(1): 65–77.

Smith, A. and Stenning, A. (2006) 'Beyond household economies: articulations and spaces of economic practice in post-socialism', *Progress in Human Geography*, 30(2): 190–213.

Stark, A. and Taylor, M. (2014) 'Citizen participation, community resilience and crisis-management policy' *Australian Journal of Political Science* 49(2): 300–315.

Thain, C. (2009) 'A very peculiar British crisis?: institutions, ideas and policy responses to the credit crunch', *British Politics*, 4(4): 434–449.

UNHCR (2015) 'Europe: Syrian asylum applications' [online]. Available from: http://data.unhcr.org/syrianrefugees/asylum.php [Accessed 14 December 2015].

White, R.J. (2009) 'Explaining why the non-commodified sphere of mutual aid is so pervasive in the advanced economies' *International Journal of Sociology and Social Policy* 29(9/10): 457–472.

Williams, A., Cloke, P., May, J. and Goodwin, M. (2016) 'Contested space: the contradictory political dynamics of food banking in the UK' *Environment and Planning A* 48(11): 2291–2316.

Wilson, M. (2013) *Everyday Moral Economies: Food, Politics and Scale in Cuba.* Oxford: Wiley-Blackwell.

Part I

Sharing in and through crisis

Throughout this collection we explore the fluid, discursive and prefigurative capacities of both sharing and crisis, anchored not in specific ideas or disciplinary traditions, but encompassing a variety of practices, politics and possibilities. In this first section we therefore seek to bring sharing and crisis into closer dialogue, and to consider the ways in which they may intersect. This includes how crises can penetrate, punctuate or proliferate sharing, how sharing may be a means of addressing or getting by in crisis, and sharing in spite of crisis.

This necessitates thinking about sharing and crises as situated in and across particular times and places, foregrounding spatial and temporal context: that crises by their very nature are underpinned by rhythm, momentum and change. But this is not to say that practices of sharing in and through crisis always and inevitably lead to entirely distinct experiences. Rather, as the chapters in this section indicate, despite the range of crises explored – including urban, ecological, financial and social – both uncanny commonalities and stark divergences cut across the four cases.

A deeper consideration of sharing as it intersects with crisis also reveals the need to move beyond fixed and often romantic assumptions of human interaction in crisis-stricken times; that sharing is a singular and uniformly expected, 'natural' response with certain social and economic limits. Moreover, the authors urge us to look beyond human-centred approaches. As they identify, relationships with other living and material things, the more-than-human elements that make up the world around us, are also crucial elements of sharing in and through crisis.

2 'It feels connected in so many ways'

Circulating seeds and sharing garden produce

Laura Pottinger

Introduction: saving and swapping seed

Ideals of sharing and giving freely are significant aspects of gardening. Belk (2010) defines sharing as a distinct consumer behaviour, free from reciprocal expectations and distinct from gifting since no debt is imposed upon the recipient. Diverse economies (Gibson-Graham 1996; 2006) built around sharing and gifting are evident in the circulation of seeds, plants, crops, tools and labour among gardening neighbours, friends and family, and in the support and ethical negotiation between individuals and wildlife co-habiting growing spaces (Smith et al. 2015; Smith and Jehlička 2013; Platten 2013; Ellen and Platten 2011). Disposition of excess garden produce amongst known individuals efficiently avoids wastage, is thrifty and supports social relationships.

Contemporarily in the global North, organised plant swaps, gleaning groups and seed exchanges have developed around purposeful redistribution of garden produce (Campbell 2012). Seeds embody millennia of human endeavour, ideas about place, heritage, history and future, yet are small, portable, easily exchangeable items (Ellen and Platten 2011). Organised seed swaps have emerged globally in response to declining agrobiodiversity (Campbell 2012). Such events connect 'seed savers' (gardeners who grow vegetables, select and save seed to provide subsequent generations of plants for themselves and others), extending diverse economic relations to spatially disparate growers, and aligning everyday practices with political, environmental and social concerns.

Seedy Sunday is an annual seed swap, held in Brighton on the South coast of England. Initiated in 2001 and inspired by North American seed exchanges which have a longer history (Campbell 2012), Seedy Sunday draws seed companies, gardening groups, environmental activists and food producers together in a day-long event. The focal point is the seed swap table. Some seeds are donated by volunteers and swap attendees, and one packet of seed can be exchanged ('swapped') for either another packet or fifty pence. These include commercial and home-saved fruit, vegetables, herb and ornamental flower seeds. At Seedy Sunday 2013, over 3000 people attended to swap seeds, listen to talks and visit commercial and community stalls.

The *Heritage Seed Library* (HSL), based in Warwickshire, UK, is a seed saving network run by the charity 'Garden Organic'. HSL conserves around 800 varieties of heritage vegetable seeds. For a yearly subscription of around £20 members choose six packets of seeds from HSL's catalogue. Some seed is produced at HSL, but much is provided by volunteer 'seed guardians': gardeners based around the country who save a particular variety (or several varieties). Guardians are given instructions regarding isolation, selection and drying of seeds, which are then posted back to HSL in autumn. Seeds are stored here at low temperatures and humidity to maximise viability, before being sent to members in spring.

This chapter contextualises seed saving within broader debates on diverse economies (Gibson-Graham 1996; 2006) and argues sharing practices hold political significance in light of growing corporatisation and regulation of seeds and natures (Castree 2003; Demuelenare 2014; Pautasso et al. 2013). Following discussion of the political and theoretical context of seed exchange, and the methodological approach adopted to research sharing relationships, I explore the inherent reciprocities (expectations of return or exchange, imagined and realised) as garden produce is circulated within and beyond organised 'sharing' networks in the UK. Examining the social, emotional, and interpersonal dimensions of garden cultivation and exchange reveals mundane practices of seed sharing are connected by individuals to diverse ethical and political commitments and motivations (Phillips 2013; Turner 2011). The empirical discussion draws out the interrelationship of these factors with attempts to resist, defy or creatively rework consumption and provisioning in light of multidimensional crises: moments of potential difficulty and danger demanding a response, in systems of food and seed production and distribution. I argue seed sharing can be understood as an ethical and political practice that challenges dominant social relationships predicated by consumerism and commodification.

Multidimensional crises in the seed landscape

In 2011, the international seed market was worth $34,495 million (US), with 75.3% controlled by just ten multinationals (ETC Group 2013). It is claimed consolidation of the seed industry amongst a few companies has accelerated loss of biodiversity and heritage varieties (Kloppenburg 2004; Phillips 2013; Shiva 1993; Stickland 2008). Commercial seed production is geared towards industrial, pesticide dependent, predominantly hybrid[1] seed, capable, for example, of providing supermarkets with uniform vegetables that can withstand extensive transportation. Deppe (2000: xv) suggests, "bred into the varieties are the values of their creators – that more is always better, that monocultures are best, and that pollution, biodiversity and sustainability don't matter."

Compounding this potential crisis for biodiversity, the 'EU Common Seed Catalogue' effectively criminalises sales of unregistered seed (Kastler 2005;

Purdue 2000). European seed legislation determines how seed and plant propagative material may be marketed, and is based on registering and certifying stable varieties exhibiting distinctness and uniformity (UPOV 2015; Winge 2015). Initially intended to protect consumers and ensure accountability (Louwaars 2002; Winge 2015), this legislation has negative consequences for crop diversity, small-scale seed producers and distributers, due to time and cost implications of testing and registering rare cultivars (Purdue 2000).

Perhaps ironically, these restrictions have stimulated diverse economic practices between gardeners. Legalities dictating that unregistered seed cannot be *sold* demand contemporary seed swaps distribute seeds in either non-monetary transactions, or for cash 'donations'. Though sharing economies developed around seed are framed as socially and environmentally just alternative consumption practices, they are not merely a reaction to emergent political, economic and ecological crises or wider anxieties about disconnected food systems (Morris and Kirwan 2010; Pottinger 2013). Rather, their instigation, maintenance and framing interweave a range of everyday concerns, enthusiasms, practicalities and sociabilities (Barnett et al. 2011), whilst contributing to a kind of 'quiet' environmental and social activism (Askins 2014; Smith et al. 2015; Smith and Jehlička 2013).

Saved and swapped seed is presented as supporting biodiverse ecologies, challenging corporate control and connecting like-minded growers into communities of intent (Demeulenaere 2014; Pautasso et al. 2013; Phillips 2013). Furthermore, saved seeds are said to gradually adjust to local conditions, fare better in organic systems than those produced for industrial agriculture, and offer increased choices for small-scale growers (Phillips 2008; Stickland 2008). Against the backdrop of increasing corporate control of seed, which has marginalised home seed production in the industrialised global North (Campbell 2012), it is argued practices of saving and exchanging constitute political acts (Nazarea 2005; Phillips 2013). Significantly, ideals of sharing and non-monetary exchange reinforce seeds as communal resources and responsibilities rather than private property (Carolan 2007; Castree 2003; Purdue 2000). As Phillips (2008: 16) notes, "[s]eeds' abilities to reproduce, and seed-savers' encouragement of this ability, allow escape from efforts to control and profit from seeds." The materialities, temporalities and propagative capacities of open-pollinated[2] seeds mean they hold great potential to underpin diverse economies centred on non-monetary exchanges of plant material (Deibel 2013; Gibson-Graham 2006; Leyshon et al. 2003).

Though a robust body of work examining the political economy of seed production and consumption has critically interrogated issues of biotechnology, commodification and patenting (Deibel 2013; Kloppenburg 2004; Shiva 1993), recent contributions foreground relationships between individual gardening practices and wider political issues, particularly in the global North (Aistara 2014; Demeulenaere 2014; Müller 2014; Phillips 2008, 2013). Phillips (2013: 7) links neoliberalisation of the Canadian seed industry with the "ethico-political engagement" inherent within individuals' practices with seeds, and Müller (2014: 40) presents a persuasive argument for attending to how gardeners "engage with seeds ... in a 'warm' relation of intimacy and care". The affective and emotional experiences of seed sharing offer a rich terrain for geographers to better understand how these 'warm relations' might require, motivate and sustain particular sets of ethical subjectivities and relationships.

Unpicking what makes *sharing* in particular meaningful to growers, in relation to and beyond the multidimensional crises outlined above requires consideration of the distribution of seeds, but also cuttings, seedlings and excess produce; and of how individuals form meaningful attachments to and through plant material (Brook 2003; Ellen and Platten 2011; Turner 2011). Shared practices and spaces of garden cultivation provide fertile ground for elucidating the emotional and affective dimensions of diverse economies and for exploring how crises in the wider political economy of seeds are made meaningful to practitioners through mundane consumption practices. As well as bringing into view existing diverse economic forms (Gibson-Graham 1996; 2006), the findings validate current arguments that responsibilities and practices of care for environments are entangled with the everyday, emotional and interpersonal (Barnett and Land 2007; Hall 2011).

Sharing in seed saving practice

This discussion draws on research conducted in 2013 with forty seven individuals participating in 'sharing' economies based around garden produce: 'seed savers' affiliated with Seedy Sunday or HSL, in the UK. These included seed swap volunteers, organisers and attendees; seed guardians; and others working on seed issues. This provided a heterogeneous sample through which to investigate wide-ranging non-monetary exchanges and alternative forms of consumption, from shared spaces of community gardens and allotments, to produce exchanged for cash 'donations'. Belk (2010) argues sharing is a distinct, if under-acknowledged form of everyday non-monetary exchange, and a fundamental consumer behaviour which creates and strengthens bonds between people. In Belk's typology, sharing differs from commodity exchange and gift-giving in that there are *no* reciprocal expectations. Though participants often described redistribution of garden produce as 'sharing', connoting ideals of giving free from self-interested expectations, in practice there is frequent slippage between the three different forms of consumption outlined by Belk (2010), influenced by context, relationship of transactors and types of things transacted. Whilst Belk (2010: 718) attempts to delineate their unique reciprocities, he concedes that "[t]he lines between gift giving, sharing, and commodity exchange are imprecise".

Much existing work on sharing relates to domestic contexts. Valentine and Hughes (2012) and Klocker et al. (2012), for example, consider negotiation of shared domestic spaces and resources, addressing internet gambling and extended family households, respectively. Whilst such studies illustrate the tensions and emotional dimensions of maintaining individuality within the family home, this investigation of seed savers' practice uncovers how relatively individual gardening pursuits are socialised and imagined as practiced with spatially disparate others. Renewed interest in contemporary sharing economies suggests closer inspection of the extension of intimate sharing relationships beyond immediate kinship groups in purposeful events or networks (Albinsson and Yasanthi Perera 2012). Studies of disposal and divestment of goods, including food (Cappellini 2009), clothing (Gregson and Beale 2004), and family heirlooms (Curasi et al. 2004) prove fruitful here in theorising the intersection of thrift, sociability and notions of "extended self" (Tian and Belk 2005; Belk 2010) as items circulate within and beyond the household. This reveals the significance within "practices of discard" (Crewe 2011: 27), as Cappellini (2009: 367) notes: "it is not only in consuming that we underline our belonging within society, rather it is also through divestment that we reaffirm such a belonging – in particular through our choice of conduits".

Though I draw predominantly on Belk's (2010) definition of sharing, it is not without critique. Arnould and Rose (2015: 10) argue Belk's formulation has an overly 'utilitarian, transactional focus' finding his notion of 'extended self' depends on an egocentric model of social action. The authors instead propose the concept of *mutuality*, which, they suggest, encompasses 'a normative expectation of how actors in a given situation ought to behave' (2015: 11), is *not* altruistic but rather 'entails belief in the reciprocal tie that is manifest in future acts of giving by the receiving party' and 'presupposes the inclusivity of a shared social fabric amongst the actors' (2015: 15).

Significant in this engagement with mutuality, indicated in Kropotkin's (1902) earlier theory of mutual aid, is the recognition that reciprocity extends across time and space. More recently, McKie et al.'s (2002: 918) discussion of time-space and care work proposes the notion of 'caringscapes' as a "way of imagining the spatial-temporal nature of everyday life, which is more usually taken as a simple, unexplored given". Also relevant is Barnett and Land's (2007: 1073) questioning of the preoccupation with delineating self-interested and altruistic behaviour in moral geographies. The authors stress their interrelationship though the notion of 'generosity', which they argue is a fundamental and "constitutive practice of sociality, community, and being together". The related, yet distinct concepts of mutuality, generosity and reciprocity refine Belk's conceptualisation by drawing out the multidirectional and temporally expansive nature of sharing and gifting. As Arnould and Rose (2015) propose, addressing normative expectations of seed saving communities is crucial to understand what makes savers' practices meaningful in light of the multidimensional crises outlined above.

Whilst participants did not form a clearly outlined, geographically situated community or social movement, they were loosely connected by episodic moments of exchange. These moments helped foster imaginings of seed saving and seasonally clustered tasks as shared amongst a wider, dispersed network of gardeners. The ethnographic methodology entailed serial interviews, and my participation in seed saving and exchange. I volunteered as a seed guardian, cultivating endangered tomatoes for HSL, and swapped seeds grown in my own allotment. The spaces of research ranged from private backyards, allotments and community gardens, to kitchens, market stalls and organised swap events. Sharing and gifting were significant practices in all these spaces, exhibited in differing formations, often with complex, more-than-material reciprocities.

The following discussion interrogates contemporary expressions of the ideals of sharing and gifting as they are extended within organised networks. It addresses collective aspects of seed swapping, considering how feelings of "communality and connectedness" (Weinberger and Wallendorf 2012: 16) develop in light of political, economic and ecological issues around food and seed. I unpick the complex reciprocal dimensions of seed saving and exchanging practices, and outline how reciprocities manifest in temporally staggered, material, emotional and interpersonal rewards entail anticipating and imagining gifts being passed forward to others. These reciprocities are rarely rationally calculating, but other-regarding, generative of community and meaningful interpersonal relationships, and embedded within ordinary concerns and enthusiasms (Barnett and Land 2007; Hall 2011). Exchanges between gardeners are shown to entail expectations of similar actions in others (Albinsson and Yasanthi Perera 2012), and generation of diverse economies, ethical subjectivities and relationships.

Sharing in ordinary concerns, enthusiasms and sociabilities

Whilst conducting fieldwork I was drawn into complex, temporally extended sharing and gifting relationships with participants. These ranged from those part of everyday relations of care in gardens and allotments, to swap events and organised seed exchange networks, where clearer reciprocal expectations were apparent. Within growing spaces seedlings, cuttings, crops and seeds were routinely circulated (Ellen and Platten 2011; Platten 2013). Several participants explained items were free to take when left on communal paths between allotment plots, or designated spaces at community gardens. This redistribution appears closer to one-sided, altruistic sharing (Belk 2010) because it affords the possibility of anonymity. As I will show, however, though ideals of giving free from expectation of material (particularly monetary) return surfaced frequently, unpicking seed savers' narratives and observed practices indicates complex reciprocities, expectations and emotional investments are entangled with ideas about giving freely and practicing generosity (Barnett and Land 2007).

Gardeners' purposeful distributions of produce extend beyond territorially defined communities of allotments or organised networks. Seed guardian Emma (30–39, Greater Manchester) leaves bags of rhubarb on a neighbour's doorstep; allotment neighbours Cathy (50–59, Greater Manchester) and Nathan (20–29, Greater Manchester) take produce to the local pub and save windfall apples for the manure man's horses. Examining the spaces of these interactions brings into view the social networks that sharing and gift-ing relations are embedded within, and the types of recipients sought out and embroiled in practices of generosity (Barnett and Land 2007; Smith and Jehlička 2013).

Clive and Cathy recently became seed guardians. They share their allot-ment with two beehives and often Nathan, who visits from the neighbouring plot. Clive takes some produce into work, but also donates excess to charities and food banks for redistribution:

> [Y]ou need to share it. You don't need to bulk keep it, or anything like that. If we grow excess, we share it, we take it all out, and as much as we can, we don't want to let it rot either. You know, it's a sin. So any excess that you've got. Send it out. And if you have to, make the effort to do that, amongst your neighbours, your friends.
> (Clive, allotment holder and seed guardian, 60–69, Greater Manchester)

'Sharing' food is both obligation and pleasure. It's a 'sin' to hoard food or passively 'let it rot', and Clive argues gardeners have a responsibility to 'make the effort' to 'send it out'. Giving produce away means Clive avoids nega-tive emotions felt watching valued produce decay, as well as facilitating social relationships.

The interrelated everyday ethical (Hall 2011) concerns of maximising affordable access to varied, interesting plants with avoiding waste means individuals develop creative arrangements to both divest of and source gar-den produce. New seed guardian Nathan has found innovative money saving sources to pursue his enthusiasm for collecting. Walking in Nathan's allot-ment reveals the extended biographies (Appadurai 2014) of his plants, and diverse social relationships that take root and are tended in his allotment:

> [T]hese lavenders here I got six for … or, we got twelve for … 9.99 on QVC […] because I used to help out in a resource centre before it closed. And the girl put a two with me, she got six, and I got six. They've come on like I don't know what. They were only plug plants.
> (Nathan, allotment holder and seed guardian, 20–29, Greater Manchester)

Nathan's gardening practices and his stories recruit others into an extended sharing dynamic. He splits seed packets with neighbour Cathy, and persuades neighbours to collect newspaper coupons:

CATHY: I've bought different seeds, and we've had a lot of good offers, haven't we Nathan? I mean we had newspaper offers. I mean, he's the coupon collecting king. He really is.

NATHAN: Daily Mail, Daily Mirror. I collect so many tokens. I was getting the next-door neighbours to get the newspaper, just to get the tokens.

(Cathy, allotment holder and seed guardian, 50–59, Greater Manchester; Nathan, allotment holder and seed guardian, 20–29, Greater Manchester)

In tandem with consumptive desires for acquiring and collecting seeds, redistributing excess helps individuals overcome concerns with hoarding and waste, by avoiding practical and emotional discomforts associated with decaying food or squandered potential. The emotional labours and strategic approaches to acquiring and disposing of garden produce suggest, as others note, that consumption can be an invested form of craft (Campbell 2005) or work (Ulver-Sneistrup et al. 2011).

Though divested produce was often explained as reducing waste, gardeners also deliberately sowed extra seeds to provide young plants to give away (Ellen and Platten 2011; Platten 2013). Though some sold a small proportion of their produce, the socially generative dimensions of deliberately produced excess should not be understated. Barbara, a seed swap organiser and volunteer explains the emotional and affective rewards derived from swapping seeds, both informally with allotment neighbours and at organised events. She describes feeling 'connected' with local and distant places and natures through seed saving practices which link 'like-minded' individuals:

> I'm swapping flower seeds with my neighbour who grows the funny gourds. And mange touts [with] the neighbour on the other side. It goes on all the time. And, um, it feels connected. You know, it feels connected in so many ways. And also, it's just, the joy of, um, avoiding the commercial world, in relation to seeds. [...] Keeping it out of the commercial field as it were, and making it a community owned thing. So it's connection with the land, with the plants, with the community. Like-minded souls.
>
> (Barbara, allotment holder and seed swap organiser, 60–69, Brighton and Hove)

In Barbara's narrative the political, economic and ecological rationales of conscious, alternative consumption, 'avoiding the commercial world' and connecting with the environment intertwine with associations with a 'like-minded' community. Interpersonal practices of generous exchange connect with efforts to resist and creatively rework consumption practices in light of corporate concentration and disconnected food systems.

Similar sentiments arose in conversations with long-standing seed guardian, Jean, as she explained how sharing seeds helps address ecological issues of narrowed biodiversity:

> [I]t's no use having everything all in one place, there. No, I share it with other people who are like-minded, you know, [the local] horticultural society, the allotmenteers, that kind of thing, so its spread in this area [...] As long as they've been outed further, that was the whole idea.
>
> (Jean, allotment holder and seed guardian, 80–89, Greater Manchester)

Jean's acts of sharing amongst local gardeners illustrates the interrelationship of practices of sociability in communities of intent with broader hopes for conserving rare varieties. This extract indicates, however, there is some selectivity in Jean's 'sharing', as seeds are strategically distributed to those who are 'like-minded'.

Examining seed savers' exchange arrangements reveals gardeners orchestrating multifarious sharing and gifting opportunities to divest of excess, maximise diversity and maintain bonds with other growers (Belk 2010). These everyday ethical dimensions are entangled with individuals' negotiations and responses to wider ecological, political and social concerns. Non-monetary exchanges facilitate the practice of ideals of giving freely. They are imagined as taking place within wider communities of intent, and entail expectations that seeds, plants, and diverse economic relationships will be continued. Unusual seeds, cuttings and food products, particularly those difficult to source commercially are passed on to encourage others to cultivate, indicating reciprocities that are complex, generalised, temporally delayed and more-than-material, as I now discuss.

Expectations of continued care and circulation

As meaningful relationships developed throughout the research, I was given numerous items by participants that acknowledged our common enthusiasms and gardening interests. Susan, a retired Cheshire dairy farmer and seed guardian, gave seeds, courgettes, quince, offered to cut me pea sticks, and made sure we foraged enough fruit from nearby hedgerows to try her sloe gin recipe. Standing in the outbuilding holding her apple harvest, she gestured to the brimming shelves and said: "[w]hatever you can eat, manage, cope with, give away. You can take with you." Notable in her generous offer of what I could 'manage' and 'cope with', however, is a sense I might be relieving something of the burden of wasted crops. Furthermore, Susan's produce comes with an expectation that I too should give excess to friends or family. As Chevalier (2014: 57) notes, in situations where there is a meaningful relationship between giver and receiver, "when a present is given, there is indeed a transfer of possession but not a complete transfer of ownership, which, in a way, becomes joint". The process of producing and distributing entails both interpersonal negotiation in the private relationship between giver and receiver, *and* a sense that through correlated expectations of sharing beyond the dyadic relationship, garden produce becomes a commonly owned resource. This partial transferral and broadening of ownership of plants, produce and seeds as they are shared and gifted is implicated in reciprocal expectations about continued care and circulation.

The perishable nature of Susan's apples implies a relatively urgent responsibility to share, and corresponding reciprocities that are vague, generalised, and relating to mundane concerns of thrift, waste and sociability outlined earlier. Exchanges of seeds, particularly rare, precious or heirloom varieties, exhibited differing reciprocities, and at times appeared closer to gifting or commodity exchange in Belk's (2010) typology. This is particularly evident when looking beyond everyday relations of care and reciprocity in gardens and allotments to consider organised seed swaps, circles and other collectives in more detail. Though seeds are ultimately perishable, their unique materialities, temporalities and propagative capacities result in exchanges with clearer expectations.

Seed guardian Anita explains that along with sending seeds to HSL, she targets gifts to others likely to continue their cultivation and propagation:

> [W]hat I do to pass them on to other people, you know, in very tiny quantities, is to say look, this is precious, this is what to do with it. I think that's important.
>> (Anita, gardener and seed guardian, 30–39, Greater Manchester)

Similarly, seed guardian and community garden organiser Louise stresses her role entails giving seeds away to widen their ownership (Chevalier 2014). This safeguards rare varieties both by physically spreading seeds, but also promoting practices of saving and swapping:

> [Y]ou're kind of like a little protector really of that variety of seed. And, you then try and encourage everyone else. If you do give a packet of ten seeds away to your friends, you'll tell them to save from them and spread them.
>> (Louise, community garden and seed circle organiser, 40–49,
>> Nottinghamshire)

Louise's gifts entail reciprocal expectations that others will grow, multiply and disperse her seeds further. Significantly, given the reproductive capacities of seeds (Phillips 2008) their possession does not preclude others from growing and therefore sharing ownership and responsibility for their conservation. 'Outing' seeds through gifting is crucial to spreading risk and managing seeds as common resources. Giving away treasured varieties also serves as a gentle prompt, a 'quiet' activism (Askins 2014; Smith et al. 2015; Smith and Jehlička 2013) encouraging conservation and further non-monetary economies.

Hopes and expectations of seeds' continuation are also apparent beyond the dyadic gifting relationships and reciprocities outlined in Anita and Louise's strategic bequests (Curasi et al. 2004). Organised swap events like Seedy Sunday complicate these more straightforward gifts (Albinsson and Yasanthi Perera 2012), and entail a spectrum of transactions ranging from seeds purchased for 50 pence (ostensibly commodity exchange) (Belk 2010), to unbalanced, unidirectional flows of plant material, labour, and expertise shared by enthusiastic seed savers and volunteers. Barbara, who organises a seed swap and promotes local seed circles, contributes many seeds each year, including some which hold particular appeal:

> I save a pea called Prew's Special, which is a wonderful heritage variety. And I always put some into Seedy Sunday, and every year I look to see if

any come back. [...] [M]aybe they do and then get snapped up again, I don't know ... but I have never actually seen any come back. I wish they would.
(Barbara, allotment holder and seed swap organiser, 60–69, Brighton and Hove)

Analogous to desires expressed by Anita and Louise are Barbara's hopes and wishes that others grow, save and swap the progeny of her plants. Though Barbara's repeated sharing of her favourite peas entails less specific or targeted expectations, Barbara imagines the seeds circulating and returning to be distributed amongst the Seedy Sunday community, and seeks out material evidence as she looks for them on the swap table each year.

Seed guardian Louise elaborates on the satisfaction in knowing her seeds have been propagated:

I like to see other people growing my seeds, and then, like, someone was growing Wild Pigeon beans this year. And I was a seed guardian for that five years ago. So the seeds I grew, now my friend [is] growing through a completely different route. [...] And then she was saving those for one of my seed circles this year. So I'm gonna get it back, the babies of the ones that I've saved.
(Louise, community garden and seed circle organiser, 40–49, Nottinghamshire)

Through her voluntary work guarding seeds and organising local and virtual seed circles (organised saving and swapping collectives), Louise sees how her acts have enabled and motivated others to save and reciprocate. Pride and satisfaction for Louise accrues less in material counter gifts of seeds, but rather in knowing the practice of saving and swapping, about which Louise is passionate, has been continued.

Returning to the everyday spaces and practices of cultivation underscores the importance placed by savers on the extended social lives (Appadurai 2014) of swapped plants and seeds. As Crewe (2011: 44) suggests, '[t]hings rarely hold value in themselves as objects but act as material memory joggers to an emotional state or moment that their owners want to recapture.' Whilst others note the significance of garden plants in maintaining cultural connections or memories of distant places (Brook 2003; Nazarea 2005), they also facilitate imaginings of futurity and hopes for generating collective, cultural memory (Smart 2007; Curasi et al. 2004).

Somewhat akin to Hill's (2013) depiction of the 'spectral' quality of historical objects, Carolan's (2007) research found savers recognised seeds as 'living histories', connecting to those who had previously protected them, and to future generations. Whilst walking together in allotments and gardens, participants relayed to me not only how they had acquired seeds and plants, but stories of their plants' onward journeys: cuttings fed into public gardens (Jean, allotment holder and seed guardian, 80–89, Greater Manchester,) or passed to knowledgeable gardeners (Anita, gardener and seed guardian, 30–39, Greater Manchester); varieties now grown at the opposite end of the allotment (Cathy, allotment holder and seed guardian, 50–59, Greater Manchester) or the other side of the world (Louise, community garden and seed circle organiser, 40–49, Nottinghamshire).

Nick organises a local swap and sells seed packets for small charitable donations when opening his garden to the public each year. As we packaged seed together for the forthcoming swap event, Nick imagined his seeds' continued existence and cultivation:

> I … really like the idea that you give, or … sell for charity, essentially you give them to people, who want them, and you know they're going to sow them. It's not like a … jar of something, or a paperweight, or a bookmark. Or something which is just going to get dusty and thrown away. You know, it will, they will be sown. […] Because that's what gardeners do with seeds.
>
> (Nick, gardener and seed swap organiser, 40–49, Brighton and Hove)

As well as finding pleasure fulfilling the desires of others by offering 'gifts' *wanted* by the receiver, Nick's seeds are imagined continuing beyond the transaction and mere possession, as he states 'they will be sown'. Unlike the heirloom objects strategically gifted in Curasi et al.'s (2014) analysis, the propagative capacities of seeds (Phillips 2008) combined with gardeners' enthusiasms and seasonally repeated practices converge to structure Nick's expectations of the continued, agentive social lives (Appadurai 2014) of his seeds.

Also imagining seeds' continuity, Claire, who cultivates a large garden and orchard alongside her partner, describes feeling responsible for saving as many seeds as possible:

> I don't eat any of mine normally. I just grow the whole lot … to save. Um, so I think, I sort of feel […] that you've achieved something because it's … it's something that's perpetual. You think well, you're giving something back that's going to go out many fold to lots of people. […] But also they're going to carry on, you know, for years hence … so I think you get that sense of achievement from doing it as well. It goes on and on and on … and obviously keeps that particular strain going for years.
>
> (Claire, gardener and seed guardian, 40–49, Derbyshire)

Claire relinquishes the pleasure of eating her pea crop so the maximum quantity can be returned to HSL, which she explains by referencing their 'perpetual' nature. Her sense of 'achievement' hinges on their widest possible distribution. Like other gardeners drawn upon here, Claire's practices of care and nurture in her garden 'carry on' through plant material stretched over time and space. Seed savers' 'extended selves' (Belk 2010; Tian and Belk 2005) are projected, imagined and circulated as their seeds are propagated and shared by others. These extended selves are difficult to disentangle from the wider community of like-minded gardeners, environments and natures in which sharing and exchanging practices are located (Arnould and Rose 2015).

Conclusion

Sharing is fundamental to everyday allotment and gardening culture, enabling connections with people, places, and times to be sustained, imagined, and remembered (Ellen and Platten 2011). Swapped seeds form material and cultural connections not only in dyadic relationships of giving and receiving (Belk 2010), but in the affective and emotional resonance of gardening 'with' a wider community (Albinsson and Yasanthi Perera 2012). Exchanges of plant material confer only a partial transfer of ownership (Chevalier 2014), and thus extend gardeners' individual practices spatially and temporally. 'Ownership' incorporates collective obligations to nurture, share and spread seeds, thereby extending the scope of caring responsibilities. Seed sharing therefore represents a collective, ethical and political practice that challenges the commodification of food and seed.

These findings have important implications for theorising diverse economies and activist practice premised on non-monetary exchange, by highlighting how everyday ethical (Hall 2011) and interpersonal dimensions of cultivation, consumption and divestment (Cappellini 2009; Crewe 2011) work to both shape and perform practices of care for environments and others (Barnett et al. 2011; Smith and Jehlička 2013). The case of seed saving illustrates clearly that individuals understand, rework and problematise everyday consumption and cultivation in the context of complex challenges of biodiversity loss, corporate control and disconnected food systems. Giving away excess addresses concerns with hoarding, waste and thrift, and mitigates risk of losing cherished varieties. Responses to the multidimensional crises in seed and food production are intimately bound with practices of sociability, mutuality and generosity (Arnould and Rose 2015; Barnett and Land 2007; Smith and Jehlička 2013).

Although seed savers spoke about 'sharing' and giving freely, exchange relationships were laden with complex more-than-material reciprocities and rewards, manifest within anticipations of mutual care and circulation (Arnould and Rose 2015). These subtle variations in reciprocal expectation indicate further analysis might further interrogate tensions emerging as intimate, domestic sharing arrangements are scaled-up or framed by explicitly activist rationales (Albinsson and Yasanthi Perera 2012). Furthermore, the collective responsibilities and subjectivities instigated and required by sharing practices identified here have broader application. Seed savers felt their acts of generosity helped generate, perpetuate or maintain alternative, non-monetary economies amongst extended communities of like-minded gardeners. These findings speak to a spectrum of consumption, environmental and social justice challenges, including issues around food waste, community gardening and food cooperatives. They also suggest that sharing food, plants and other items might be a productive strategy for developing collective action around a broad range of concerns extending beyond food production and distribution (Albinsson and Yasanthi Perera 2012; Wilson 2013). The interpersonal, reciprocal and imaginative dimensions of consumption and cultivation emerge as significant motivations for ethical, sustainable and activist practice.

Notes

1 Produced by cross-pollination. Controlled hybrids can result in desirable, uniform characteristics in the first generation (F1), but subsequent generations do not retain this consistency, making them less suitable for home seed saving.
2 Non-hybrid/F1 seeds that breed true to type can be saved relatively easily by home-gardeners and are said to increase biodiversity.

References

Aistara, G.A. (2014) 'Actually existing tomatoes: politics of memory, variety, and empire in Latvian struggles over seeds', *Focaal* 2014(69): 12–27.
Albinsson, P.A. and Yasanthi Perera, B. (2012) 'Alternative marketplaces in the 21st century: building community through sharing events', *Journal of Consumer Behaviour* 11(4): 303–315.
Appadurai, A. (Ed.) (2014) *The Social Life of Things: Commodities in Cultural Perspective*. 12th edn. Cambridge: University Press.
Arnould, E.J. and Rose, A.S. (2015) 'Mutuality: critique and substitute for Belk's "sharing"' *Marketing Theory* 21(4): 254–263.
Askins, K (2014) 'A quiet politics of being together: Miriam and Rose', *Area*, 46(4): 353–354.
Barnett, C. and Land, D. (2007) 'Geographies of generosity: beyond the "moral turn"' *Geoforum* 38(6): 1065–1075.
Belk, R. (2010) 'Sharing', *Journal of Consumer Research*, 36(5): 715–734.
Brook, I. (2003) 'Making here like there: place attachment, displacement and the urge to garden' *Ethics, Place and Environment*, 6(3): 227–234.
Campbell, C. (2005) 'The craft consumer: culture, craft and consumption in a post-modern society' *Journal of Consumer Culture*, 5(1): 23–42.
Campbell, B. (2012) 'Open-pollinated seed exchange: renewed Ozark tradition as agricultural biodiversity conservation' *Journal of Sustainable Agriculture*, 36(5): 500–522.
Cappellini, B. (2009) 'The sacrifice of re-use: the travels of leftovers and family relations' *Journal of Consumer Behaviour*, 8(6): 365–375.
Carolan, M.S. (2007) 'Saving seeds, saving culture: a case study of a heritage seed bank', *Society and Natural Resources'*, 20(8): 739–750.
Castree, N. (2003) 'Commodifying what nature?' *Progress in Human Geography*, 27(3): 273–297.
Chevalier, S. (2014) 'Turning commodities into presents', *Journal of Classical Sociology*, 14(1): 54–64.
Crewe, L. (2011) 'Life itemised: lists, loss, unexpected significance, and the enduring geographies of discard', *Environment and Planning D: Society and Space*, 29(1): 27–46.
Curasi, C.F., Price, L.L. and Arnould, E.J. (2004) 'How individuals' cherished possessions become families' inalienable wealth', *Journal of Consumer Research*, 31(3): 609–622.

Deibel, E. (2013) 'Open variety rights: Rethinking the commodification of plants', *Journal of Agrarian Change*, 13(2): 282–309.

Demeulenaere, E. (2014) 'A political ontology of seeds: the transformative frictions of a farmers' movement in Europe', *Focaal*, 2014(69): 45–61.

Deppe, C. (2000) *Breed your own Vegetable Varieties: The Gardener's and Farmer's Guide to Plant Breeding and Seed Saving*. Vermont: Chelsea Green Publishing.

Ellen, R. and Platten, S. (2011) 'The social life of seeds: the role of networks of relationships in the dispersal and cultural selection of plant germplasm', *Journal of the Royal Anthropological Institute*, 17(3): 563–584.

ETC Group. (2013) 'Putting the cartel before the horse ... and farm, seeds, soil, peasants, etc: who will control agricultural inputs, 2013?' *ETC Group Communique*, 111.

Gibson-Graham, J.K. (1996) *The End of Capitalism (As We Knew It): A Feminist Critique of Political Economy*. Oxford: Blackwell.

Gibson-Graham, J.K. (2006) *A Postcapitalist Politics*. Minnesota: University Press.

Gregson, N. and Beale, V. (2004) 'Wardrobe matter: the sorting, displacement and circulation of women's clothing' *Geoforum*, 35(6): 689–700.

Hall, S.M. (2011) 'Exploring the "ethical everyday": an ethnography of the ethics of family consumption' *Geoforum* 42(6): 627–637.

Hill, L. (2013) 'Archaeologies and geographies of the post-industrial past: Landscape, memory and the spectral' *Cultural Geographies*, 20(3): 379–396.

Kastler, G. (2005) *EU seed laws in Europe: locking farmers out*. Available at: https://www.grain.org/article/entries/541-seed-laws-in-europe-locking-farmers-out (Accessed: 15 August 2015).

Klocker, N., Gibson, C., and Borger, E. (2012) 'Living together but apart: material geographies of everyday sustainability in extended family households', *Environment and Planning A*, 44(9): 2240–2259.

Kloppenburg, J.R. (2004) *First the Seed: The Political Economy of Plant Biotechnology, 1492–2000*. 2nd edn. Cambridge: University Press.

Kropotkin, P. (1902) *Mutual Aid*. London: William Heinemann.

Leyshon, A., Lee, R. and Williams, C.C. (eds.) (2003) *Alternative Economic Spaces*. London: Sage.

Louwaars, N.P. (2002) 'Variety controls', *Journal of New Seeds*, 4(1–2): 131–142.

Morris, C. and Kirwan, J. (2010) 'Food commodities, geographical knowledges and the reconnection of production and consumption: The case of naturally embedded food products', *Geoforum*, 41(1): 131–143.

Müller, B. (2014) The seed and the citizen: Biosocial networks of confiscation and destruction in Canada. *Focaal*, 2014(69): 28–44.

Nazarea, V.D. (2005) *Heirloom Seeds and their Keepers: Marginality and Memory in the Conservation of Biological Diversity*. Tucson: University of Arizona Press.

Pautasso, M., Aistara, G., Barnaud, A., Caillon, S., Clouvel, P., Coomes, O.T., Delêtre M., Demeulenaere E., De Santis P., Döring T., Eloy L., Emperaire L., Garine E., Goldringer I., Jarvis D., Joly H., Leclerc C., Louafi S., Martin P., Massol F., McGuire S., McKey D.B., Padoch C., Soler C., Thomas M., Tramontini S. (2013) 'Seed exchange networks for agrobiodiversity conservation: a review', *Agronomy for Sustainable Development*, 33(1): 151–175.

Phillips, C. (2008) 'Canada's evolving seed regime: relations of industry, state, and seed savers', *Environments: A Journal of Interdisciplinary Studies*, 36(1): 5–18.

Phillips, C. (2013) *Saving More than Seeds: Practices and Politics of Seed Saving*. Surrey: Ashgate Publishing, Ltd.

Platten, S. (2013) Plant exchange and social performance, in Ellen, R., Lycett, S.J. and Johns, S.E. [eds.] *Understanding Cultural Transmission in Anthropology: A Critical Synthesis*. Oxford: Berghahn Books, 300–319.

Pottinger, L. (2013) 'Ethical food consumption and the city', *Geography Compass*, 7(9): 659–668.

Purdue, D. (2000) 'Backyard biodiversity: seed tribes in the west of England', *Science as Culture* 9(2): 141–166.

Shiva, V. (1993) *Monocultures of the Mind: Perspectives on Biodiversity and Biotechnology*. London: Zed Books.

Smart, C. (2007) *Personal Life*. Cambridge: Polity.

Smith, J. and Jehlička, P. (2013) 'Quiet sustainability: fertile lessons from Europe's productive gardeners' *Journal of Rural Studies* 32: 148–157.

Smith, J., Kostelecký, T. and Jehlička, P. (2015) 'Quietly does it: questioning assumptions about class, sustainability and consumption', *Geoforum*, 67: 223–232.

Stickland, S. (2008) *Back Garden Seed Saving: Keeping our Vegetable Heritage Alive*. Bath: Eco-Logic Books.

Tian, K. and Belk, R.W. (2005) 'Extended self and possessions in the workplace', *Journal of Consumer Research* 32(2): 297–310.

Turner, B. (2011) 'Embodied connections: sustainability, food systems and community gardens' *Local Environment* 16(6): 509–522.

Ulver-Sneistrup, S., Askegaard, S. and Kristensen, D.B. (2011) 'The new work ethics of consumption and the paradox of mundane brand resistance' *Journal of Consumer Culture*, 11(2): 215–238.

UPOV (2015) *The UPOV system of plant variety protection*. Available at: http://www.upov.int/about/en/upov_system.html#what_is_a_pv (Accessed: 25 February 2015).

Valentine, G. and Hughes, K. (2012) 'Shared space, distant lives? Understanding family and intimacy at home through the lens of internet gambling' *Transactions of the Institute of British Geographers*, 37(2): 242–255.

Weinberger, M.F., and Wallendorf, M. (2012) 'Intracommunity gifting at the intersection of contemporary moral and market economies' *Journal of Consumer Research*, 39(1): 74–92.

Wilson, A.D. (2013) 'Beyond alternative: exploring the potential for autonomous food spaces' *Antipode* 45(3): 719–737.

Winge, T. (2015) 'Seed legislation in Europe and crop genetic diversity', *Sustainable Agriculture Reviews* 15: 1–64.

3 Malleable homes and mutual possessions

Caring and sharing in extended family households as a resource for survival

Chris Gibson, Natascha Klocker, Erin Borger and Sophie-May Kerr

Introduction

Families in contemporary urban settings in the Minority World face multiple interrelated and complex predicaments. Austerity policies aimed at reducing government budget deficits have eroded basic service provision and harshened economic outlooks in ways that place added stress on family life (Hall 2016). The spectre of environmental crisis looms large, and a suite of policies is increasingly targeting households as change agents (Head et al. 2013). Meanwhile, within cities, housing is becoming ever more unaffordable. Demand for new dwellings has outstripped population growth due to a confluence of socio-demographic trends that contribute to shrinking average household sizes: population ageing, high rates of divorce and delayed age of family formation (Wulff et al. 2004). In Australia, where the authors live and work, one-quarter of households now contain just one person (ABS 2012). Similar socio-demographic processes, with associated urban, social, sustainability and spatial planning implications, have unfurled throughout Europe, the United Kingdom and North America (Buzar et al. 2005, Rérat 2012). Families are at once subject to such intersecting external pressures, and are key "agents of urban transformation" (Buzar et al. 2005: 413) with influence over environmental and socio-economic trends. Crises are multiple, and are often mutually reinforcing, or held in tension, as when trade-offs emerge between financial (or temporal) poverty, caring duties, and desires to reduce environmental burden (Gibson et al. 2013). Families are a fundamental, everyday social unit where such tensions are played out and resolved.

Extended family living – in which various configurations of adult children, parents, grandparents, siblings, aunts, uncles and grandchildren reside under one roof – has been the norm for human society for millennia, and remains so in much of the Majority World. Yet it became considered 'unusual' in the Minority World in the modernist age of the nuclear family. More recently, extended family living constitutes a statistically slight, but growing, counter-trend to shrinking household sizes in the Minority World, where extended families increasingly cohabit in single households, for a mix of reasons. Although overshadowed by the overall demographic shift to smaller average household sizes, rates of extended family living have risen in the US, Europe and Australia in recent years due to financial crisis, high housing costs, marital breakdown (and remarriage), delayed age of home leaving, population ageing and the growing presence of migrants from countries where extended family living is common (Allan et al. 2011; Keene and Batson 2010). An increasing number of adult children have remained in (or returned to) the parental home (Stanes et al. 2015). With an undersupply of housing and rising property prices, combined with rising youth unemployment, precarious working arrangements and increasing years spent in education, this trend is likely to continue.

The formation of larger household units such as these presents opportunities to contemplate what kinds of future living arrangements are possible in an austere and more ecologically volatile world, and whether they are less resource intensive. The current persistent state of global recession amplifies – and complicates – possibilities and implications of sharing in extended family households (cf. Hall 2015). Austerity measures currently unfurling in Greece, the UK and elsewhere, coupled with structural adjustment programs that punish poor households for national economic mismanagement, are likely to further fuel extended family household formation. We certainly do not intend here to advocate for austerity measures that regressively impact on the vulnerable, nor do we accept the social injustices contained therein. Nevertheless, hardship and sustainability are increasingly interwoven in light of ecological crises. Reductions in energy and resource use and overall material consumption are part of the necessary conversation to be had in response to climate change (Head et al. 2013), implying a degree of constraint with regard to material affluence. Increasingly, austerity discourses are being pinned to anti-consumerist sentiments as part of sustainability campaigns (Brammall 2011). Extended family living in many ways encapsulates a vision of what such material constraint in the home may look like, amidst hardship and ecological crisis.

In such circumstances, poverty and sustainability frequently interact to produce 'inadvertent environmentalisms' (Hitchings et al. 2015) where overly pro-environmental concerns may be less immediate than hardship in generating more sustainable practices. At the same time, financial and time poverty have been identified as dilemmas that prevent household investment in energy-reducing technologies, and that deepen dependence on unsustainable transport, food and consumer goods (cars, fast food, poor quality clothing), exacerbating environmental crises (Head et al. 2013). Rather than blame low-income households for apparently unsustainable practices, as is so often implied in media discourse, analysis should centre on the social and material conditions within which families juggle everyday decisions and pressures (Evans 2011). The nexus between socio-economic and environmental crises thus provides a distinctive context within which to identify and theorise noteworthy sharing practices.

To understand sharing in Minority World extended family households, and amidst complex interplays of socio-economic and environmental crises, this chapter builds on ethnographic work with extended family households in Australia. Distinct patterns of sharing were documented at the height of the global financial crisis, and at a time when climate change had become the preeminent national political issue (upon which a Federal election had been decided). Our ethnographic research took place in an industrial region suffering disproportionately from recessionary economic forces, and which had often born the blame as a 'carbon central' location contributing more to the problem of climate change than to solutions. In this context we sought to explore how unheralded sharing practices evolved among cohabiting extended families.

Our research intersects conceptually with the growing literature on practices of sharing, gifting and pooling of material resources (Ozanne and Ballantine 2010). We visit Belk's (2010: 715) conceptualisation of sharing as the dissolution of 'interpersonal boundaries posed by materialism and possession attachment through expanding the aggregate extended self'. Belk (2010: 720) has described 'mutuality of possession' as an important characteristic of sharing, differentiating unselfconscious acts of sharing from gift giving or non-monetary commodity exchange. Counter to arguments that modern life is defined by individualism and weakening kinship and familial ties (Duncan and Smith 2006), we observe through everyday sharing practices an abundance of instances of unconditional familial love and care, nonreciprocal sharing, and pooled resources (the use of which within extended families renders money irrelevant). Adding to this, the significance of such sharing practices is magnified given the sustainability dimension. At the same time, we confront what may be the observed limits to such boundary dissolution, as a consequence of the interplay of new and old household technologies, home designs, and persistent norms of privacy and self-identity. Identifying such limits is, we argue, important for further consideration of the potential of extended family living to promote sharing cultures in ways that cultivate collaboration and reduce resource burden.

These limits also point towards the agency of *space* in sharing arrangements. Building on Belk's (2010) conceptualisation of sharing, Griffiths and Gilly (2012) have argued the characteristics and dimensions of sharing space demand further attention. Griffiths and Gilly focus on sharing of public spaces, but literature on geographies of the home (see e.g. Dowling and Power 2012) remind us that the sharing of spaces within homes are also worthy of further attention, as the making of home and the cultural and material spaces of family and domestic practices ultimately shape and are shaped by available space. In particular, emerging alternative forms of co-habitation (cohousing, extended family households, share houses, urban consolidation etc.) bring to light the ways in which the shared occupation of space is practiced within domestic/private spheres (Munro and Madigan 1999). The physical spaces within the home and the social relations contained within them provide an important ground for understanding how individuals negotiate their daily lives through sharing practices.

With this in mind, we consult findings from our research to consider three important questions: Do larger households share space, appliances, clothes and other material things in ways that obviate the need for greater levels of consumption? How might we theorise such sharing practices amidst socio-economic hardship? Does sharing within larger familial households constitute an unheralded resource for survival in times of economic and ecological volatility? Conducted in 2010 at the height of the global financial crisis, our research below is informed by threads of scholarship on home and the household as a space of social life and relations of care (Cox 2010; Tarrant 2013), on everyday material sustainability practices (Lane and Gorman-Murray 2011), and on vernacular capacities to respond to economic and environmental crisis (Hall 2016). Pushing Belk's theorisation further, we argue that sharing extends the self through material objects in ways that are shaped by particular times of crisis and disruption, and in distinct physical contexts.

A note on definitions and method

We have deployed an expansive and inclusive definition of extended family living. As understood in this chapter, an extended family household is a nuclear family unit that has been extended to include three generations, or the families of more than one sibling. Extended family households may also be called multigenerational households, or multiple family households (Liu et al. 2013). Our definition includes – but is not limited to – adult children returning to the parental home (with or without their spouse and own children) and elderly parents living with an adult child. Each of these configurations brings together *related* individuals in a manner contrary to the 'norms' of nuclear (or single-parent) family living, and decreases the overall number of dwellings required. Our working definition of family was one defined by kinship and inter- and intra-generationality, rather than a families of choice approach that might include friends (though we acknowledge that families of choice are equally relevant and warrant research in the contexts of intersecting economic and environmental crises).

We follow Reid et al. (2010) and Blunt (2005) in defining a 'household' as a social unit occupying a single place or space of residence, notionally bounded by a physical structure, but constituted by social, cultural and economic relations that connect life within the home to processes, technologies and communities beyond. At the same time, we note that while there are some similarities between families and households, the two do not necessarily map onto one another.

Two key methods were used: semi-structured in-depth interviews with 17 participants from ten extended family households, and home tours (see Klocker et al. 2012 for further detail). Interviewees were recruited variously: four were volunteers from a prior survey we conducted on household sustainability (for further details, see Waitt et al. 2012); one was recruited via a Facebook group; and five via snowballing. All were located in Wollongong and southern Sydney. Interviews conducted in May–July 2010 explored how decisions about material resources and household spaces were made, and the values upon which decisions were based. Interviewees were asked about the highlights and challenges of extended family living, and what had motivated that arrangement. They were also asked how they shared and distributed space, appliances, consumables, transport and household tasks.

Households involved in our study included older family members who could not, or did not want to, live alone; and parents of young children who struggled to balance paid work and caring responsibilities. Our interviewees were primarily female (13 participants were women) and offered a multigenerational perspective (aged between 18 and 70 years). We interviewed whoever was willing to talk within a household, and sought representatives of different generations, though in many cases adequate representation across age groups was not forthcoming or feasible (for instance, it was not possible to interview children without breaching conditions set by our university ethics committee). Our sample was by no means representative of Australia's socioeconomic and cultural diversity – though some families were low-income and others comfortably middle-income, and four had migrant (Italian) backgrounds. All but one of the dwellings was owner-occupied. Our empirical discussion seeks to spotlight distinctive but unheralded sharing practices within these extended family households, and to identify limits to cultivating sharing practices amongst extended family households within the exigencies – and *spaces* – of everyday life.

Do larger households share in ways that reduce resource burdens?

The extended family households in our study contained an average of 4.3 occupants compared to a national average of 2.6 per household. As energy use and waste production per capita are inversely related to household size (Liu et al., 2003), these larger-than-average households foster economic savings and environmental benefits – without even trying (cf. Hitchings et al. 2015). Direct per capita energy consumption was curtailed when household members shared appliances and tasks; and also by heating, cooling and lighting one home (not two or three). Indirect energy consumption (stemming from the embodied energy contained in objects as a legacy of their extraction, production and transport) was also reduced by sharing and reusing material objects within the home, rather than purchasing separate items for discrete dwellings.

Identified examples of such sharing practices highlight the central role of material domestic space. Amongst our interviewees, the need to maintain some semblance of privacy within large households prompted a range of complicated boundary-making strategies around particular household spaces and activities (and the material objects entailed therein). As we argue below, close physical proximity enabled types of sharing that are difficult over greater distances. Equally, it led household members to be resolute in retaining some spaces and material objects for individual consumption.

The physical form of dwellings – and the specific nature of the spaces available to each family 'unit' within those dwellings – fundamentally affected the daily lives of the households in our sample, and their capacities to share. Physical space prompted household negotiations over the 'ideals and practicalities of entangled and mutual dwelling' (Nansen et al. 2011: 712). Some extended family households spent time together in living spaces (especially lounge rooms and kitchens) and did not substantially modify their dwellings. Usually, this was because the arrangement was short-term and there was insufficient space within the dwelling to create separate living spaces. Other extended family households – typically those in longer-term extended family living arrangements – effectively lived together but apart by duplicating 'communal' areas (e.g. kitchens, lounge rooms). There were key differences in the organisation of household spaces between the two household types.

In contrast to living spaces, laundry rooms and washing machines were universally shared across both types of extended family household – a classic example of Belk's 'mutuality of possession'. The act of washing laundry together is emotionally significant and linked to an ethic of care (Kaufmann 1998). From a sustainability perspective, embodied energy is saved by purchasing just one washing machine, and direct energy use is curtailed by running full loads of combined washing. Minimising half-loads is also significant for water use – a crucial issue where we write from in southeast Australia. Here, chronic water shortages have, at various times, led to domestic water-use restrictions. Shared laundry practices were thus both an unceremonial act of resource pooling – facilitated by the decision to share a dwelling – and a notable sustainability benefit.

Householders also shared clothing, which was passed between family members as needed. Leanne previously bought clothes regularly, but now shared her daughter's: "I'll come and try Jodi's on and then I'll go back to the shop after that if I can't find anything". Clothing was also shared in Pauline's house: "Melissa [adult daughter] and I would often share clothes. Megan and Patricia [sisters] share. So it does the rounds". Formal dresses, suits and other clothes for special occasions became mutual possessions, because "the girls can't see the point in buying something that they will only wear once or twice". Reuse and proximate sharing enabled fewer purchases to be made, reducing waste and overall consumption (Horne et al. 2011). Reuse is more likely to occur through familial and social networks, over short distances and via convenient, readily accessible channels (Lane et al. 2009). While also possible when family members live in separate homes, extended family living provides a particularly fertile setting for such exchanges.

In addition to clothing, the affordances of close physical proximity in shared domestic spaces were apparent in relation to cooking practices. Ingredients, kitchen appliances and food leftovers were circulated through household spaces, often in an explicit attempt to minimise waste. In those extended family households where separate kitchen spaces were present (half of our sample), proximity meant that household members did not have to double up on little-used kitchen appliances (sandwich toasters and pasta cookers) and they could make a last-minute dash up or downstairs to grab a missing ingredient. Leftover food was passed within and across family 'units' within the household because, as Marion stated, "It just makes sense to share it around rather than throwing it out. Food is too expensive to throw out". All of these (seemingly minor) acts of sharing, made possible when individuals live under one roof, mitigated financial hardship, but also cumulatively contributed to reduced material consumption.

Beyond clothes and food, other material resources were subject to mutual possession, nonreciprocal exchanges and inalienable familial relationships. Reflecting the general practice in Australian detached home-building since World War II, most homes featured car garages (including double and even triple garages) that had long since housed cars, and instead became important 'libraries' of dormant material goods and sentimental possessions. Material goods that were considered to have retained their use value as objects, irrespective of their newness/oldness, or their exchange value as second-hand goods, were stored in garages *en masse*: fridges, lounge suites, bookshelves, exercise bikes, vacuum cleaners, golf clubs, coffee tables (cf. Woodward 2015). Such practices are not unique to extended family households, but appeared more prevalent; the scope and complexity of the collections contained in garage 'libraries' were more ambitious than typically found in smaller families. Returning adult children (after divorce or travel) frequently stored their own separate, duplicate possessions in such garages. Garages were meticulously catalogued repositories of resources with implied shared ownership. Household members across generations could dip into, borrow and take stored items for their own rooms, or if they eventually moved back into their own separate premises – without the need for monetary exchange or expectation of reciprocity. Book, CD and DVD collections were often merged within main living spaces – resulting in larger, cherished libraries of diverse titles with more reading and listening options, especially for children. By extending the use value of goods, such sharing practices offset future anticipated financial outlays for new purchases, and inadvertently reduced future environmental burdens.

For the households involved in our study, the capacity to endure and enjoy extended family living hinged upon the ability to separate certain domestic spaces to achieve independence, privacy and harmony. Extended families were resolute about not sharing some spaces and objects. Across all the extended family households, there was universal reluctance to share televisions. Screens functioned as anchors for retreat from 'crowded' communal areas, and were used to maintain privacy. Multiple bedrooms were nonnegotiable – most had one bedroom per household member (including children). Where extended family household arrangements were short-term (e.g. adult children 'getting back on their feet' financially, or following travel or a relationship breakdown), daily rhythms tended to intersect more closely. Living spaces were jointly occupied, with attendant elevated levels of object sharing. A common strategy for maintaining a semblance of privacy was spending more time in personal spaces (e.g. in bedrooms). Where the extended family living arrangement was longer-term (e.g. elderly parents moving in with adult children), family members carefully created and maintained their own distinct spaces (Klocker et al. 2012). This mode of living was powerfully influenced by a culturally driven predilection for 'space'. The overarching dwelling was effectively shared, but the spaces in which everyday life is lived were 'cordoned' off.

In order to achieve such physical separation (in contexts of close proximity), longer-term extended family households sought dwellings with self-contained units, or which could be modified to create separate living spaces. Several interviewees noted that difficulties would arise if bathrooms were shared across nuclear and extended families – due to conflicting schedules and divergent cleanliness standards. For Marion, separate kitchens maintained harmony: "there's that old Chinese proverb, 'two women living under the same roof is disharmony' ... separate the kitchens ... then you're right." Gail, who had a kitchenette in her daughter's house, noted that being able to cook for herself made her 'granny flat' feel "much more like home". In part such concerns were a practical extension of varying time schedules and dietary preferences, but they also reflect the more-than-functional significance of kitchens as spaces of identity formation, creativity, gendered ethics of care, status and leisure (Meah 2014). Households with separate kitchens usually shopped, cooked and ate separately. Those with one shared kitchen shopped and cooked for the whole group, although family members sometimes ate at different times.

How might we theorise sharing practices amidst hardship?

At the time of our interviews in 2010 hardship was deeply felt by families throughout the country as a consequence of exposure to global economic crisis. Industries that were highly exposed suffered most – prominently tourism and manufacturing – and regions with concentrations of investment in those industries were especially hard hit. The bulk of our participants lived in southern Sydney and nearby Wollongong region, where such conditions prevailed.

Our participants cited two key motives for extended family living: financial imperatives and caring requirements, whether for elderly parents or young children (cf. Keene and Batson 2010). Environmental sustainability was neither a motive, nor volunteered as a positive outcome of the arrangement. When asked to describe what they enjoyed about their living arrangements, interviewees cited financial necessities and benefits, and opportunities to build caring and supportive familial relationships.

One participant, Jodi, "made the decision to move home to help Mum with the mortgage. I'd rather pay Mum rent than pay someone else rent". Another, Melissa (a single mother), "came back from America five months pregnant [laughs], so that was a good start. I couldn't get a job or anywhere to live so I stayed with Mum until Sophie was four months old, and then we moved out". Melissa subsequently quit her job to start a home-based childcare enterprise, but then amidst economic downturn

> lost the house and the day care and everything. I got into some debt so I moved home until I can catch up. Every time I catch up I get another setback. So I'm still trying to get back on track … And it's good for me financially. I can't afford rent on my own.

Rarely did the owner-occupying members of the extended family ask for full rent to cover mortgage costs; a small amount of board was typical, "just basically to help out with the groceries, it's not really going towards the house as a rental cost. Basically just paying for the food for the week and maybe help out with the electricity bill or the phone bill" (Michael). Sharing homes in this way extended bonds of family care in times of hardship, without the need for or expectation of reciprocity.

Extended family living also meant improved quality of life amidst financial constraints. Wendy explained:

> My mum was getting to the stage where she would have to move from her townhouse, as she one day would not be able to manage the stairs. So it was really a matter of pooling our financial resources so that we could have a house that Mum could live in as well. We were also anticipating that she would have increasing caring needs. So it was really just a matter of financial and caring convenience I guess.

Her husband, Wes, elaborated:

> Well for me, I guess it is different for both of us. What is on top of the list is that we got a beautiful house because we were able to combine our finances … We would have been in a much smaller house somewhere if we hadn't have done it like this.

In many cases, financial stress was a combined factor along with recently returning from travel, childcare needs, employment constraints or the desire to strengthen family bonds. One nuclear family had been living in Japan for about 8 years when they decided to move back to Australia, but could not afford to rent privately due to high housing costs and full-time study:

> It was a big risk moving back. I quit a job in Japan to move back so financial security was a big thing. So we had a choice to move in with my parents … At that stage we had a two-and-a-half-year-old and we thought it would give my parents a chance to bond with our son, and also it was more of a financial choice. Plus my wife is from Taiwan so she has no family here … My parents live in a two-bedroom townhouse, and it was a bit small. But they accommodated us too. They knew about our financial situation.
>
> (Mark)

In Michael's household, he and his adult sister (with her children and husband) moved back in with their parents in order to save money, and also to make complex everyday rhythms of work, childcare and family time run more smoothly:

> my sister was living in Corrimal in a three-bedroom house and when their son [Luke] came along, my sister was still working at the time and John was working as well. Grandparents are the best babysitters you can find, so just for my mum to drive all the way out to Corrimal to look after Luke, or for my sister to drop him all the way out to Dapto [20 kilometres away] was a bit of a mission. John is working Monday to Friday, ten hours a day and my sister is still juggling work around. So to have us all in the one household made it a lot easier for all parties, and it's really been really nice. Mum and Dad get to see Luke pretty much every day and watch him grow up. I think they both love it as well.

Hardship, while thus often a catalyst for extended family household formation, was not isolated from other factors and needs, including caring duties and time constraints.

Sharing as emotional support, and as an unheralded resource for survival

Extended family households generate living spaces with potentially more capacity to foster sharing and pooling practices, thus cultivating noncapitalist circuits of exchange of material goods and services in ways that reduce environmental burden, and respond to conditions of hardship and resource scarcity. Moreover, the household is a critical scale at which families encounter disruption and adjust while balancing competing pressures of everyday life (Collins 2015). In this important space, we argue, it is possible to observe practices that are, amidst economic and ecological volatility, "a catalogue of resources for survival" (Gibson et al. 2015: 420).

Amongst our study participants, marriage breakdown and losing a job were frequent precursors to extended family household formation – major disruptions in life with accompanying financial reverberations. Emotional spaces of sharing enabled compassion and companionship. One couple lived in an extended family household for 2 years prior to the interview after their son's marriage broke down acrimoniously:

> He had a marriage breakdown and they were in Western Australia, so he came home for a couple of years … It gave him the opportunity to save up for a house. He wouldn't have been able to do it while he was paying rent … he had no furniture or appliances when he moved in here. Just his clothes … The two years he stayed here, gave him the opportunity to save for the house and have the settlement finalised, because that takes time.
>
> (Neil)

Our participants felt comfort, and even joy, at hearing extended family members laugh through walls, floors and ceilings; likewise help was within reach if an elderly parent fell, or a young mother was at her wits' end with a screaming child in the middle of the night. Such everyday relations of care amidst disruption were intensified in close proximity – an important resource for a climate changing future where, for instance, heat waves will be more frequent and severe and where living alone will become a heightened vector of vulnerability (Farbotko and Waitt 2011). Melissa, a single-mother, lived with her own mother and adult sisters: "If I feel like I am losing it [at the child], I'll call mum, and mum will come down". Gail was widowed in recent years and subsequently moved in with her adult daughter, Gabrielle's, family. She commented, "One thing I like is that I can hear them up there". And Gabrielle, in turn, reflected:

> She [Gail] was in her own house for a little while after Dad died ... and we were both worried about if she was a bit lonely ... now we don't need to worry. We know that she is downstairs and if she wants to she'll come and say hello.

Extended family living fostered a sense of connectedness and contentment. Marion, who lived with her husband and adult daughter Patricia (together with Patricia's husband and two children), reflected:

> [I]t's a really nice way to live ... there's always somebody in this house so the kids don't come home to an empty house ... I think that's really lovely ... Before my father died, he lived here too, and so he was being cared for by the whole group ... He died here in this house which is what he wanted to do ... he had the emotional support around him.

Such narratives of care within and across generations were typical and widespread (cf. Tarrant 2013) and indicate the degree to which familial bonds beyond the 'conventional' nuclear family remain strong, even in an age of shrinking average household sizes (cf. Duncan and Smith 2006). Sharing a dwelling proved a most fundamental means to cement and express such bonds. Extended family living brought with it tensions, arguments over parenting methods, television shows and cooking. But importantly, in the face of increased future volatility – both economic and environmental – extended family living also provided a means to deepen family relationships and to cope with disruption and change.

Conclusions

In many areas of policy (sustainability, taxation, population planning) households are treated as black boxes – freestanding social units operating only at the local, domestic scale – filled with people and inert 'stuff' that is merely 'consumed' (Head et al. 2013). We by contrast have sought to explore 'configurations of people and material things whose social and ecological relations are diverse, shifting and complex' (Head et al. 2013: 2). The 'stable' and persistent dimensions of household materiality – the physical dwelling, furniture, objects, bodies, rooms – are more-than-material items, 'inscribed with meanings, values and beliefs' that reflect and reproduce ideas about family (Blunt, 2005: 507), and are central to capacities to share. The configuration of domestic space is "not a neutral backdrop for the performance of daily life" (and attendant sharing practices), but an active participant in that performance (Nansen et al. 2011: 711). How these spaces, and objects within them, are configured into shifting practices of sharing – in times of personal hardship or during more widespread financial and/or ecological crises – remains an ongoing empirical question to which we have sought to respond here (cf. Jarvis 2013; Williams 2008).

Although sharing (of resources, space, time) is a fundamental human behaviour, it is all too regularly overlooked by academics and policymakers because it is subtle, and often takes place in the interior of the home as part of 'mundane' everyday routines (Belk 2010). Acts of sharing are at once mundane, familiar, accessible and feasible; as well as exciting, powerful and potentially transformative. Extended family households are one increasingly important social setting within which people dissolve materialist boundaries via practices inferring mutuality of possession. Homes are shared and physically altered to absorb ageing parents, or when adult children return in times of financial hardship or residential uncertainty, as an expression of unconditional love and care. Accumulation of duplicated but still useful goods, meanwhile, comes to be seen not as pathological 'hoarding' but as a 'library' of resources with implied shared ownership. Such spaces of sharing signify not just a means to practical ends around material possessions, but broader dispositions and ethics of care. As Rosie Cox (2010) has powerfully argued, "If we accept that we are dependent on others we are better able to acknowledge our collective dependence on the Earth". One expression of this in everyday life is the unheralded sharing of material spaces and resources within families.

Nevertheless extended family households also reinscribe certain boundaries around the private self (through, for instance, television ownership and screen viewing practices). What is or isn't shared – and how – does not merely reflect the human-to-human relationships contained within the home, but how family members negotiate mutual possession, move, store and redeploy objects, and alter the material landscapes of the house, as well as their own relationships (cf. Munro and Madigan 1999). Cultural values relating to the "social, temporal, and spatial fabric of daily life", along with social pressures to accomplish 'normal' ways of living and to perform certain identities within the home, constrained the capacities of our interviewees to share and pool some material resources (Hand et al. 2007: 669, 672). Tensions emerged from our empirical example around duplication (common areas, household fixtures and fittings), and separation of energy-using practices (e.g. cooking separately).

Understanding everyday practices in light of both hardship and environmental concerns benefits from such tensions being brought into the open.

Nevertheless domestic structures, spaces and relationships are simultaneously acted upon by a competing value-set based on an ethic of care within (but not limited to) family settings (Tarrant 2013). Such issues are of growing interest within the broader consideration of social welfare, urban management and sustainability initiatives, as the state increasingly absolves itself of responsibility for providing youth, aged and disability services and encourages care for relatives within the home (Tarrant 2010). Extended family household formation also illustrates how people pool resources in times of hardship, in ways that allow them to maintain a higher 'standard' of living in material terms. Pushing Belk's theorisation further, we can see that sharing extends the self through material objects in specific ways in the temporal context of hardship and disruption, and within the physical context of homes, with particular rooms and dimensions (cf. Munro and Madigam 1999). Such contexts ultimately shape capacities to share, with accompanying affordances that refract – and test – familial relationships.

References

ABS (2012) *2011 Census QuickStats – Australia*. Canberra: Australian Bureau of Statistics.

Allan, G., Crow, G. and Hawker, S. (eds.) (2011) *Stepfamilies*. Basingstoke: Palgrave Macmillan.

Belk, R. (2010) 'Sharing' *Journal of Consumer Research* 36: 715–734.

Blunt, A. (2005) 'Cultural geography: cultural geographies of home' *Progress in Human Geography* 29: 505–515.

Brammall, R. (2011) 'Dig for victory! Anti-consumerism, austerity and new historical subjectivities' *Subjectivity* 4: 68–86.

Buzar, S., Ogden, P. and Hall, R. (2005) 'Households matter: the quiet demography of urban transformation' *Progress in Human Geography* 29: 413–436.

Collins, R. (2015) 'Keeping it in the family? Re-focusing household sustainability' *Geoforum* 60, 22–32.

Cox, R. (2010) 'Some problems and possibilities of caring' *Ethics, Place & Environment* 13: 113–130.

Dowling, R. and Power, E. (2012) 'Sizing home, doing family in Sydney, Australia' *Housing Studies* 27(5): 605–619.

Duncan, S. and Smith, D. (2006) 'Individualisation versus the geography of 'new' families' *21st Century Society* 1: 167–189.

Evans, D. (2011) 'Blaming the consumer – once again: the social and material contexts of everyday food waste practices in some English households' *Critical Public Health* 21: 429–440.

Farbotko, C. and Waitt, G. (2011) 'Residential air-conditioning and climate change: Voices of the vulnerable' *Health Promotion Journal of Australia* 22: S13–14.

Gibson, C., Farbotko, C., Gill, N., Head, L. and Waitt, G. (2013) *Household Sustainability: Challenges and Dilemmas in Everyday Life*. Cheltenham: Edward Elgar.

Gibson, C., Head, L. and Carr, C. (2015) 'From incremental change to radical disjuncture: rethinking household sustainability practices as survival skills' *Annals of the Association of American Geographers* 105: 416–424.

Griffiths, M. and Gilly, P. (2012) 'Sharing space: extending Belk's (2010) "sharing"' *Journal of Research for Consumers* 22: 1–24.

Hall, S.M. (2015) 'Everyday ethics of consumption in the austere city' *Geography Compass* 9: 140–151.

Hall, S.M. (2016) 'Everyday family experiences of the financial crisis: getting by in the recent economic recession' *Journal of Economic Geography* 16(2): 305–330.

Hand, M., Shove, E. and Southerton D. (2007) 'Home extensions in the United Kingdom: space, time and practice' *Environment and Planning D* 25: 668–681.

Head, L., Farbotko, C., Gibson, C., Gill, N. and Waitt, G. (2013) 'Zones of friction, zones of traction: the connected household in climate change and sustainability policy' *Australasian Journal of Environmental Management* 20: 351–362.

Hitchings, R., Collins, R. and Day, R. (2015) 'Inadvertent environmentalism and the action-value opportunity: reflections from studies at both ends of the generational spectrum' *Local Environment* 20: 369–385.

Horne, R., Maller, C. and Lane, R. (2011) 'Remaking home: the reuse of goods and materials in Australian households' in Lane, R. and Gorman-Murray, A. [eds.] *Material Geographies of Household Sustainability*. Aldershot: Ashgate, 89–111.

Jarvis, H. (2013) 'Against the "tyranny" of single-family dwelling: insights from Christiania at 40' *Gender, Place & Culture* 20: 939–959.

Kaufmann, J. (1998) *Dirty Linen: Couples and Their Laundry*. London: Middlesex University Press.

Keene, J. and Batson C. (2010) 'Under one roof: a review of research on intergenerational coresidence and multigenerational households in the United States' *Sociology Compass* 4: 642–657.

Klocker, N., Gibson, C. and Borger, E. (2012) 'Living together, but apart: material geographies of everyday sustainability in extended family households' *Environment and Planning A* 44: 2240–2259.

Lane R. and Gorman-Murray, A. (2011) *Material Geographies of Household Sustainability*. Aldershot: Ashgate.

Lane, R., Horne, R. and Bicknell, J. (2009) 'Routes of re-use of second-hand goods in Melbourne households' *Australian Geographer* 40: 151–168.

Liu, E., Easthope, H., Burnley, I. and Judd, B. (2013) 'Multigenerational households in Australian cities' *7th Australasian Housing Researchers' Conference*, Perth WA, http://business.curtin.edu.au/local/docs/ahrc13/Multigenerational-households-in-Australian-cities-evidence-from-Sydney-and-Brisbane-at-the-turn-of-the-twenty-first-century.pdf

Liu, J., Daily, G., Ehrlich, P. and Luck G. (2003) 'Effects of household dynamics on resource consumption and biodiversity' *Nature* 421: 530–533.

Meah, A. (2014) 'Reconceptualising power and gendered subjectivities in domestic cooking spaces' *Progress in Human Geography* 38: 671–690.

Munro, M. and Madigan, R. (1999) 'Negotiating Space in the Family Home' in Cieraad, I. [ed.] *At Home: an Anthropology of Domestic Space*. Syracuse: New York, 107–117.

Nansen, B., Arnold, M., Gibbs, M. and Davis, H. (2011) 'Dwelling with media stuff: latencies and logics of materiality in four Australian homes' *Environment and Planning D* 29: 693–715.

Ozanne, L.K. and Ballantine, P.W. (2010) 'Sharing as a form of anti-consumption? An examination of toy library users' *Journal of Consumer Behaviour* 9: 485–498.

Reid, L., Sutton, P. and Hunter, C. (2010) 'Theorising the meso level: the household as a crucible of pro-environmental behaviour' *Progress in Human Geography* 34: 309–324.

Rérat, P. (2012) 'Housing, the compact city and sustainable development: some insights from recent urban trends in Switzerland' *International Journal of Housing Policy* 12: 115–136.

Stanes, E., Klocker, N. and Gibson, C. (2015) 'Young adult households and domestic sustainabilities' *Geoforum* 65: 46–58.

Tarrant, A. (2010) 'Constructing a social geography of grandparenthood: A new focus for intergenerationality' *Area* 42: 190–197.

Tarrant, A. (2013) 'Grandfathering as spatio-temporal practice: conceptualising performances of ageing masculinities in contemporary familial carescapes' *Social & Cultural Geography* 14: 192–210.

Waitt, G., Caputi, P., Gibson, C., Farbotko, C., Head, L., Gill, N. andStanes, E. (2012) Sustainable household capability: which households are doing the work of environmental sustainability? *Australian Geographer* 37, 45–55.

Williams, J. (2008) 'Predicting an American future for cohousing' *Futures* 40: 267–286.

Woodward, S. (2015) 'Hidden lives of dormant things: cupboards, lofts and shelves' in Casey, E and Taylor, Y [eds.]. *Intimacies: critical consumption and diverse economies*. Basingstoke: Palgrave Macmillan.

Wulff, M., Healy, E. and Reynolds, M. (2004) 'Why don't small households live in small dwellings? Disentangling a planning dilemma' *People and Place* 12: 58–71.

4 Reciprocity in uncertain times

Negotiating giving and receiving across time and place among older New Zealanders

Juliana Mansvelt

Relations of reciprocity and care are simultaneously intimate and personal, and shaped by social and political contexts. As local and global economies shift in response to economic crises, what it means to both provide for others and receive from others inevitably shifts. Expectations and expressions of reciprocity reflect the social and material conditions one is exposed to throughout the lifecourse. Consequently, the capacity to reciprocate is not simply a matter of individual choice, but is influenced by personal and material well-being and access to and opportunities to receive and give commodities, time and service in place. Political, social, economic, familial and personal changes which occur over one's lifecourse impinge on both expectations of, and capacity to reciprocate care and time. In the context of concerns about population ageing the worth of older people is understood in relation to their contribution and involvement in society (Morrow-Howell and Wang 2013). In this context, expectations to volunteer, give help and participate in communities through active engagement may place an additional burden on those who struggle to balance giving and receiving as part of a reciprocal moral economy embedded in networks of family and friends, local communities, health agencies and the state.

Though many people aged over 85 may have experienced economic hardship through the Depression and rationing in World War II, and many older people have experienced the insecurity of unemployment and under-employment through their lifetimes, new forms of insecurity in a period of austerity may be emerging as many older New Zealanders wonder whether they have sufficient resources to support any health, social, housing or familial crises they may face (Mansvelt et al. 2014). These changes are particularly pronounced as New Zealand (NZ) experienced a rapid shift from welfare state provision to neoliberalism. Prior to the Fourth Labour Government taking power in New Zealand in 1984, there were indications that the relative stability of the Welfare State was being shaken. Pressures to make NZ's economy and borders more porous to global capital, investment and migration flows, and to remove protectionist measures on agriculture and industry, underpinned many of the Fourth Labour Government's measures to restructure NZ's economy and claw back national debt. Underpinned by neoliberal policies – the hollowing out of the welfare state post 1984 was rapid and unsettling for many New Zealanders. With neoliberalisation came challenges to 'cradle to the grave' State provision of and entitlement to services. This included the extension of 'user pays' for a range of health, education, transportation services, market rates for state housing rentals, and increasing emphasis on the voluntary sector as a provider of safety-net care and advocacy services. Kelsey (2015) believes that the rapid changes associated with the application of neoliberal State policies over the last 30 years, the global financial crisis, the decline in manufacturing and the increasing significance of the financialisation in wealth creation have created a climate of uncertainty for many New Zealanders. This has resulted in rising inequality and unsustainable levels of household and national debt (Kelsey 2015). As a consequence, older people remain in an ambiguous position – empowered to make 'good' and responsible consumer choices to age well, but in a context in which their future economic, physical and ontological well-being may be increasingly uncertain.

This shift to viewing older people in terms of market consumers has also influenced experiences of ageing in New Zealand. Previous understandings of ageing in terms of decline and dependence (Mansvelt 1997) have been increasingly challenged by an emphasis on active ageing, with one's later years depicted as a time of productivity, engagement and contribution (Pond et al. 2010; Rudman 2006). Reflecting international ageing policy trends, the NZ Government's Positive Ageing Strategy (Ministry of Social Development 2001) strongly promotes activity, contribution, and connection as part of ageing well in place. Alongside this, state agencies such as the Office of Senior Citizens and the Retirement Commission promote individual responsibility and the necessity of making wise choices and saving for one's retirement. Policies on positive and active ageing favour ageing trajectories that are self-sufficient in terms of finance and need for care and ignore the inevitability of change as people age. While the security of NZ's comparatively generous universal superannuation remains, the entitlement age was adjusted from 60 to 65 between 1992 and 2001. Responsibilities for older people to age well are shaped in the context of debates about the intergenerational equity and affordability of NZ superannuation as the older population increases (Hurley et al. in press). Together changes in state support, uncertainty about future levels of superannuation, and imperatives on individuals to be self-managing, active citizens who contribute to society as they age well 'in place' (rather than in assisted care settings), provide the backdrop for older people's framings of giving and receiving as part of reciprocity in the 2000s (McDonald et al. 2007).

Moral economies and reciprocity in later life

Reciprocity as returning gifts of time, commodities and service can be regarded as a social force which underpins forms of economic and social exchange in society (Offer 2012). Reciprocal giving has been shown to be a part of older people's sense of independence and their connectedness (Breheny and Stephens 2012; Heenan 2010). Altruistic motivations and the giving of support or assistance to others rather than receiving support has also been shown to be directly related to better mental and physical health outcomes (Stephens et al. 2015). Thus the moral economies of reciprocity can have significant discursive effects – both in terms of expectations of giving and receiving, and in the relative amounts and balances seen as necessary to do so appropriately. Reciprocity can be practiced 'in kind'; a material gift may be reciprocated by acts of service or giving of time. Relations of obligation may be fulfilled in other forms such as guidance, protection, esteem and loyalty (Daniels 2009). The reciprocal act of returning the 'gift' in whatever form, may not be immediate but occur over a longer time-frame (Bowlby 2012; Moody 2008), and to different recipients as part of a wider social and moral contract for older people (Buys and Miller 2006). Consequently, examining the complex practices which comprise reciprocity, and the ways in which they may be balanced across time and place is important to understanding how moral economies of reciprocity operate.

Giving and receiving things, help, and time are not neutral exchanges but are shaped in the context of moral economies which place normative expectations around acts of reciprocity. McKie et al.'s (2002) work on caringscapes has implications for understanding these relations of reciprocity. McKie et al. argue that caring occurs in place and across time, with both current and anticipated needs implicated in arrangements of care (McKie et al. 2002). Taking a caringscapes approach draws attention both to the practical activities of caring, as well as the feelings and subjective positionings of people both in the provision and receipt of care across different temporal and spatial contexts. These expectations inform the relative balance of giving versus receiving. Funk (2012) argues that the moral norm of reciprocity itself can be a significant dimension of one's identity as a participating citizen. This tension is particularly marked in terms of neoliberal older citizens, expected to contribute and reciprocate to maintain their worth in an ageing society (Mansvelt 1997) yet subject to precariousness of health and social care services needed to support participation in civic life. For example, older people who have traditionally volunteered to community organisations may feel uncomfortable if their health or finances no longer enable them to do this. This shift can mean viewing themselves as dependent and primarily as recipients of health care and community services. Reciprocity and contribution for older people are further complicated in the face of the neoliberal hollowing out of the State as these services recede. Increased encouragement for older people to contribute to communities through the voluntary sector sits alongside the State disciplining of the sector though necessitating voluntary groups to develop levels of professionalisation, accountability, evaluation and auditing if they are to fulfil State contracts for such services (Grey and Sedgwick 2013).

Thompson (2013) argues that social identity is critical to how people make sense of their place in the world, and that a sense of reciprocity is a significant part of older people's identity, well-being, and purpose in life. Place is also critical in shaping reciprocity and moral norms around the social exchange of benefits. What may be appropriate to give and receive in one context can differ significantly in another context. For example, we would anticipate differing expectations for how reciprocity might operate in familial and intergenerational households, or in arrangements where older people are renting in communal accommodation. Consequently, places are not simply settings for social relations through which reciprocity is experienced, but are fully implicated in the way in which reciprocity may be understood, manifest and practiced. When the material environment of a dwelling, for example, becomes filled with medical equipment, this can alter not only one's sense of 'home' but also challenge existing household relations and norms around the giving and receipt of care (Wiles 2005). McKie et al. (2002: 910) argue for the importance of examining "the context of particular places, institutions or physical bodies with their distinctive histories, memories, meanings and patterns of social interaction" in understanding care. Relations of reciprocity in later life similarly require a spatial and temporal context; they occur across time and in place.

The studies: stories of coping and aspirations – narratives of reciprocity

The data on which the excerpts for this paper are drawn are taken from three studies related to the social geographies of everyday life, and the ways in which material and individual well-being, consumption, and place intersect. The data for all of these studies was analysed thematically (Braun and Clarke 2006) and participants quoted in this chapter have been identified by pseudonym, age and study number.

Study 1 explored the relationships between consumption, ageing, and place (Mansvelt 2013). Three in-depth qualitative interviews of 1–2 hours' duration were held with each of the twelve participants at 1-, 2- and 3-month intervals in 2009 and 2010. Research interviews focused on the experiences and practices surrounding household consumption, examining acquisition, maintenance, accommodation, reuse and wasting of groceries, clothing and electrical appliances, commodities chosen for differing their different positional status, modes of shopping and use (Mansvelt 2012). Participants were selected across a range of living standards, from 55- to 70-year-old participants who had volunteered to be interviewed in the Health, Work and Retirement Survey (Towers, et al. in press).

Study 2 was a large qualitative research project (2009–2012) focussed on developing a measure of living standards for older New Zealanders (Breheny et al. 2016). Semi-structured interviews of approximately 60 minutes duration were used to examine the capabilities provided by economic resources from the perspective and experience of 153 participants aged 63–93 years. Participants were recruited by community interviewers to represent a range of socio-economic status, ethnic groups, and geographic locations across New Zealand. These interviews explored spending and saving, managing financially, and participation in social networks (including volunteering and community contribution) in a range of urban and rural areas across New Zealand.

Study 3 (2009–2012) explored how older New Zealanders (aged 65–96) engaged and interacted with a range of organisations. These organisations included a range of voluntary, private sector and publically funded agencies including banks, hospitals, retail outlets, charities and recreation groups. Nineteen 'home-based elders' – older people who had difficulty leaving home for mobility or health reasons without the assistance of others – were recruited and interviewed for approximately one hour (Mansvelt and Zorn 2012).

Across all three studies, participants framed a responsibility to contribute to the lives of others, both proximate and distant, as part of a wider social and moral contract. This obligation stemmed not only from the 'give and take' that was expected as part of one's membership of families, organisations and communities, but as part of a naturalised and normative order of things as one aged. For many individuals, giving and contributing in various forms – through formal volunteering and informal helping and acts of service for family, friends and communities was an important part of their self-esteem and well-being (Morrow-Howell et al. 2003). Many older people saw themselves as having a responsibility to help others as part of being a contributing New Zealand citizen, and recognised that 'retirement' posed additional obligations and opportunities to reciprocate as one had more time available.

Reciprocity as community contribution: it's what makes this place ...

Reciprocity was often imagined in terms of 'community', an imagined geography that could signify local, regional and national place contexts. Throughout the three studies contribution to community was an expected part of one's citizenship. With a good income in retirement, Alison (age 60, study 1) had both the resources and the time to continue to give to her local community. When asked about all her volunteering, she shrugged it off and noted that she was also the recipient of her neighbours' care, a natural and normal part of how her local community was constituted. In the quote that follows the interviewer reinforces the notion of reciprocity as embedded in neighbourhoods, but Alison goes further to argue that such exchanges of neighbourly care are a very 'New Zealand thing'.

INTERVIEWER: Like your baking, my neighbours give me beans, so it's a nice sort of you know.
ALISON: "That's very New Zealand".

Alison's response and that of the interviewer, not only minimised her extensive volunteering as part of the way things are in New Zealand but also framed Alison's giving as part of a place-based reciprocity that comprised "kiwi" culture. Locating these norms and expectations in place rather than in individual practices makes them more permanent. Though people in this location may change, reciprocity will endure. Alison's comment about "That's very New Zealand" also frames her baking contributions as a natural, normal part of citizenship. Such norms of reciprocity were also significant in creating meaningful places in Crystal's (age 59, study 1) talk. Crystal gave fruit and vegetables to her neighbours, helped clear lawns in her vicinity after a storm, sewed for local charity shops, and gave to those who needed 'a hand' in the local area. She and her husband lived in a rural area where they knew everyone in their locality.

> Well I'm a great believer in waving out to people, always saying hello to somebody and being, just going and seeing your neighbours, I mean standing on the street and having a yap and that and then one comes, another one comes, and you always find that yeah you can draw people in and it's nice to know that they've got a baby two doors down and that and if they need a hand they know where they can come and you know, things like that and I, I feel that it's missing a lot and I think that's where town scares us a bit too because you just don't have that.

Crystal situates herself at the centre of a set of emplaced relations, with others moving towards and away from her in sequence. Crystal bemoaned that notions of reciprocity were not as strongly expressed in towns and cities, a belief based on their discursive construction of the rural (in contrast to the urban) as a caringscape comprising known others (Barnett and Land, 2007), an imagined geography which underpinned their hesitancy in considering a shift into town should they need to do so as they aged. These anxieties can also be understood in terms of movement from a place where relations of reciprocity have been accumulated. In the context of increasing vulnerabilities as people age, the places where reciprocity is grounded become increasingly important. Crystal also alludes to the moral economies of her rural community, noting that in such a community – time, resources and greetings are not only freely exchanged, but that social expectations of assistance are able to be expressed freely – the family with the baby *know* where they can come for help.

In such circumstances, it was common for participants to note the benefits of reciprocity extending beyond the individual. For example, Crystal believed her efforts were part of creating a sustainable moral economy which allowed the benefits of gifting time and resources to accrue to needy others:

> Yeah …, like going over to the neighbours and offering to prune their tree and end up cleaning out their gardens and that, which is really

self-satisfying. It helps them, and you know, and that but, yeah, then there's always an ulterior motive like the Scouts get a donation or something so you know you're doing one thing for another.

Besides the intrinsic satisfaction she gains from helping others, Crystal also alludes to the existence of normative expectations surrounding reciprocity as constituted collectively in local places. In referring to possible 'ulterior motives for helping' she explained how assistance to her neighbours was often reciprocated in the form of donations to the local branch of Scouts which she was associated with.

Thus in neighbourhoods and localities, people become known as givers and recipients of care relations, with the balance of giving and reciprocating unevenly expressed, but able to be reconciled within a shared sense of community. In a previous interview Gary (age 67, study 1) had talked with a sense of pride about the pleasure he derived from engineering and fixing things and the fact that he was able to help those in the neighbourhood who lacked such abilities. Here he demonstrates the wider ways in which reciprocity is distributed across communities:

> Nerida come over last, yesterday, she's got one of these fly things you know it sprays, she couldn't get it to go … So I check the battery … so I put it in and I go there [to her house], … they got a little button on the side of them, you got to just push it down three times and it goes "fissht", and then she's (the flyspray dispenser) away and that's it. [She says] "Oh thank you very much!"
>
> So then, I was sitting there yesterday, last night, and the girl up the, up [the road], she walks in with a $10 gift voucher. And I thought "what's that for?" She said "Oh, you take my mail when I've been away" … and "You've done this?!" I thought!

In recounting this story of fixing a spray can for which he receives only personal thanks, followed by receiving a gift voucher for another unrelated act of care, Gary documents how reciprocity is demonstrated across a range of acts in his community of residence. While the giving of the gift voucher (a form of economic value) might complicate the reciprocal relation through reconfiguring care-giving as a contractual relationship, Gary's indication of his surprise when a neighbour's daughter gives him a voucher for which the value outweighs his notion of the effort expended speaks to norms of reciprocity. Though giving and receiving exist in reciprocal relation, explicit and stated expectations of receiving kindness in return for care given may denigrate the altruistic motives individuals' desire to express. Thus Gary's talk makes known to the interviewer this personal and moral norm of not expecting that his individual act of kindness will be reciprocated. At the same time he reinforces discourses of reciprocity framed around 'communities' as places of giving and receiving which are comprised of multiple and individual acts of reciprocity. Gary's and many other participants' narratives illustrate the ways in which norms around reciprocity are shaped in particular places. However, there are indications that neoliberal policies may reduce the capacity of individuals to engage in their communities (Talbot and Walker 2007). As a consequence, inclinations and capacities to give and receive in local communities may be manifested unevenly across places, shaped in the context of the material attributes of places and influenced by place histories and meanings (Hanibuchi et al. 2012).

Lydia (age 59, study 1) notes how at the beach settlement where she lives, her neighbours look out for one another, and food is shared freely, a familial tradition which she and her sister continue to perform as they grow older:

> Certainly, at the beach, there is quite a bit of that, like my neighbour, cause, that I took the baking across to, she'll, she'll ring up and say "I've put a roast on and my kids" ... [then] on Sunday night [she says], "Will you and Roger come over and help us eat it?". [Interviewer: Oh wow!].....
> So, so you know frequently that'll happen or, or you know I got back from, must have been about my first or second night back and she comes over with a bottle of wine and some nibbles, you know yeah, so it's just that really nice community.

Lydia expressed the give and take that makes the beach settlement a desirable place to dwell, noting the frequency of reciprocal acts of kindness. It was common throughout the three studies for localities (be they urban neighbourhoods, rural areas, beach settlements, or retirement communities) to be constituted as places which encourage the expression of reciprocity and in turn to be defined as meaningful places because of the reciprocity that exists. Across these examples, the speakers frame the expectation for reciprocal arrangements as founded on characteristics of their places, at times in relation to other places that lack these characteristics. Situating the expectations and the practices of reciprocity to community characteristics has advantages for older participants, as they are able to rely on distributed obligation rather than personal expectations between individuals. Framing reciprocity in terms of 'the way we do things around here' provides more stability and predictability in terms of exchange of resources, time and care than individualised relations of reciprocity. Older people can also situate themselves as building a sense of community through encouraging a sense of reciprocity in new community members. The solidification of relationships based on trust and reciprocation can further promote a sense of social obligation in communities (Brown et al. 2014). Thus imagining and experiencing and producing localities as community through talk and practice may underpin older people's sense of being and self-identity in the world – enabling them to feel at home in place, part of the social world and contributing positively to their well-being (Coleman and Kearns 2014).

Reciprocity as a lifecourse norm: giving back and paying forward

Moral economies of reciprocity are formed across the lifecourse. Accounts of reciprocity were frequently framed in relation to past experiences and imagined futures. A sense of giving back, of the imperative to give as one had received, was present in many interviews. Giving to others whether financially or in help was seen as way of demonstrating gratefulness for the blessings already received in life, as Amelia's (age 86, study 2) quote demonstrates:

> I do help if I can. I always give to charities I believe in, even if it's only two or three dollars. Because I think I am quite lucky really.

Participants were keen to demonstrate the exercise of reciprocal obligation – giving as they have received; here Seth gives to recognise God's overwhelming generosity:

> God gives us money in the big box, but we only give God money in the spoon
>
> (Seth, age 70, study 2)

In these quotations reciprocity is part of a moral economy in which participants saw their obligation to reciprocate in thanks for benefits accrued to them over the lifecourse. For some participants this was framed in terms of thankfulness to God couched in notions of charitable citizenship (Cloke 2002), whereas for others this was in terms of good fortune understood more generally. A temporal form of 'caring at a distance' (Barnett and Land, 2007), generosity towards unknown others was manifest in terms of both 'giving back'. A desire to 'give back' emerged out of recognition that participants had experienced favourable life outcomes and also from a belief that they had the physical, financial, intellectual or social capability to do so, to use the 'gifts' they had been provided with to be contributing and productive citizens.

The responsibility of 'giving back' using gifts and talents developed during the lifecourse was also connected to the increased availability of time in retirement and the desire to be active as (Catherine, age 73, study 3) notes:

> And you talked about volunteer interests. Okay I'm a volunteer with the [town] Citizens Advice Bureau. [Int:*Great*] And I'm a volunteer knitter for three groups in the city.
> *So how often do you do the Citizens Advice, go along to, to …*
> Oh well you have to have a duty at least once a week. I mean that's only two or three hours, but I sometimes will fill in quite happily cause I've got time on my hands. Then you have training once a month and then you do updating of the data base on the phone at home, like about 50 phone calls, which I've got time to do.

Catherine gladly gave her time as she enjoyed giving back and feeling she was utilising skills gained during her working life. Her engagement in voluntary activity provided a sense of achievement, contribution and autonomy as she grew older.

For other participants an ability to give was framed in relation to 'paying forward', arising from the recognition that they might need resources, care or help in the future as they aged. Fred for example talks about the air ambulance service which flew his granddaughter to hospital noting that he "might need them one day". Many participants gave examples of paying forward into voluntary health and social care services which were linked to particular health conditions. Fred's comment again demonstrates the ways in which notions of reciprocity are situated in place; for many New Zealanders living distant to a major hospital (or those who engage in outdoor activities in remote areas) means urgent medical attention may require an air-ambulance. By donating to the service, Fred notes how obligations to reciprocate can extend into the future times and places:

> Because of [my granddaughter], the air ambulance … we give them a modest donation and the reason I do that is probably twofold – a. I might need them one day but more importantly they flew [my granddaughter] to Auckland hospital.
>
> (Fred, age 68, study 2)

It was not uncommon for participants to acknowledge the potential need for a charity or service, and their contribution in case the eventuality of this need should arise. Neil, for example, used the analogy of 'putting money in the bank' to describe his desire to contribute to hospice services. That such a desire should be seen as a reciprocal exchange was expressed most strongly by Barbara, who was at pains to state that she is not 'generous' but has given over the years to charities which she has had need of (arthritis) and because of the (relative) certainty that she may get Alzheimer's disease:

> I tended to donate to what I was involved in like the Arthritis. I've always donated to Alzheimer's cos it's going to happen sooner or later, I'm not what you call very generous, no.
>
> (Barbara, age 74, study 2)

This temporal flexibility of the expectations regarding reciprocity allows older people to maintain a sense of contribution over a long time period and across a range of domains and across generations (Bowlby 2012), removing the requirement to manage reciprocity in terms of specific interpersonal relationships. In participants' constructions of reciprocity stretched across time and space, temporalities of care and concern (McKie et al. 2002) were also couched in the context of austerity and a reduction in centrally funded health and social services. Through such actions, older people use the social norms of reciprocity to justify distributed support of health and social care provision more aligned with earlier welfare state provision. In this way, participants attend both to their own future vulnerabilities in terms of being recipients of such services and recognise the vulnerability of the services themselves in the context of neoliberalism. Though, in their talk about giving back or paying forward some participants referred to circumstances which made reciprocating difficult. Most participants were able to maintain a sense of parity across their lifecourse; however, for a minority of participants imperatives to reciprocate as part of being an autonomous and contributing citizen were conflicting – it was at these times participants articulated a sense of reciprocity 'out of balance'.

Reciprocity out of balance: when receipt outweighs contribution

In underpinning a sense of an active, contributing, responsible and autonomous self, notions of reciprocity help frame identity and citizenship for people as they age. However, notions of giving back, and paying forward and of contributing to the maintenance of community pose issues for those who are unable to conform to norms of giving and receiving as balanced across time and place. Those in the position of receiving care, and who for financial, health or social reasons were unable to give and contribute as they would wish, did considerable discursive work in their interview narratives to remove the weight of signification associated with moral expectations to care, contribute to communities and help others. Keith's (age 77, study 3) mobility was severely restricted, and he explained the difficulties associated with what he saw as a critical balance between giving and receiving:

> I get far more pleasure out of giving, or doing something for somebody than I do out of, don't say I don't appreciate receiving something …
>
> *INT: No. I know what you're saying but it's that giving and I can see that's …*
>
> It's giving something that is far more important or it gives me a better feeling than actually receiving something.

Keith's sense of autonomy and independence was challenged by needing to receive the care of others when he struggled to contribute in kind, making it hard for him to receive such care easily.

Across all participants in varying living situations, gifting of time, commodities, and resources shaped the public narrative of the morally good citizen and individual, be they parent, partner, friend or relative. Narratives of giving as part of caringscapes were a conduit for the representational transformation of self and a means of demonstrating love and care to friends and across familial generations. Pam's (age 81, study 3) declining health and mobility meant she was no longer able to contribute outside the home as she had done previously – her possibilities for reciprocity had narrowed to the space of the home and helping her paid caregiver, but this was also becoming increasingly challenging:

> I help, I help her. Well at least I do other things. Some, you know I'll always, if there are dishes on the bench and often now I say I'll do these

Jan [the caregiver], and I always quite like to do my own washing, and hang it out, unless there's something wrong you know. Only thing that seemed to really bug me these days is I get very, very sort of low on energy.

Even though Pam's care was a paid contractual arrangement, so strong was the imperative to reciprocate, Pam was willing to do whatever she was capable of in order to show care in return. Pam's desire to do so was also a significant part of her self-identity as independent, contributing and self-managing citizen.

As older people begin to feel the balance of giving and receiving shifting, they are placed in a difficult position. After being widowed a few months previously, Peta (age, 64, study 1) was having difficulty managing financially. These difficulties meant she could no longer provide money or transport necessary to volunteer for her local social sport club.

> And so all my 'Sports club' mates I, and I says well I'll get the meat, tell me how much meat you want and he said, I said "Did I say you had to pay for?" and I feel so, I'm lucky in a way, but then I feel so embarrassed and I said, I said I'll buy some, he said yes well you, you do all the baking.

As a consequence of her unbalanced situation, Peta narrated a sense of herself as both 'lucky' (a undeserving recipient) and 'embarrassed' (a person who should be giving). Peta managed her inability to contribute financially through the statement that she would contribute through her time and effort in baking. Like many older people in her interview Peta narrated a sense of stoicism and coping demonstrated by her reluctance to acknowledge her need or desire for help and in stating her intention to overcome her financial challenges on her own (Mansvelt 2012). Given that a relative imbalance in giving and receipt is hard to accept, Peta does considerable discursive work in her interview to reframe herself as a giver, with her family now 'paying back' for the care she has given them over the years. Whilst acknowledging "you don't add these up", Peta manage an accounting of sorts to alleviate the position of needing to receive more help than she can presently reciprocate:

> They [her children] keep saying to me, "Payback time, oh it's payback time" and I said you know "If I get it all together add it all", well you see you don't add things up … And my kids go, "Mother don't be so proud". And I said it's not being proud.

Poor health was another factor in participants' expression of the undesirability of assumed balances between giving and receipt of commodities, time and care. When asked whether she engaged in any voluntary work, Grace (age 88, study 3) replies:

> Unfortunately not, no cause this, I regret this very much. I feel I'm useless. I can't do anything for anybody now. I couldn't even go and help a neighbour out you know because I just can't see. But …

> *But you would have liked to (it says here) if you could. You'd like to volunteer to ..?.*
>
> Oh I would. I would help. You know over the years I used to be on the Plunket Committees and School Committees and different things like that that, I'm no use now.

Being in poor health, blind and unable to leave home demonstrates the intersection of temporal and contextual factors in defining the limits to Grace's reciprocity. The temporal flexibility of moral economies of reciprocity were unable to be drawn upon in Grace's framing of her limited self-worth and lack of value as a contributing citizen. In positioning of herself as 'useless', she highlights the limits of the capacity of past acts of reciprocity to accommodate present and future circumstances. Grace is unable to see how she could contribute in order to either reciprocate acts of care or pay them forward. Although the notion of 'paying forward' was common among those anticipating being net beneficiaries of support in the future, as older people moved from a position of paying in to drawing down accumulated help, they struggled to accommodate this change. Anticipating care in their turn was a moral position in earlier old age, but receiving such care often did not play out as anticipated. An irreconcilable imbalance in giving and receipt was not surprisingly expressed by those who had the most limited capabilities of reciprocating whether for health or economic reasons, raising issues of how a sense of pleasure, participation, contribution, autonomy and self-worth can be achieved for those who are unable to reciprocate.

Conclusion

This analysis demonstrates how building social identity on reciprocity is fraught in one's later years. Reciprocal social relationships are an important part of well-being (McMunn et al. 2009) but as this analysis demonstrates they can also be an area in which the sense of self is diminished as one ages. Participants sought to narrate a sense of balance across communities and over the lifecourse with regard to practices of paying forward and giving back. At times this balance was maintained through such rhetorical strategies as denying need, giving out of excess or blessing, justifying current receipt by past reciprocal acts, or by referring to lifecourse or familial expectations. Where current and future possibilities for giving time, money or resources was unachievable, participants struggled invoke this flexible and temporal accounting of reciprocity in order to maintain a sense of self-worth, contribution and autonomy. For many New Zealanders, contribution and altruism is framed as part of New Zealand culture. Giving, gifting, sharing and receiving time, commodities and care are important in the construction of familial and individual subjectivities and in building meaningful places. Discourses of 'positive ageing' and 'consumer citizenship' are both produced and reflected in place through notions of imagined community and practices of reciprocity. The moral norms associated with reciprocity thus have material effects and affects – they are both outcomes and influencers of material environments, embodied practices and constructions of ethnicity, gender, class, and age across time and place.

It is important to recognise the heterogeneity of older people and the ways in which reciprocity and notions of paying back and forward may be reconstituted as one ages and finds oneself in different material, familial and health circumstances. Chances to age actively through contribution of time, services and commodities are not equally accessible to all. Consequently, versions of positive and successful ageing may ignore structural and personal differences such as income, poor health and mobility, lack of access to community services (Breheny and Stephens 2012). Older people carry socioeconomic inequalities experienced during early life into retirement age and beyond (Jatrana and Blakely 2014). Constructions of reciprocity are framed in the context of wider shifts in expectations over the lifecourse. Neoliberalisation shifts responsibility for care from the state to the voluntary sector and communities. Given this, individuals, families and communities develop strategies to build community-based relations of reciprocity and provide for one another across time in the context of changes in health and capacity. As Lynch (2007) argues, there is nothing inevitable about arrangements of care and solidarity; political and social contexts can both support and inhibit relations of care and reciprocity. Shifting expectations regarding responsibilities for self-care and the care of others influence intimate care work as well as wider temporal and spatial caringscapes. Furthermore, economic, social and material inequalities are exacerbated by spatial inequalities. Differences in built environments, places and regions (such as between urban and rural areas) and in the discourses and norms of reciprocity associated with them can influence the expectations and the capabilities of older people to give, share and contribute time and resources, creating geographies of inclusion and exclusion. Our study has not only demonstrated that expectations of giving and receiving may shape norms of nationhood in places (what it means to be a New Zealander) but also that reciprocity may be an important part of how places as local communities are understood, imagined and negotiated.

Older people are not a homogenous group who participate and experience social and structural change in the same way (Wiles and Jayasinha 2013). Though the differently able, the sick and those in financial difficulty all endeavour to respond to moral obligations to reciprocate, the norms by which these are defined differ according to one's cultural, ethnic and social networks and intersectional factors such as age, ethnicity and the structural and spatial contexts in which they are located. The capability to engage in reciprocal practices and their forms vary according to socioeconomic circumstances (Conlon et al. 2014). Access to greater material wealth enables a wider range of choices and expressions of forms of reciprocity. Neoliberal discourses of productivity, individuality, self-management and responsibility, frame current imperatives to contribute, care for others (including adult family) and reciprocate. Reduced capabilities to give may further marginalise older people who cannot fulfil moral or social expectations to actively engage in and contribute to society (Pond et al. 2010, Martinez et al. 2011; Stephens et al. 2015). Consequently the intersections between the material and the moral aspects of gifting economies influence not only the forms reciprocity might take and normative notions of 'balance' – but they also frame the possibilities and limitations for all to age well in place, particularly in uncertain times.

References

Barnett, C., and Land, D. (2007) Geographies of generosity: Beyond the "moral turn". *Geoforum, 38*, 1065–1075.

Bowlby, S. (2012) 'Recognising the time–space dimensions of care: caringscapes and carescapes' *Environment and Planning A*, 44: 2101–2118.

Braun, V. & Clarke, V. (2006) 'Using thematic analysis in psychology' *Qualitative Research in Psychology* 3(2): 77–101.

Breheny, M., & Stephens, C. (2012) 'Negotiating a moral identity in the context of later life care' *Journal of Aging Studies, 26*(4): 438–447.

Breheny, M., Stephens, C., Henricksen, A., Stevenson, B., Carter, K., & Alpass, F. (2016) 'Measuring living standards of older people using Sen's Capability Approach: development and validation of the LSCAPE-24 (Living Standards Capabilities for Elders) and LSCAPE-6' *Ageing and Society, 36*(2): 307–332.

Brown, T. C., Forsyth, C. J., & Berthelot, E. R. (2014) 'The mediating effect of civic community on social growth: The importance of reciprocity' *The Social Science Journal* 51(2): 219–230.

Buys, L, B., & Miller, E, M. (2006) 'The meaning of "active ageing" to older Australians: Exploring the relative importance of health, participation and security' Paper presented at the *39th Australian Association of Gerontology Conference*, Sydney.

Cloke, P. (2002) 'Deliver us from evil? Prospects for living ethically and acting politically in human geography' *Progress in Human Geography*, 26(5): 587–604.

Coleman, T., & Kearns, R. (2014) 'The role of bluespaces in experiencing place, aging and wellbeing: Insights from Waiheke Island, New Zealand' *Health and Place* 35: 206–217.

Conlon, C, Timonen, V., Carney, G. & Scharf, T. (2014) 'Women (re)negotiating care across family generations: intersections of gender and socioeconomic status' *Gender & Society* 28(5): 729–751.

Daniels, I. (2009) 'The "social death" of unused gifts' *Journal of Material Culture* 14(3): 385–408.

Funk, L. M. (2012) '"Returning the love", not "balancing the books": talk about delayed reciprocity in supporting ageing parents' *Ageing & Society*, 32(4): 634–654.

Grey, S., & Sedgwick, C. (2013) 'Fears, Constraints, Contracts: The democratic reality of New Zealand's voluntary sector' presented at the *Community and Voluntary Sector Forum*, University of Wellington 26th March.

Hanibuchi, T., Murata, Y., Ichida, Y., Hirai, H., Kawachi, I., & Kondo, K. (2012) 'Place-specific constructs of social capital and their possible associations to health: A Japanese case study' *Social Science & Medicine* 75(1): 225–232.

Heenan, D. (2010) 'Social capital and older people in farming communities' *Journal of Aging Studies*, 24(1): 40–46.

Hurley, K., Breheny, M., & Tuffin, K. (in press) 'Intergenerational inequity arguments and the implications for state-funded financial support of older people' Ageing & Society.

Jatrana, S., & Blakely, T. (2014) 'Socio-economic inequalities in mortality persist into old age in New Zealand: study of all 65 years plus, 2001–04' *Ageing & Society* 34(6): 911–929.

Kelsey, J. (2015) *The Fire Economy: New Zealand's Reckoning*. Wellington: Bridget Williams Books.

Lynch, K. (2007) 'Love labour as a distinct and non-commodifiable form of care labour' *The Sociological Review*, 55(3): 550–570.

Mansvelt, J. (1997) 'Working at leisure: critical geographies of ageing' *Area* 29(4): 289–298.

Mansvelt, J. (2012) 'Consumption, ageing and identity: New Zealanders' narratives of gifting, ridding and passing on' *New Zealand Geographer* 68(3): 187–200.

Mansvelt, J. (2013) 'Situating Ageing, Consumption and Materiality through the Life-Course' in Nicolas, A. and Flaherty, I. [eds.] *Growing Up Growing Old. Trajectories of Times and Lives*. Freeland: Inter-disciplinary Press, 195–215.

Mansvelt, J., Breheny, M., & Stephens, C. (2014) 'Pursuing security: economic resources and the ontological security of older New Zealanders' *Ageing and Society* 34(10): 1666–1687.

Mansvelt, J., & Zorn, T. E. (2012) 'The problems and possibilities for home-based elders in New Zealand' *Sites* 9(1): 107–132.

Martinez, I. L., Crooks, D., Kim, K. S., & Tanner, E. (2011) 'Invisible civic engagement among older adults: Valuing the contributions of informal volunteering' *Journal of Cross-Cultural Gerontology*, 26: 23–37.

McDonald, R., Mead, N., Cheraghi-Sohi, S., Bower, P., Whalley, D., & Roland, M. (2007) 'Governing the ethical consumer: identity, choice and the primary care medical encounter' *Sociology of Health & Illness* 29(3): 450–456.

McKie, L, Gregory, S., & Bowlby, S. (2002) 'Shadow times: the temporal and spatial frameworks and experiences of caring and working' *Sociology*, 36(4): 897–924.

McMunn A., Nazroo J., Wahrendorf M., Breeze E. and Zaninotto P. (2009) 'Participation in socially productive activities, reciprocity and well-being in later life: baseline results in England', *Ageing and Society*, 29, 765–782.

Ministry of Social Development (2001) NZ Government's Positive Ageing Strategy. Retrieved from http://www.msd.govt.nz/about-msd-and-our-work/publications-resources/planning-strategy/positive-ageing/.

Moody, M. (2008) 'Serial reciprocity: a preliminary statement' *Sociological Theory* 26(2): 130–151.

Morrow-Howell, N., & Wang, Y. (2013) 'Productive engagement of older adults: elements of a cross-cultural research agenda' *Ageing International* 38(2): 159–170.

Morrow-Howell, N., Hinterlong, J., Rozario, P. A., & Tang, F. (2003) 'Effects of volunteering on the well-being of older adults' *The Journals of Gerontology Series B: Psychological Sciences and Social Sciences* 58(3): S137–S145.

Offer, S. (2012) 'The burden of reciprocity: processes of exclusion and withdrawal from personal networks among low-income families' *Current Sociology* 60(6): 788–805.

Pond, R., Stephens, C., & Alpass, F. (2010) 'Virtuously watching one's health: older adults' regulation of self in the pursuit of health' *Journal of Health Psychology* 15(5): 734–743.

Rudman, D.L. (2006) 'Shaping the active, autonomous and responsible modern retiree: an analysis of discursive technologies and their links with neo-liberal political rationality' *Ageing and Society* 26(2): 181–201.

Stephens, C., Breheny, M., & Mansvelt, J. (2015) 'Volunteering as reciprocity: Beneficial and harmful effects of social policies to encourage contribution in older age' *Journal of Aging Studies* 33(0): 22–27.

Talbot, L., & Walker, R. (2007) 'Community perspectives on the impact of policy change on linking social capital in a rural community' *Health & Place* 13(2): 482–492.

Thompson, S. (2013) *Reciprocity and Dependency in Old Age: Indian and UK perspectives* [https://archive.org/details/springer_10.1007-978-1-4614-6687-1]. New York: Springer.

Towers, A., Stevenson, B. and Breheny, M. (in press) 'The health, work and retirement longitudinal study' in Pachana, N. [ed.], *Encyclopedia of Geropsychology* (Vol. Longitudinal and Centenarian Studies). New York: Springer.

Wiles, J. (2005) 'Home as a new site of care provision and consumption' in Andrews, G.J., & Phillips, D.R. [eds.] *Ageing and Place: Perspectives, Policy, Practice*. London and New York: Routledge, 70–109.

Wiles, J.L., & Jayasinha, R. (2013) 'Care for place: The contributions older people make to their communities' *Journal of Aging Studies* 27(2): 93–101.

5   Relationships, reciprocity and care
Alcohol, sharing and 'urban crisis'

Mark Jayne, Gill Valentine and
Sarah L. Holloway[1]

Introduction

This chapter advances the application of social and cultural theory to understanding alcohol, drinking and drunkenness by exploring the moral and ethical relationships which constitute alcohol consumption and sharing in everyday life.[2] We begin by generating a dialogue between writing on 'constructive' drinking, and literature focused on alcohol-related urban encounters. In doing so, we show that focusing on relationships, reciprocity and care offers an important antidote to long-standing political, policy, popular and academic pathologisation of alcohol as contributing to an 'urban crisis' of violence and disorder. We then pursue this argument with reference to emotional, embodied and affective geographies relating to practices, politics and possibilities of an urban 'counter public' generated around alcohol-related practices and experiences.

The findings presented in this chapter are based on fieldwork conducted as part of a wider study titled 'Drinking places: where people drink and why', which explored attitudes towards, and practices of, alcohol consumption by adults in the UK.[3] Participant observation in public spaces and commercial venues, as well as 60 in-depth interviews that reflect socio-economic diversity and a range of attitudes to, and experiences of alcohol were undertaken. All the interviews were recorded, transcribed, and analysed using conventional social science techniques. To ensure anonymity, the interviewees were allocated pseudonyms that have been used in the analysis and publication of transcript data.

Urban encounter and constructive drinking

From the birth of the modern city in the late eighteenth and early nineteenth centuries, alcohol has been depicted in political, popular and policy terms as a key driver of social unrest, criminality, violence, disorder and so on (Jayne et al. 2006; Kneale 2001). In academic debate, such focus and concern can be contextualised by writing from sociologist Georg Simmel (1903: 15), who argued that as urban modernity flourished and expanded at a rapid pace, city dwellers developed a "blasé attitude" and an "aversion ... to strangers" that could lead to conflict and tension. More recently, a range of influential authors have highlighted how urban diversity, congestion and 'throwntogetherness', liveliness and improvisations of city living ensures that urban encounter is fraught with potentially positive and negative outcomes (see Amin 2012; Jacobs 1961; Lefebvre 1996; Massey 2005; Thrift 2005). For example, in the contemporary city, Valentine (2008) highlights how encounters in public space can positively charge prejudice, whilst Bunnell et al. (2012) and Kathirevelu (2013) suggest how 'friendships', whether long-standing or fleeting, are ritualised and contextual, but are nonetheless constituted through moments of trust, reciprocity and sharing.

To a large degree, many of these same arguments have played out in writing about alcohol and the city. For example, Mass Observation's *The Pub and the People* (1987 [1937–1943]) was initiated in response to the 'moral panic' around alcohol consumption that emerged in the late eighteenth and early nineteenth centuries. More specifically, Mass Observation was a response to dissatisfaction with the way in which drinking was reported in official statistics, and concern that political, policy and policing measures to curb drunkenness failed to grasp the experience and context of drinking. Mass Observation studies of pub life were undertaken in the UK in Bolton, Blackpool, Plymouth, Liverpool and Fulham and participants noted that alcohol was not the sole reason for public drunkenness, and that pub sociality encouraged a relaxing of sober self-control even for those who were not drinking (Kneale 2001). Indeed, pubs were considered by their patrons to be spaces for relatively intimate social relations, and encapsulated within this were associations of drunkenness with commensality, trust and reciprocity. Observers noted practices such as drinking rates, where groups all drank at the same speed and took similar sized sips in order to ensure social bond and equivalence between drinkers. This highlighted the ways in which drinking was a way of creating and transforming social relationships with associations of drink as being bound up with trust, relaxing of formal social relations and sharing.

For example, the working-class drinking practice of 'rounds' and 'treating' one another reproduced social ties and obligations, and hence drinking can be seen to have played an important role in making connections between people. Drink was equated with social worth, trust and fraternity. The formation of crowds of people, drunk and not-so-drunk, engaging with one another and with other users of public space was also seen as a key feature of drunken behaviour. In particular, the promenading of people after closing time, in large but temporary groups was shown to be a key component of urban drinking that was a form of dialogue, an engagement that held out the offer of diversity and heterogeneity.

However, Kneale (1999) argues that during the nineteenth century, public debate surrounding the construction of public space was to a large degree bound up with public opinion that was attuned to a new sensitivity to the social context of drinking, the role of the drink trade and rituals of conviviality.

Kneale shows that discussion of the place of drink in temperance documents between 1856 and 1914 highlights two different geographical imaginations of public space. He suggests that a customary sense of public space based on drink as a form of sharing and gift exchange was becoming marginalised. This was defined by the political tenets of liberal democracy, adhering to the characteristics of the public sphere as a space where individuals are aware of their responsibilities as citizens. In striving to replace social and community-based relations with more abstract and political senses of citizenship and democratic rights, the temperance movement in particular played a part in remaking understandings of public space as a mirror of the public sphere. Drinking in public spaces and the drink trade were defined as problematic and constitutive of a broader 'urban crisis' and geographical and scientific knowledge played their part in legislating and guiding state action against such unruly and socially 'problematic' practices and behaviours (see Jayne et al. 2006; 2011a).

More recently, the landmark publication of the book *Constructive Drinking*, edited by Mary Douglas (1987), was also influential in further challenging researchers to move beyond a research agenda dominated by the limiting theorisation of the pathologising of alcohol consumption and depictions of alcohol-fuelled urban violence and disorder. Douglas advocated the need to address theoretically and empirically the everyday social relations and cultural practices bound up with drinking. Moreover, other important publication prior to, and following, *Constructive Drinking*, such as McAndrew and Edgerton's *Drunken Comportment* (1969), Harrison's (1971) *Drink and the Victorians*, Malcomson's (1973) *Popular Recreations in English Society 1700–1850*, Girouard's (1975) *Victorian Pubs*, Clarke's (1983) *The English Alehouse: A Social History 1200–1830;* Schivelbusch's *Taste of Paradise* (1992) and Burnett's *Liquid Pleasures: A Social History of Drink in Modern Britain* (1999) touched on similar terrain. Following this groundbreaking writing, a voluminous amount of academic research has offered theoretical and empirical insights into the discursive and differential construction of 'constructive' drinking with reference to diverse urban spaces, cultures and identities around the world. Such writing has been vital in laying the foundations for studies of alcohol consumption which point to practices, politics and possibilities of urban encounters that are underpinned by reciprocity, care and sharing rather than constitutive of an 'urban crisis' (see Jayne et al. 2011b; Jayne and Valentine 2015b).

Alcohol and urban 'counter publics': sharing emotions, embodiment and affect

Contemporary theoretical and empirical work has built on understanding of symbolic and social practices relating to alcohol, drinking and drunkenness to highlight how reciprocity, care and sharing can be better understood with reference to shared emotions, embodiment and affect (see Jayne et al. 2010; Jayne et al. 2006; Wait et al. 2011; Valentine et al. 2013). Working from the viewpoint that "[q]uestions about how emotions are embodied and located merit further elaboration in the context of typical and less typical everyday lives" (Davidson et al. 2005: 5), in parallel with studies that investigate affect as "a sense of push in the world ... a notion of broad tendencies and lines of force" (Thrift 2004: 60), theorists have made significant progress in advancing understanding of how embodied emotions and affect are intricately connected to specific contexts and practices relating to alcohol consumption.

While the diversity of embodied, emotional and affective geographies of different social groups requires sustained research, here we want to focus on similarities of shared experiences of alcohol consumption across social groups that contrasted starkly with popular and political representations of 'urban crisis'. Indeed, while it is important to bear in mind Leyshon's (2008) depictions of unequal social relations surrounding drinking and Jayne and Valentine's (2015a) engagement with 'actually existing' alcohol-related violence and disorder, the vast majority of respondents in our study described alcohol consumption in terms of positive emotional, embodied and affective senses of being able to find 'belonging' through both sharing practices (such as buying rounds, 'getting dressed up for a big night out', being a designated driver, being 'out on the pull' and so on) as well as highlighting other examples of shared experiences, to which we now turn.

Throwntogetherness and feeling 'at home'

While some participants in our research suggested that you could feel 'out of place', or fearful, in venues and public spaces by appearing to be too old or too young, or by visiting venues they didn't know well; and while others feared gendered, racist, subcultural, embodied, or homophobic comments and violence, the majority of respondents in our research talked about being able to develop strategies which allowed them to feel 'at home' because of alcohol consumption. Such responses were aligned with closeness, for example, to people they may have known for many years, to friendships that emerge for just a few minutes, and brief interactions with strangers on the street. The diversity of such relations was expressed in the following quotes, where (not so) intimate social relations offer people a sense of community, corporeal participation and shared experience – and are a key factor in facilitating the 'togetherness' of a night out for close-knit groups or a broader sense of shared experience with other drunken revellers:

> it's the atmosphere and the fun that I want, it's, the alcohol helps to sort of relax you but it is pure, it is a secondary part of it, it's talking, it's actually the conversations with friends that, that I like.
>
> (55–64, Male, NS-SEC 1)

And people you don't know from Adam ... you can sit and talk to them for half an hour blah blah blah and it's really nice to talk to people just like ... it's, you just go oh ... hello how are you?

(25–34, Female, NS-SEC 1)

I go in the pub, I don't mind going in the pub on my own. Or to meet, to, on the off chance that somebody I know will be in there. And I can, you know catch up on, on some news. ... You don't feel as though, oh I haven't been, I haven't been there for like you know sort of like, a week, I'd better go in quick in case everybody's forgotten, forgotten who I am you know, that sort of, that sort of thing. I think sometimes you feel, you almost feel as though you're committed to the pub, you want the pub to succeed. But the other side is the sort of camaraderie that's, that you, you sort of, you know miss. The, it's like a sort of camaraderie and it's also a sort of a mutual thing, sort of help, help thing, there's always help.

(45–54, Male, NS-SEC 4)

Respondents acknowledged that such feelings of belonging and social interaction were to a large degree facilitated by alcohol. Mirroring findings from Mass Observation, our research highlighted that drinking loosens inhibitions, offers the opportunity for creative and innovative thinking, allows the opportunity to say things you might not usually – all of which were considered as part of the pleasure of drinking. Indeed, the feeling of abandonment and being able to 'lose' yourself, was often expressed in terms of an enjoyment of the suspension of 'real time' into 'pub time' – of whiling away the hours – or in terms of heightened sexual desire and enjoyment of loud music and spectacular lighting.

For example, respondents talked (either affectionately or in terms of embarrassment) about having 'beer goggles' – of finding others interesting to talk to, or attractive and sexy – of being less judgemental of strangers, and of being able to overcome social boundaries. Many described this as emotionally liberating.

The effects of alcohol and performance of shared experiences which cemented 'closeness' emerged in a number of ways – from listening to friends' drunken silliness, rants and melancholy as well as drunken conversations with strangers. In addition to this the spatial/physical proximity of people consuming alcohol achieved by the extended time spent sitting or standing together while drinking, in public and domestic spaces was regarded as important, whether as part of a group, or one-to-one discussions (see Mehta and Bondi 1999). Thus, alcohol consumption combined with the time spent in particular spaces facilitates interaction providing key space-times for uninterrupted and often candid communication, about sharing problems, worries, good news, future plans and so on.

However, this was not always convivial. All respondents acknowledged that emotional talk could involve confrontations, loosing one's temper, being argumentative, belligerent, stubborn and so on. For some, this happened when alcohol amplified an existing mood or offered an opportunity to express long running feelings about certain people or topics:

> But if mentally, you're really up for it and you want to be you know bit a devil, lairy and have a good night then, yeah, that. I really think that it's all down to what sort of mood you're in … Yeah, if you drink gin. Then tears, but that's great though, because. It's great, because it's hilarious the next day, it's. Liz, Liz has been my best friend since I was 16 years old. And we're really close friends and we know each other really well, [laughs] We'll sit there and just cry and cry and cry and she's just like, and you know at the time, you think oh there's something wrong with me, I can't stop crying, and it's like, it's connected to your hormones and everything but it's quite healthy sometimes … To let it all out and it's fine … Sometimes I can be really mouthy in a horrible way to people. I just get really … and I'm just being vile to people. Very cutting …
>
> Interviewer: And do you ever have to apologise the next day or do you feel guilty about it?
>
> Well, yes and that happened to me a couple of weeks ago, actually, I got really drunk and I was really out of order with a friend of mine, and I woke up the next morning, I really cringed. And I rang him straight away, I said I'm really sorry and he said oh no it's fine, don't worry about it.
>
> (25–34, Female, NS-SEC 1)

> Your capacity to make an arse of yourself, you can drink and drink when you're out the house and just in the past I've done that and I don't know, just I'd got to the point where I just didn't like waking up the next day thinking what have I done and what have I said? Even though it was none, just that sort of, that feeling you get the next day after ale.
>
> (25–34, Male, NS-SEC 5)

As with the intensified conviviality, these heightened conflicts and tensions relate to the freedom of expression achieved through drinking. In many instances this results in what some people referred to as 'beer fear' – the uncomfortable feeling of trying to remember what might have happened or been said the night before – and is tempered by an emotional reciprocity, where bad behaviour, melancholy and so on is more often than not forgiven amongst friends. However, the ability to discount such behaviour as being 'down to the drink' was also acknowledged as bringing people together and strengthening relationships, of getting to know the best and worst of people through their drunkenness, of shared expressions both good and bad of peoples' behaviour and providing opportunities for terms of remembering, forgiving and forgetting.

These stories are useful in considering how geographies of emotions, embodiment and affect can challenge contemporary political, policy and popular depictions of alcohol related violence and disorder in urban public spaces (Jayne et al. 2006; Jayne and Valentine 2015a). For example, drinking and rowdiness can be theorised in terms of what Alan Radley (1995: 9) suggests is a "world of sensations, of movement, of the loss and recovery of physical control", or what he calls the "collective body-for-fun". This shows alcohol, drinking and drunkenness "is not merely the private, subjective enjoyment of the body, but also a symbolic transformation of feeling with the body … That is to say, they [drinkers] inhabit an imaginary world of their own making, central to which is their comportment and that of their fellows" (Radley 1995: 11). The street, loud and busy, ensuring transactions between people, places and things and the ability to interpret and navigate this milieu, is clearly an important feature of a night out. In these terms, interpreting, participating in, and enjoying the 'the buzz' and spectacle of a night out are facilitated and enhanced by alcohol (which in turn, enhances the experience of drinking):

> I've always liked a pub crawl, I've always liked you know walking between places and going into a fresh place and having a look round, seeing fresh people and seeing who's about and having a quick one and moving on. I much prefer to do that on a big night out then stay in one place, if you're, if you're just out on a midweek night, having a few pints, that's fine, stay in the same place … But on a night out, I always think it's more exciting to do a bit of trawl. It's just walking between the two, as well, you know, it's the, the whole experience. Well I think there is an undercurrent of the potential of meeting new people but I think it's also just the sort of, the kinetic energy and the, and the vibrancy that, that it brings. I hate empty streets and empty bars and empty pubs, it's horrible, depressing.
>
> (35–44, Male, NS-SEC 1)

> I mean the difference with England and with the continent. You know now whether it's because the climate conditions I don't know. Where they can just go out and have a quick glass of wine. And off they go and they're quite happy with it. Our culture demands. Sort of entertainment, excitement. Buzzing and all this business like you know. Dancing and all that, it, it all relates to it you know.
>
> (55–64, Male, NS-SEC 7)

Emotional, embodied and affective sharing economies

Such comments reveal that Nigel Thrift's (2004) conceptualisations of the "affective register of cities" are central to understanding contemporary geographies of drinking and drunkenness. When considered alongside feelings of sharing, belonging, closeness and connectivity, the experience of a 'big night out' is clearly facilitated by a mix of alcohol, adrenalin, endorphins, affect, shared emotions and interaction with (non)human actors:

> There's just nothing like that feeling you get on a Friday night … it's like a freedom that you don't get at other times. You might go out to the cinema, or for a meal during the week, even for a beer or two, but on Friday and Saturday its different … I don't get much time to see my mates, I work hard and I'm often tired but on a Friday you get a buzz … You look good, you've got your best gear on, there's nothing like that feeling that you've the whole weekend ahead of you to do what you want and the time to do it, and recover from the hangover … and that everyone about your age feels the same … you don't have to get up to work so you can go out and get pissed … drink what you want, do what you want, go where you want … and everyone on the streets is the same … when else do you get that freedom to walk … mess around, see and be seen … be part of thousands of other people who are just having a good time … you feel part of it, its yours and you feel the places you go are aimed at you and they way you want to live. After a hard week at work it's exactly what I need.
>
> (18–24, Male, NS-SEC 5)

Thinking about the assemblages that are brought together by drinking alcohol in the city (and in acknowledging differences between various commercial venues such as different types of pubs and nightclubs, public spaces and various social groups) allows a focus on the milieu, context and surroundings that relate to certain structural and aesthetic registers that offer insights into specific geographies of alcohol, drinking and drunkenness. Such theorisation is vital to understanding the shared emotional, embodied and affective nature of individual and collective drinking. Moreover, Sara Ahmed's (2004: 146) depiction of transpersonal 'affective economies' relating to the circulation between objects and signs, as an 'emotional ripple', is also pertinent. Applying these conceptions to alcohol consumption and relationships, reciprocity, care and sharing allows understanding of affects, feelings and emotions that emerge from a set of assemblages that intermix the biological, technical, social and economic – of different alcoholic liquids, people of different social groups, with different tolerances to alcohol, in different moods, in different venues and public spaces, responding to policing and legislative regimes and so on.

For example, Ahmed (2004) describes how collective emotions offer an intensification of processes of individuation which is potentially multiple and always/already part of assemblages that foster distributions of specific emotions and singular affects. Indeed, Ahmed argues that such affects are central to contemporary debates over the privatisation of public spaces in Western cities, where fear is attached to certain bodies, and where certain affects and emotions are individuated through relations of conflict and co-operation, within and between humans (often raced, classed and gendered bodies) and non-humans. Such arguments add important more-than-representational perspectives to understandings of the 'moral panics' that have loomed large in political and popular discourses relating to the drunken and disorderly working class, and more recently women and young people. As noted earlier, these discourses, circulating since the late eighteenth century, have sought to structure drinking behaviour through models of good citizenship (Leyshon 2005; 2008).

Contrary to such discourses, alcohol consumption nonetheless offers 'contingency, unpredictability and change' into the world (Ahmed 2004: 156), and in these terms drunken emotions work to secure collectivities through the way in which the bodies of others are read and encountered in more-than-representational ways. While it is a useful question to investigate such contradictions further and to consider how "emotions work to align some subjects with some others and against others" (Ahmed 2004: 25), there is also work to be done to consider how drinking and drunkenness plays a crucial role in the 'surfacing' of individual and collective bodies and enabling relationships, reciprocity, ethics of care and sharing. For example, emotions associated with drinking can be argued to align individuals with collectives – or bodily space with social space – through "the very intensity of their attachments" that alcohol and drunkenness offer (Ahmed 2004: 26). In these terms, rather than locating emotion in 'the individual' or 'the social', it can be argued that alcohol consumption allows responsiveness to and openness towards the worlds of others, that involves an interweaving of the personal with the social, and the affective with the mediated, which offers specific opportunities for drinkers to engage in relationships, reciprocity, care, sharing practices and experiences with friends and strangers in commercial and public spaces in a way that they may not do if they haven't been drinking alcohol (Ahmed 2004: 28).

Drunkenness can thus be seen as bound up with emotions, embodiment and affect that 'can be performative; they both repeat past associations as well as generating their object' (Ahmed 2004: 32). Moreover, as Dewsbury (2000: 493) suggests, performativity of events can be considered irretrievable and involve kinetic astonishment: "it is performativity therefore to think/act on real existences in opposition to the possibility of existence being pronounced by a priori ideas: it is the 'earthiness' of daily tasks, the encounters for our tears and laughter, and our corporeal needs that etches out the conceptual". Such theorisation rings true with respondents' reasons for consuming alcohol as a project of experimentation, of allowing venturesome couplings with regard to shared practices and experiences, of being creative and 'letting go'. Such arguments also offer tentative explanations of how individuals with differing levels of intoxication differently 'fit in' with drunken geographies, and also how, when high levels of alcohol are consumed in different cities around the world, a very specific set of emotional and affective registers, assemblages and performativities emerge to ensure different 'intoxicated urban geographies' (with variations within city spaces too).

Returning to consider the long-standing 'moral panics' and depictions of 'urban crisis' that circulate around urban drinking, the work of Nigel Thrift (2005) in describing cities on the brink of catastrophe is insightful. For example, alcohol consumption can be closely associated with representations of a pessimistic view of the moral and ethical life of cities that Thrift describes as 'a fear economy'. Nonetheless, despite such temporal practices, politics and possibilities of foreboding, where around the corner there is something to be feared, Thrift also argues that such politics amplifies the sense that around every corner is an opportunity. With such conditions in mind, Thrift argues that 'prosocial' everyday forms of kindness can be installed in cities as a value that goes beyond 'simple' civility, by adopting kindness as a social and aesthetic technology of *belonging to a situation* rather than as an organic emotion (Thrift 2005: 144). Thrift (2005: 139), nonetheless, argues that achieving sociality does not mean that everything has to be rosy and that alongside acts of kindness and compassion can be active dislike and outbreaks of violence, malign gossip, endless complaining, and a full spectrum of jealousy, petty snobbery, personal deprecation and so on. As Thrift concludes, cities bring people and things together in manifold combinations that don't always sit comfortably with one another (2005: 140).

However, while Thrift warns against a 'starry-eyed' search for such conditions, our respondents have explicitly outlined how alcohol consumption facilitates such sociability and enables relationships, reciprocity, care and sharing. In these terms, urban alcohol consumption is not dominated by 'a fear economy' but rather is constituted by diverse 'sharing economies'. Indeed, there are strong resonances in the research findings to claim that drinkers can be argued to be 'a counter public' with convivialities and sharing practices and experiences arising out of "a mutable itinerate culture, based around an urban politics of assembling intimacies, kindness and compassion, relating to an understanding of a range of social and aesthetic technologies of belonging" (Thrift 2005: 145). As the quotes throughout the chapter show, although alcohol enables respondents' specific modes of social interaction and friendship based around 'light-touch gatherings' (Thrift 2005: 146) such interactions can also include kinds of negative emotions, tensions and competition, which can heighten rather that lessen social divides. Nonetheless, respondents clearly talked about alcohol fuelled friendships and relationships, a sense of moral community coalescing around alcohol consumption and drunkenness that includes practical affective politics with explicit mobilisations of affect around drunkenness that allow a use of urban space in ways that will produce new understandings of the moment (Thrift 2008: 147).

This stands in contrast to Thrift's description of the "drunken mayhem of British cities on a Saturday night ... [in terms of an] undertow of spite, a thin veneer of altruism at its thinnest" (2005: 141). In these terms, Thrift's interpretation is closer to political, policy and media representations. Indeed, even those respondents who did express concern over 'feeling out of place' or fear of alcohol-related violence and disorder recognised that such anxiety was overwhelmingly related to 'second-hand stories' and media representations of violence and disorder rather than their own experiences (see Valentine 2008). Moreover, while others have described alcohol and drunkenness as an accelerator to violence for people (mostly men but increasingly women) who feel ontologically insecure due to feelings of economic and social marginalisation, job insecurity and so on (Winlow and Hall 2006), respondents in our study accepted that violent behaviour occurred, and that they attempted to be vigilant; of those who regularly visited commercial venues, none felt fearful enough for such concern to dampen the enjoyment of their night out (see Jayne and Valentine 2015a). Danger, unpleasantness, frustration, resentment, anger and fear thus tend to be a marginal feature with the majority of our respondents' drinking experiences being more concerned with 'positive' relationships, reciprocity, of care for drunken friends and overwhelmingly shared experience, reciprocity and care for strangers.

In these terms, Thien's (2005) 'contours of intimacy' is particularly useful in highlighting how alcohol allows temporary suspension of social norms of 'closeness' and interaction. Encounters between bodies, objects and spaces, and the impacts of those encounters that bear on the body's capacity to act or be affected, can be thought of as a "vitality, or potential for interaction" (Massumi 2002: 35). It is clear that for our respondents, consuming alcohol represents a specific "technology of the self", that

> permit[s] individuals to effect by their own means, or with the help of others, a certain number of operations on their bodies and souls, thoughts, conduct and ways of being so as to transform themselves in order to attain a certain state of happiness, purity, wisdom, perfection or immortality.
>
> (Foucault 1988: 18)

This enables relationships, reciprocity, care and sharing practices and experiences specifically constituted through alcohol, drinking and drunkenness.

Conclusion

This chapter has highlighted how alcohol, drinking and drunkenness enable shared practices and experiences including a sense of 'throwntogetherness' and 'belonging' that enables relationships with friends and strangers based on an ethic of 'transformation' and 'care'. In these terms, when Pile (2010) asks whether people – and not just political elites – can manipulate affect, it is clear than alcohol, drinking and drunkenness is used to generate particular embodied, emotional and affective experiences which while varying between individuals nonetheless creates collective drunken mind-body-worlds (Venn 2010).

While there are social differences and power relations bound up in emotional, embodied and affective geographies our research shows that there are also similarities and connectivities that bind drinkers together as a 'counter public' enabling interaction with people, space and place in a way that is intimately (dis)connected from sober experiences. In parallel with Dewsbury's (2000: 21) description of affect as phenomenon, our research has also highlighted that alcohol allows shared experience of the materialities of the world; with drunkenness allowing volumes of space, touch, rhythms, the movement of air, flows of blood and adrenaline to be heightened or dulled in order to be specifically different from their 'normal' everyday experiences. Alcohol, drinking and drunkenness allow a felt intensity which produces understanding before it can be signified and articulated – or, as Dewsbury suggests, "a field of sensible experience full of unqualified intensity" (2009: 21).

These findings show that alcohol is consumed by people because it offers a unique and explicit connection both 'within' and 'outside' the body allowing people to become "subjects which are caught and situated as bodies with radiating ripples and circuits of feeling, intensity, response and sensation ... [via] flows that wrap into and fold out of our bodies" (Dewsbury 2009: 21). In particular, alcohol allows drinkers to experience, negotiate and perform shifting emotions (over a few minutes, hours and longer time periods), including subjectivities that are multiple, emergent diverse and complex, bound up with bodily sensations and affective experiences that are challenging, at times unpredictable, fun, sad, and often un-rememberable 'intoxicated geographies'. Of course, developing an understanding of our emotional, embodied and affective lives in ways that account for the differences between each of these as well as understanding of how they work together in both personal and shared collective experiences is a big challenge. In this chapter we have nonetheless shown that foregrounding practices, politics and possibilities of sharing offers not only fruitful avenues to pursue such an agenda but also a profound critique of academic, political, popular and policy depictions of an alcohol-fuelled 'urban crisis'.

Notes

1 We would like to thank the Joseph Rowntree Foundation for funding the research upon which this chapter is based.
2 This chapter draws on, updates and advances previous arguments made in Jayne, M., Valentine, G. and Holloway, S. L. (2011b) *Alcohol, Drinking, Drunkenness: (Dis)Orderly Spaces*. Aldershot: Ashgate; Jayne, M., Valentine, G. and Holloway, S. L. (2011a) "What Use Are Units? Critical Geographies of Alcohol Policy', *Antipode*, 44 (3): 828–846; Jayne, M., Holloway, S. L. and Valentine, G. (2006) 'Drunk and disorderly: alcohol, urban life and public space', *Progress in Human Geography*, 30 (4), 451–468; Jayne, M., Valentine, G. and Holloway, S. L. (2010) 'Emotional, embodied and affective geographies of alcohol, drinking and drunkenness', *Transactions of the Institute of British Geographers* 35 (4), 540–554; Jayne, M. and Valentine, G. (2015a) 'Alcohol-related violence and disorder: new critical perspectives', *Progress in Human Geography*, (OnlineFirst) and Jayne, M. and

Valentine, G. (2015b) 'Drinking dilemmas: making a difference?, in Thurnell-Read, T. (Ed). *Drinking Dilemmas: Sociological Approaches to Alcohol Studies*, Routledge: London.
3   For more details visit http://www.jrf.org.uk/publications/drinking-places-where-people-drink-and-why

References

Ahmed, S. (2004) 'Collective feelings or the impression left by others' *Theory Culture and Society*, 212: 25–42.

Amin, A. (2012) *Land of Strangers*. London: Polity.

Bunnell, T., Yea, S., Peake, L., Skelton, T., and Smith, M. (2012) 'Geographies of friendship' *Progress in Human Geography*, 36(4), 490:507.

Burnett, J. (1999) *Liquid Pleasures: A Social History of Drinks in Modern Britain*. London: Routledge.

Clarke, P. (1983) *The English Alehouse: A Social History 1200–1830*, London: Faber and Faber.

Davidson, J., Smith, M. and Bondi, L. (2005) (eds) *Emotional Geographies*. Aldershot: Ashgate.

Dewsbury, J-D. (2000) 'Performativity and the event: enacting a philosophy of difference' *Environment and Planning D: Society and Space*, 18: 473–496.

Douglas, M. (1987) *Constructive Drinking*. Cambridge: Cambridge University Press.

Foucault, M. (1988) 'Technologies of the self' in Martin, L., Gutman, H. and Hutton, P. [eds.] *Technologies of the Self: A Seminar with Michael Foucault*, Tavistock: London.

Girouard, M. (1975) *Victorian Pubs*. London: Yale University Press.

Harrison, B. (1971) *Drink and the Victorians*. London: Faber.

Jacobs, J. (1961) *The Death and Life of Great American Cities*, New York: Random House.

Kathiravelu, L. (2013) 'Friendship and urban encounter: towards a research agenda', Max Planck Institute for the Study of Religious and Ethnic Diversity, Working Paper 13-10.

Jayne, M. and Valentine, G. (2016) '"It makes you go crazy": children's knowledge and experience of alcohol consumption' *Journal of Consumer Culture*, (In press).

Jayne, M. and Valentine, G. (2015a) 'Alcohol-related violence and disorder: new critical perspectives' *Progress in Human Geography*, (OnlineFirst)

Jayne, M. and Valentine, G. (2015b) 'Drinking dilemmas: making a difference?' in Thurnell-Read, T. [ed.] *Drinking Dilemmas: Sociological Approaches to Alcohol Studies*. London: Routledge.

Jayne, M., Valentine, G. and Holloway, S. L. (2010) 'Emotional, embodied and affective geographies of alcohol, drinking and drunkenness', *Transactions of the Institute of British Geographers* 35(4): 540–554.

Jayne, M., Valentine, G. and Holloway, S. L. (2011a) 'What use are units? Critical geographies of alcohol policy', *Antipode*, 44(3): 828–846.

Jayne, M., Valentine, G. and Holloway, S. L. (2011b) *Alcohol, Drinking, Drunkenness: (Dis)Orderly Spaces*, Aldershot: Ashgate.

Jayne, M., Holloway, S. L. and Valentine, G. (2006) 'Drunk and disorderly: alcohol, urban life and public space', *Progress in Human Geography*, 30(4): 451–468.

Kneale, J. (1999) '"A problem of supervision": moral geographies of the nineteenth-century British public house', *Journal of Historical Geography*, 25(3): 333–348.

Kneale, J. (2001) 'The place of drink: temperance and the public, 1956–1914', *Social and Cultural Geography*, 2(1): 43–59.

Lefebvre, H. (1996) *Writings on Cities* (translated by E. Kofman and E. Lebas), Oxford: Blackwell.

Leyshon, M. (2005) No Place for a Girl: rural youth, pubs and the performance of masculinity in Little J, Morris C (eds) *Critical Studies in Rural Gender Issues*, Altdershot: Ashgate, 104–122.

Leyshon, M. (2008) '"We're stuck in the corner": Young women, embodiment and drinking in the countryside'. *Drugs: Education, Prevention and Policy*, 15(3): 267–289.

Malcomson, R. (1973) *Popular Recreations in English Society 1700–1850*. Cambridge: Cambridge University Press.

Massey, D. (2005) *For Space*. London: Sage.

Mass Observation (1987 [1937–1943]) *The Pub and the People*. London: The Cresset Library.

Massumi, B. (2002) *Parables for the Virtual Movement Affect Sensation*. London: Duke University Press.

McAndrew, C. and Edgerton, R.B. (1969) *Drunken Comportment: A Social Explanation*. London: Nelson.

Mehta, A. and Bondi, L. (1999) 'Embodied discourse: On gender and fear of violence', *Gender, Place and Culture*, 6(1), 67–84.

Pile, S. (2010) 'Emotions and affect in recent human geography', *Transactions of the Institute of British Geographers*, 35: 5–20.

Radley, A. (1995) 'The elusory body and social constructionist theory', *Body and Society*, 1: 3–23.

Schivelbusch, W. (1992) *Tastes of Paradise*. London: Pantenen.

Simmel, G. (1903) 'The metropolis and mental life' in Kasinitz, P. [ed.] *Metropolis: Center and Symbol for Our Times*. New York: New York University Press.

Thien, D. (2005) 'Intimate distances considering questions of Us' in Davidson J, Smith M and Bondi L (eds) *Emotional Geographies*. Aldershot: Ashgate, 191–204.

Thrift, N. (2008) *Non-Representational Theory*. London: Routledge.

Thrift, N. (2005) 'But malice aforethought: cities and the natural history of hatred' *Transactions of the Institute of British Geographers*, 30(2): 133–150.

Thrift, N. (2004) 'Intensities of feeling towards a spatial politics of affect' *Geografiska Annaler Series B Human Geography*, 86: B1, 57–78

Valentine, G. (2008) 'Living with difference: reflections on geographies of encounter' *Progress in Human Geography* 32: 323–337.

Valentine, G., Jayne, M. and Gould, M. (2013) 'The proximity effect: the role of the affective space of family life in shaping children's knowledge about alcohol and its social and health implications' *Childhood: a Journal of Global Child Research* 21(1): 103–118.

Venn, C. (2010) 'Individuation, relationality, affect: rethinking the human in relation to the living' *Body and Society*, 16(1): 129–161.

Waitt, G., Jessop, L. and Gormann-Murray, A. (2011) '"The guys in there just expect to be laid": Embodied and gendered socio-spatial practices of a "night out" in Wollongong, Australia' *Gender, Place and Culture*, 18(2): 255–275.

Winlow, S. and Hall, S. (2006) *Violent Night*. Oxford: Berg.

Part II

Sharing, the economy and sharing economies

This second section disentangles what we see as key and sometimes competing components of conceptualising sharing and the economy. We propose that there are multiple ways of thinking, doing and combining sharing and the economy, which are not limited to contemporary notions of 'the sharing economy'. Together, these chapters challenge, trouble or move beyond strict compartmentalisations and definitions, and broaden out theoretical scope and discussion so as to better reflect sharing as ordinary economic practice.

This is not to say that 'the sharing economy' is to be dismissed, for we are alert to the momentum of ideas and creativity that this sphere presents. Instead, it is that we do not see this as the only way of sharing in an economic sense, and indeed nor do our authors. The chapters herein exemplify the diversity of thinking and doing sharing, the economy, and sharing economies, even within initiatives in 'the sharing economy'. Most importantly, they provide colourful illustrations of how these can meet, merge and mingle in the lived realities of everyday life.

With examples that include the sharing of spaces, things, experiences and moments, sharing and the economy can be seen anew. We see that sharing is not always a neat fit with the economic, that the interception of emotions, values and taste can rouse tensions and conflict over what is being shared and how such sharing is organised. Thinking through how different forms of sharing encounter one another also makes way for thinking through the relationships upon which sharing can be built or build, reminding us that sharing is a much a social practice as it is an economic one.

6 Home for hire

How the sharing economy commoditises our private sphere

Paula Bialski

Since the rise of the sharing economy in recent years, mass media (the *Economist* (2013), *The New York Times*, and the *Guardian* (2014), to name a few), have scoffed at the word 'sharing' and questioned the term 'economy' – critiquing the do-goody, fluffy nature in which the term 'sharing,' arrives at your consciousness first, hiding the term 'economy', and making the whole practice "seem selfless" (Singer 2015). The term 'sharing economy' was first associated with online technologies that match providers or owners of certain goods (like a couch to sleep on) or services (like dog walking) with consumers – allowing users to access goods and services without the necessity of ownership. That being said, these recent mass media discourses have promoted an understanding that this form of 'sharing' is indeed much akin to an economic exchange. What has not been presented thus far is a critique of that which is being 'shared' or sold, and how this form of economy is helping capitalise on spheres of life which have formally been off limits to monetisation. This chapter is about the ways in which recent transformations in economic life – through the phenomenon of short-term apartment 'sharing' or renting – have placed some of the most intimate and private spheres for purchase: namely, the home and everything that comes with it: privacy, intimacy, candidness, and authenticity.

For the past 7 years, I have been conducting fieldwork in a number of sharing economy and related sites – including CouchSurfing, Airbnb, and various ride-sharing networks. During one of my most recent moments in the field, I noticed something was awry with how public the 'home' has become. I was 15 minutes into my visit to the San Francisco headquarters of the sharing-economy giant of short-term apartment renting, Airbnb. My host was leading me through the giant hallways, colourful hammocks and co-working desks, until my eyes slowly focused on one specific detail – a conference room. I looked inside its glass walls and pressed my palms up to get a better look. My gaze stopped at a bed covered in a bright duvet, accentuated by a bold coloured shelf filled with used books lining the wall. Next to the door near my hands, a photo hung above the standard boardroom sign-up sheet. I focused in and saw 'Milan' labelled across the door, with a small 5x3 photo of the bedroom inside hanging above it. I turned around and looked at my host.

He smiled. "Our boardrooms are modelled after real listings." I looked back inside. I suddenly started imagining the couple in Milan who shared that bed. I was with them during their morning coffee, and overhearing their pillow talk at night. It was this Silicon Valley "unicorn" that helped bring millions of people into the bedrooms of other strangers, and they were highlighting the power of this process as they appropriated one of these bedrooms for their staff meeting room.

With the rise of social media, the call to "share!" has more or less become an imperative (Benkler 2004; Leistert and Röhle 2011). Peer-to-peer structures are spreading into new areas of social life (Bauwens 2005); for example, in peer-production of news or movies or the so-called crowdsourcing of peer-finance through platforms such as Kickstarter. Recent years have also in particular witnessed a boom in online social networks that allow people to access goods rather than just owning them. Services such as *Mitfahrgelegenheit* for car-sharing, bike sharing schemes in various cities, or CouchSurfing and Airbnb for accommodation have created spaces for sharing one's resources with others offline. These platforms which offer access to goods rather than ownership, have been called a number of terms, including the "sharing economy" (Sacks 2011), "collaborative consumption" (Botsman and Rogers 2010), or an "economy of sharing" (Wittel 2011).

The practice of collaborative consumption can be embedded (more or less deeply) in discourses around sharing, borrowing, gift-giving, personal space, cooperation, possession, intimacy, reciprocity, and a number of other socio-economic phenomena. Collaborative consumption refers to all sorts of practices of monetised or non-monetised exchange. The latter relates to what Jenkins et al. term 'inter-personal borrowing,' further defining it as a "pervasive form of non-market mediated access-based consumption and a distinct form of exchange" (Jenkins et al. 2014: 131).

The predominant problem with the descriptions of the sharing economy thus far is that it emerged from business and marketing industries and consumer studies, and little analysis has been done to date that analyses how the sharing economy has exploited the private sphere, evoking an emotional labour on behalf of the hosts and guests. As other chapters in this volume have shown, the sharing economy may be understood to be as much about sharing as it is about entrepreneurship, with financial interests an "important factor in the formation of positive attitudes towards collaborative consumption," where "economic benefits are a stronger motivator for intentions to participate in such communities" (Hamari et al. 2016: 2055). This chapter looks at the sharing economy as part of the monetisation of private life. As such, one must take into account both the cultural and economic logics inherent in the exchange, what exactly is being 'shared,' how, and by whom. The boundaries of 'sharing' are constantly being redrawn as new forms of economy, and with it, new understandings of property are being developed. How has the sharing economy intertwined public-sphere market logics with private-sphere emotional needs?

This chapter focuses on the way in which the sharing economy encroaches upon the intimate sphere – specifically through its design choices and enforced homemaking practices – and places what was once 'the sacred' on display: ready to be rated, remodelled, and updated. This in turn creates a homogenisation of intimacy, and a branding of 'coziness.' Along the lines of previous studies on conditional hospitality, such as the work of Brandth and Haugen (2012) or Daugstad and Kirchengast (2013) on the commercialisation of home within agrotourism, I will be mainly focusing on the way in which private sphere is being sold and marketed. As such, I will be focusing on the practice and inherent complexities of 'hosting' via Airbnb.

The significance of home

In order to fully understand and critique the practice of the short-term rental sharing economy, I would first like to focus in on what exactly is being 'shared.' The case study this chapter will focus on is Airbnb – an online apartment 'sharing' marketplace, where people are able to rent out a room in their house, their entire home, or their second home, for a fee. After working with CouchSurfing for nearly 7 years, I began studying their 'sharing economy' counterpart. While the two social networks have little to do with one another organisationally, what interested me was that Airbnb and CouchSurfing both enable people to invite strangers into one's home, and both push boundaries of interaction in terms of how strangerhood was treated, intimacy and privacy were negotiated and friendship or 'friendliness' was being monetised.

In 2014, I started researching Airbnb in Germany – between hosting and guest-ing, I also watched over the shoulders of the Airbnb team in Hamburg as they conducted a public relations survey. In this survey, which was taken by 400 hosts and 700 guests in Berlin, it turned out that 63 per cent of Airbnb users rent out their primary residence. In other words, the short-term rental sharing economy is mainly about sharing one's 'home' (note that hosts often move to their partner's or family's homes for the duration of the guests' stay). The act of sharing and selling one's home is a problematic practice, and one that has not been taken into account as the sharing economy began taking over apartments and houses, particularly in global tourism capitals.

The home sphere is highly significant as a temporal and cultural construct. Rybczynski (1986: 221) explains that home is "a sense of domesticity … [or] an atmosphere of coziness". Moreover, home is also linked to "domestic comfort [which] involves a range of attributes – convenience, efficiency, leisure, ease, pleasure, domesticity, intimacy, and privacy" (Rybczynski 1986: 231). Privacy necessitates that a boundary of control is set up, delineating what is 'home' and what is outside this private space. Normally, those feeling 'at home' are in control of how 'home' is demarcated, and who enters this 'home' territory. Derrida stated that the act of opening oneself up or offering hospitality inevitably reaffirms this control: "This is mine, I am at home, you are welcome in my home" (Derrida 2000: 14). The boundaries of 'home' are thus controlled by various material objects: walls, doors, fences, name signs, etc. Goffman, who wrote extensively on interaction orders and boundaries, used the concept of 'stalls' to explore the way in which privacy, personal space, and a sense of self, is claimed. The "claim to personal space," he wrote, could be understood in the way in which people mark 'stalls' around them, or use objects to demark a boundary or territory of claim. He provided the example of a park bench – which exists in order to be claimed, if only temporarily (Goffman 1997).

Bauman explains the reason for drawing a boundary:

> Control, and the right to decide who or what is allowed to pass the border and who or what is bound to stay where they are on one side only (what items of information have the prerogative of remaining private, and which ones are allowed or decreed to be made public).
>
> (2010: 67)

Invasion of this space is generally unwanted. When exploring private space, Baumann explains that the "change in the prevailing rules of border traffic, were almost exclusively expected and feared to arrive from the 'public' side: public institutions were widely suspected of an endemic proclivity for snooping and eavesdropping" (Bauman 2010: 68).

While a further section will explore the way in which Airbnb enforces certain mechanisms of control that encroach on the private sphere, breaking territorial boundaries, space and place are central features of the experience of 'being-in-the-world' as an embodied subject, for embodiment is always experienced through spatial dimension. The human geographer Yi-Fu Tuan calls the emotional relationship with places or landscapes topophilia, or "the affective bond between people and place or setting" (Tuan 1974: 4). The emotional meaning of home has been explored by Deborah Lupton, who stated that "in contemporary western societies, the concept of 'the home' has particular resonances for the 'authentic' emotional self" (Lupton 1998: 156). The perceptions of place and space that individuals gather from their senses – the sights, sounds, smells, tastes and feel of the environment – have a potentially powerful role in the production of emotion. Just as people are able to shape aspects of their physical environment, so does the environment shape subjectivity (Lupton 1998: 152). The exact meaning of home "is physically, psychologically, and socially constructed in both 'real' and 'ideal' forms" (Somerville 1997). Moreover, the home is a "prime unexcavated site for an archaeology of sociability" (Putnam 1999: 144).

While this might seem obvious, I would like to argue that various new market forces made possible by sharing economy platforms such as Airbnb help reconfigure and redefine these spaces of sociability, and affective dimensions of authenticity, coziness, and privacy. As Germann Molz pointed out, the "global distribution of capital and commodities threaten to undermine the geographical boundedness and emotional groundedness that we tend to associate with home" (Germann Molz 2008: 325).

To uncover these sites of reconfiguration and redefinition, I want to turn to the role of the Airbnb host. The ideological and aesthetic regime of how to be a host, how to create and 'market' one's home, and in what way to interact with one's guest are all inherent parts of the short-term apartment sharing economy. Designed like a social networking website with a profile of each user, photographs, a friendship list, and a review system, Airbnb – or the so-called community marketplace – allows a user to offer accommodation for a certain price to anybody who is willing to pay the given amount. The exchange differs from a hotel booking, as the host has to first accept the guest's request. Any host can deny the rental of their space, without giving a reason to the user requesting the space – and I want to mention that Airbnb does not directly outline the terms by which the host rents out their apartment – the frequency of rental, the price, and terms of service, are generally all outlined by the host. That being said, there is a culture of hosting, a specific aesthetic regime that Airbnb promotes, and a suggested code of conduct that Airbnb promotes – all of which shall be explored in a later section of this chapter. Additionally, the exchange is not purely about hospitality – the host-guest exchange is usually based on an economic imperative – where the host relies on the income of the guest, thus, more often than not, accepting the guest's request.

In order to advertise accommodation – the host is requested to upload one or more photos of the space-on-offer, describe the space, and provide its location. When searching for accommodation in a given location, a traveller can filter the available spaces based on location in a city (limited to a certain desired district), price range, and accommodation type (whether an entire apartment, a room in a shared house, or a shared room). The offers then appear on a list as well as on a map of the city. Somebody searching for accommodation will then book the space of their choice by providing credit card details and time of arrival and departure. The host then must approve the booking via email, and arrange a time to let their guest into their house. During my fieldwork, I noted that very often, a host gives the guests keys to the apartment for the duration of their stay, and provides the guest with a small tour of the apartment.

Emerging networks of technologically mediated actors, that platforms such as Airbnb afford, "are enabling dispersed and distributed users to engage and participate in complex social webs of presence and action" (Dennis 2007: 22). The codes of conduct, as well as forms of emotional labour of presence and collaboration are part of the ways in which Airbnb users 'succeed' in the community. This participation is creating a type of participatory culture that has not been discussed before – and not in the public sphere, but on a private, intimate, home-scale. Airbnb sells itself on the same premise as the hospitality club CouchSurfing once did – that users want to experience 'home' and "don't wanna be treated as a tourist no longer" – as one CouchSurfer stated, saying, "I'm a traveller and participate in daily life when I'm CouchSurfing" (Bialski 2012).

Put on a smile

The following section will outline the way in which the private sphere is 'sold' – but I will do so by looking at the various processes by which this is done, starting with the host's 'emotional labour.' The nature and value of emotional labour for waged and unwaged economies can be traced back, most notably perhaps, to the works of Hardt and Negri (2001), and their use of the term "immaterial labour" and "affective labour." One example of affective labour, can be drawn from Hochschild's widely read book, *The Managed Heart* (2003). There, Hochschild describes the way in which airline companies sell their image through the emotional labour of their female flight attendants – namely, through their smile – and how this process moves the private, intimate, and emotional to commercial use (2003: 93). This emotional labour required by flight attendants, and the way in which this emotional labour is akin to that of the short-term rental sharing economy, can be observed in the following passage, which describes the way in which a pilot outlined the expected behaviour of his flight attendants:

> Having first established the emotional labour due him, he went on to describe what was due the passengers: "Now, girls, I want to tell you something else," he said moving slowly, with authority. "I want you to think of the cabin as the living room in your very own home. At home. Wouldn't you go out of your way to make friends feel at ease and have a good time? Well, it's the same thing in the L-1001." Then he said what other pilots were to repeat after him: "Girls. I want you to smile. Your smile is your best asset. So I want you to go out there and use it. Smile. Really lay it on. Smile." The young woman from Memphis wrote in her notebook, "Must smile."

Much like other areas of the service economy where emotional and embodied forms of labour are important (McDowell 2004), smiling and exuding "friendliness" is just one aspect of being a 'successful' Airbnb host. In the 'hosting' section on the Airbnb website (www.airbnb.co.uk/hospitality: no pagination), one can find a "Hosting Standards" section for hosts, which outlines the various procedures necessary for successful hosting. This section includes guidelines for replying to rental requests ('within 24 hours'), ways of preparing one's home to match the Airbnb 'cleanliness standard,' and expected availability (a host must be 'available for the guest when they arrive'). The help and guidance section also features a few paragraphs titled "Personality," which guide the new host through the best ways of 'presenting' oneself:

> Airbnb is made up of magical moments and hosts like you create them. Let the personality of you and your listing transform the trip experience.

While Airbnb is not being as explicit in forcing their hosts to 'smile,' this statement bares similarities with Hochschild's example of the emotional labour required from an airline company. Here, the flight attendant is the copywriter who communicated Airbnb's 'mission' through the "Help/Personality" section of the website, and the airline stewardess is the new Airbnb host. The first tip asks the host to provide their guests with the best experience through creating 'magical moments,' as if magic is an ability everyone knows how to perform, and a 'moment' can both be predicated and designed. The host is summoned to be a magician, painting the perfect travel experience for their guests. While not explicitly forcing the hosts to do so, this 'tip' is more of a call to action, implicitly stating, "If you follow these simple steps, you will gain more guests." This statement places corporate pressure on the host to engage in an emotional labour, also implying that if a host does not do so, they will not be among the 'successful' hosts. The main difference is that being a host is not like being a stewardess – who is a wage labourer earning a monthly salary. Hosts can in fact, increase the amount they earn, depending on the amount of customers they acquire. Thus, the pressure to succeed is an inherent part of the market logic of this economy.

The second statement on the 'Help' section of the Airbnb website was even more blunt:

> Make sure you maintain a helpful and polite tone, and find opportunities to personalise your communication so that you can build trusting relationships with other members of the Airbnb community.

To 'make sure' is a statement between a warning and a suggestion, one that aims to ensure the hosts keep up the emotional standards of the Airbnb community. Being helpful and polite is not a permanent state of being. It requires a certain amount of emotional labour to be helpful and polite, especially in moments when one does not feel inclined to do so (Leidner 1999). 'Building trust' is also a complex process, and one that cannot be reduced to a 'helpful and polite' tone between two actors. The website's call to share is also a call to be emotionally stable, helpful and polite. One is encouraged to 'share,' but only those emotions which are desirable – that which is personal, 'authentic,' and wins trust. Further, the hosting guidelines state,

> No one knows your space, your neighbourhood, or your city like you do. Share your favourite places with them and introduce them to your closest pals … Guests often relish unconventional travel opportunities. Teach them something local and unforgettable … You invited your guest in … now consider inviting them out! Ask your guest if they would like to join you at your favourite café, museum, or neighbourhood lounge.

Not only is the website asking the hosts to engage in a certain emotional labour, but also calls to share other immaterial goods – such as their network capital or cultural capital. By 'network capital' I mean here, the sharing of one's 'closest pals.' This call to action is indirectly forcing hosts to capitalise on their best friends, implying, "Share your best friends and you'll gain more rental capital." A close friendship is a highly delicate social relation, one that involves reciprocity, care, and consideration, and maintaining close friendships involves rituals specific to each particular dyad (Fischer 1982a, 1982b). Sharing one's close friendship circle with every guest can endanger the close friendship, and instrumentalise a relationship which was, perhaps, a means-relationship (and not one based on ends, or utility) (see Badhwar 1987; 2008; Bunnell et al. 2012).

Elsewhere (Bialski 2012), I explored how CouchSurfing – a non-monetary form of apartment sharing – was based on an economy of attention and reciprocity. Those who used CouchSurfing, sought out interactions on the move because they wanted to "see things through other people's eyes, understand their life and find ideas." These travellers also expressed that they "would never have experienced" these ideas and emotions "alone." CouchSurfing has become a way of meeting others in order to 'gain' something, and friendships created via this network seem like types of relationships centred on clearly circumscribed interests that must be fixed objectively (Simmel and Wolff 1950). Badhwar termed this type of friendship as a 'means' friendship, "a lesser friendship where the central feature is the instrumental or means value of each to the other" (Badhwar 1987: 2). An example of this sort of friendship is one in which two individuals are social as a means for further social advancement, amusement, the promotion of some cause, or even mutual edification or improvement (Badhwar 1987; 2008). Relationships created within Airbnb can be seen as 'means' relationships – where a host or guest follow the rules outlined on the hospitality guidelines section of the Airbnb website, in order to gain good reviews or other benefits or incentives such as staying an extra night for 'free'. For example, as the hospitality guidelines page suggests, the host can 'maintain a helpful and polite tone,' or introduce their guest to their 'best pals'. The process of giving, opening up, trusting, and exchanging is already conducive to a 'pure' form of sociality – a sociality which Simmel outlined as a relationship which "has no ulterior end, no content, and no result outside itself, it is oriented completely about personalities" (Simmel and Hughes 1949: 255). The sharing economy platforms such as Airbnb have an ulterior end – to earn money.

Bernstein (2007), in her ethnography of sex workers in San Francisco, explained that sex workers advertise themselves as "girlfriends for hire" and describe the ways in which they offer not merely eroticism but authentic intimate connection for hire in the marketplace. How is this any different to the authenticity that is staged through this 'sharing' economy? When Airbnb asks users to stage 'authentic' experiences, in which guests will meet their best pals, go out with the host to their favourite bars, and provide them with unforgettable experiences, we can say that Airbnb is attempting to stage an authentic friend experience, only instead of overworked high-tech professionals paying for staged sexual transactions (in the example of Bernstein's), Airbnb promises authenticity to weary travelers, tired of the same-old impersonal hotel chain.

On multiple occasions, guests I spoke to explained that they prefer to use Airbnb because of its more personal atmosphere.

In a section on prostitution in 'The Philosophy of Money', Simmel stated that the lowest level of human dignity is "reached when what is most intimate and personal for a woman ... is offered for such thoroughly impersonal, externally objective remuneration" (Simmel 2011: 112). As I already outlined in an earlier section of this chapter – the home is also considered one of the most intimate and personal spaces. In a similar way, we can imagine that Simmel would critique Airbnb's monetisation of home – that something as intimate and personal as one's home is offered for money, through impersonal, externally objective remuneration. This point calls for further research into the ways long-term hosting enforces a process or feeling of "de-homing" – in which the host feels less and less like the space they are selling, the space that is being used by dozens or hundreds of strangers, still feels in fact like the intimate and personal "home" they once experienced.

My home is your home

In the previous section, I outlined the way in which Airbnb enforces an emotional labour among hosts – emotion which helps provide access to the home, and helps simulate the feeling of home and community. In the same recent survey of Berlin hosts mentioned in an earlier section, 68 per cent of home owners using Airbnb expressed that they rented out their entire home, rather than just one or two rooms, to guests. The sharing economy in this case is indeed about 'sharing' the entire home, and thus also constitutes an emotional economy. While the previous section outlined the emotional labour that is required of a host, this section will explain the way in which a website and the host put their actual home for 'hire.' There are a number of practices, elements of the website's design, and aesthetic mechanisms, which force hosts to put their intimate sphere on display.

Firstly, the multitude of images each user reveals in order to underline the coziness and comfort offered to their guests is part of the way in which a home is sold. As an incentive for many new hosts, Airbnb will send a photographer into the home. One of my hosts in Berlin was proud that her stylish apartment was offered a free photo-shoot. She explained that these 'professional' photos are supposed to help highlight the 'listing' more – yet the website states that photos are "copyrighted to Airbnb." In having a photographer come into the host's space, and then appropriating these photos as sole property of the Airbnb company, Airbnb, de facto, invades the private sphere. In a similar vein, Bauman commented on the way in which social media invades the private sphere,

> covering it with a dense network of garrisons, spying gadgets and bugging devices, and thereby depriving human individuals or groups of individuals of the shelter offered by a private, untrespassable space; and by the same token, of their personal or group security.
>
> (Bauman 2010: 68)

This does not go to show that commercial exploitation of a private sphere is strictly a top-down process. In 'The Time Bind' (1997), Hochshild analysed the cultural transposition of emotional meaning from the sphere of domesticity to the sphere of public commerce, arguing that such symbolic inversions are a consequence of the changing material realities of both public and private spheres. Baumann argued that indeed the private sphere is now infiltrating the public, forcing itself upon others:

> Privacy is the realm that is meant to be one's kingdom, the land of one's sole and indivisible sovereignty, inside which one has full power to decide 'what and who I am', and from which one may launch and relaunch at will campaigns to have one's own decisions duly recognised and respected.
>
> (Bauman 2010: 62)

The act of 'showing off' one's home through an Airbnb profile, establishing oneself as a skilful homemaker, a stylish decorator, or somebody full of care, is also at play when building a public profile.

Yet why then emulate a sense of home? Why does 'cosiness' sell? Bensman and Lilienfeld (1979) have stressed the growing concern to achieve intimacy in modern societies, stating that "the demand for intimacy persists to the point where it is virtually compulsive." They explain this situation in terms of the alienating effects of the development of large, impersonal organisations in the modern world. Much of social life becomes run along impersonal lines. A flight into intimacy is an attempt to secure a meaningful life in familiar environments that have not been incorporated into these larger systems (Bensman and Lilienfeld 1979: 94). One can also see the opposite of cold an impersonal hotel, the warm and authentic 'real' home of an Airbnb host. During my research into Airbnb, I noted that the friendlier, cosier, more seemingly 'authentic' apartments gained more positive reviews on the website – which is linked to the authentic interiority that is being offered for pay.

This illusion of authenticity that is being offered for pay is what Berstein, in "Temporarily Yours," terms bonded authenticity. Here, she explores the way sex workers create an illusion of intimacy – where payment from the customer requires that the sex worker uphold this illusion of an "emotionally bounded erotic exchange" (Bernstein 2007: 6).

In one way or another, this illusion of authenticity, and the illusion that sharing does take place, is inherently part of the sharing exchange. During my fieldwork, I noted that the guests I interviewed disliked living in sterile apartments that "looked like hotels." The more the apartment they were staying in looked like an authentic home, or even looked like their home, the better. This authenticity is part of the economy of atmospheres that is promoted by peer-providers, and made visible through the Airbnb interface through images and listing reviews. Advertising a listing as 'home,' rather than just an apartment, room, or space, already connotes that the guest will gain an experience of a certain atmosphere – in this case, a *sense* of home. This 'economy of atmospheres' – where what is being exchange is in fact a feeling, a 'dream,' a specific atmosphere – is intrinsic in the logic of this form of sharing economy.

Throughout this chapter, it might seem that I painted the Airbnb host as somebody with no boundaries, and that Airbnb was a hegemonic infrastructure that forced all users to exploit every corner of their home. Indeed, there are mechanisms of territorialisation that manifest themselves when hosting and being a guest, and these mechanisms are enforced through various regulations and affordances that Airbnb provides. Within the Airbnb profile, a host is able to outline the nature of their 'listing,' (e.g. "the home is centrally located"), a description of the house (e.g. "There are 3 other housemates"), and what the guests can and cannot do (e.g. "The attic is off-limits"). Yet while these mechanisms exist, the paradox is that while hosts are 'free' to present their boundaries online, the emotional economy of this website, which promotes a demeanour of openness and freedom, forces users to put on a face of openness, and minimise their boundaries. Strictness and territorial behaviour lose the game and will lose 'customers'. In order to understand the Airbnb host, we must imagine them as shop owners, dusting off their shelves and putting their best, trendiest wares on display. They want every customer to admire them, every customer to want to sleep in their beds, cook in their kitchens, and sip coffees on their porches and balconies. Building up territorial boundaries in a culture of openness is a losing move. A host who puts up a possessive boundary could perhaps communicate, through their online profile: "Do not use the washing machine" or "The coffee maker is off limits." Yet this generally is not done. Not because the hosts don't feel inclined to do so, but because if they do so, they will lose 'selling power.' This is due to a number of market logics that force them to compete with other hosts who are also adhering to the same emotional and monetised economies.

Conclusions

The fact that digital media brought us a tool that helped us exploit one of our final remaining private and intimate spheres is not surprising. One can say that due to the increase in our global mobility, there is a market demand for intimacy and home. As I previously mentioned, the "global distribution of capital and commodities threaten to undermine the geographical boundedness and emotional groundedness that we tend to associate with home" (Germann Molz 2008: 325). In the past, popular culture has depicted the business traveller or the backpacker of today's hyper-mobile society as a lone nomad, travelling alone, eating alone, living in hostels or hotel rooms. In his text on home territories, David Morley underlined that in recent years, theories in postmodernity painted the image of supposedly deterritorialised culture of "homelessness: images of exile, diaspora, time-space compression, migrancy and 'nomadology'" (Morley 2000: 3). According to Morley, the concept of home often remains as the "uninterrogated anchor or alter ego of all this hyper-mobility" (Morley 2000, 3). Place itself, or "the seeking after a sense of place, has come to be seen by some as necessarily reactionary" to the "geographic fragmentation, the spatial disruption, of our times" (Massey 1991: 24).

The aim of this chapter was to investigate the mechanisms in place within the Airbnb website which help exploit the home sphere. In doing so, this analysis brought us closer to understanding the full dimensions of the sharing economy – as an economy of emotion, of intimacy, and privacy. Here I touched upon how exactly this so-called sharing economy helps exploit the home-sphere. In order paint a picture of this process, I unpacked the website's enforcement our emotional labour – which provides guests with access to our home, helping to simulate the feeling of a familiar 'home' community. I then highlighted the website's infrastructural mechanisms that place the home on display. What other dimensions the 'sharing economy' claim to share, beyond just the short-term rental websites such as Airbnb, would be interesting to investigate, in order to build a deeper critique of this 'movement.'

References

Badhwar, N.K. (1987) 'Friends as ends in themselves' *Philosophy and Phenomenological Research* 48: 1–23.

Badhwar, N.K. (2008) 'Friendship and commercial societies' *Politics, Philosophy, and Economics* 7: 301–326.

Bauman, Z. (2010) *44 Letters from the Liquid Modern World*. London: Polity.

Bauwens, M. (2005) 'The political economy of peer-production' *CTheory*. Retrieved from http://www.ctheory.net/articles.aspx?id=499

Benkler, Y. (2004) 'Sharing nicely: on shareable goods and the emergence of sharing as a modality of economic production' *Yale Law Journal* 114(2): 273–358.

Bensman, J. and Lilienfield, R. (1979) *Between Public and Private*. New York, NY: Free Press.

Bernstein, E. (2007) *Temporarily Yours: Intimacy, Authenticity, and the Commerce of Sex*. Chicago, IL: University of Chicago Press.

Bialski, P. (2012) 'Technologies of hospitality: how planned encounters develop between strangers', *Hospitality & Society*, 1(3): 245–260

Brandth, B., & Haugen, M. S. (2012) 'Farm tourism and dilemmas of commercial activity in the home' *Hospitality & Society* 2(2) 179–196.

Bunnell, T., Yea, S., Peake, L., Skelton, T. and Smith, M. (2012) 'Geographies of friendships' *Progress in Human Geography*, 36(4): 490–507.

Daugstad, K., & Kirchengast, C. (2013) 'Authenticity and the pseudo-backstage of agri-tourism' *Annals of Tourism Research* 43: 170–191.

Dennis, K. (2007) 'Technologies of civil society: communication, participation and mobilization, *Innovation: The European Journal of Social Science Research*, 20(1): 19–34.

Derrida, J. (2000) *Of Hospitality*. Stanford: Stanford University Press.

Economist (2013) 'All eyes on the sharing economy' *The Economist*. Retrieved from http://www.economist.com/news/technology-quarterly/21572914-collaborative-consumption-technology-makes-it-easier-people-rent-items

Fischer, C. S. (1982a) *To Dwell among Friends: Personal Networks in Town and City*. Chicago: University of Chicago Press.

Fischer, C. S. (1982b) 'What do we mean by "friend"? An inductive study' *Social Networks*, 3(4): 287–306.

Germann Molz, J. (2008) 'Global abode: home and mobility in narratives of round-the-world travel', *Space and Culture*, 11(2): 325–42.

Goffman, E. (1997) *The Goffman Reader*. Oxford: Wiley-Blackwell.

Guardian (2014) 'Taxi drivers in European capitals strike over Uber – as it happened' *The Guardian*. Retrieved from http://www.theguardian.com/politics/2014/jun/11/taxi-drivers-strike-uber-london-live-updates [accessed August 20th, 2014].

Hamari, J., Sjöklint, M. and Ukkonen, A. (2016) 'The sharing economy: why people participate in collaborative consumption' *Journal of the Association for Information Science and Technology*, 67(9): 2047–2059.

Hardt, M. and Negri, A. (2001) *Empire*. Cambridge, MA: Harvard University Press.

Hochschild, A.R. (1997) 'The time bind' *Working USA*, 1(2): 21–29.

Hochschild, A.R. (2003) *The Managed Heart: Commercialisation of Human Feeling*. San Francisco: University of California Press.

Jenkins, R., Molesesworth, M. and Scullion, R. (2014) 'The messy social lives of objects: inter-personal borrowing and the ambiguity of possession and ownership' *Journal of Consumer Behavior*, 13: 131–139.

Leidner, R. (1999) 'Emotional labour in service work' *Annals of the American Academy of Political and Social Science*, 561(1): 81–95.

Leistert, O., & Röhle, T. (Eds.). (2011) *Generation Facebook: Über das Leben im Social Net*. transcript-Verlag.

Lupton, D. (1998) *The Emotional Self*. London: Sage.

Massey, D. (1991) 'A global sense of place' *Marxism Today*, 38: 24–29.

McDowell, L. (2004) 'Work, workfare, work/life balance and an ethic of care' *Progress in Human Geography*, 28(2): 145–163.

Morley, D. (2000) Home Territories: Media, Mobility and Identity. London; New York, NY: Routledge.

Putnam, T. (1999) 'Postmodern home life' in Cieraad I (ed.) *At Home. An Anthropology of Domestic Space*, Syracuse, NY: Syracuse University Press.

Rybczynski, W. (1986) *Home: A Short History of an Idea*. New York, NY: Viking Penguin.

Sacks, D. (2011) 'The sharing economy' *Fast Company* 155: 88–93.

Simmel, G. and Hughes, E.C. (1949) 'The sociology of sociability' *American Journal of Sociology* 55: 254–261.

Simmel, G. and Wolff, K. (1950) *The Sociology of Georg Simmel*. Toronto: Free Press.

Simmel, G. (2011) *Georg Simmel on Individuality and Social Forms*. Chicago: University of Chicago Press.

Singer, N (2015) 'Twisting words to make "sharing" apps seem selfless'. *The New York Times*, August 8, 2015. Retrieved from https://www.nytimes.com/2015/08/09/technology/twisting-words-to-make-sharing-apps-seem-selfless.html.

Somerville, P. (1997) 'The social construction of home' *Journal of Architectural and Planning Research*, 226–245.

Tuan, Y-F. (1974) *Topophilia: A Study of Environmental Perception, Attitudes, and Values*. Englewood Cliffs, NJ: Prentice-Hall.

Wittel, A. (2011) 'Qualities of sharing and their transformations in the digital age' *International Review of Information Ethics*, 15: 3–8.

7 'Hand-me-down' childrenswear and the middle-class economy of nearly new sales

Emma Waight[1]

Community provisioning and middle-class mobilities

Technological innovation, societal changes and the rise of consumer culture are all considered responsible for a society structured more around the individual, than the community (Hovland and Wolburg 2010). In Western societies, the contemporary consumer is more likely to rely on supermarkets or online shopping to fulfil their basic needs (and consumer desires) as opposed to their local family and neighbours, who historically would have relied on one another to assist in family provisioning and care work, particularly in times of austerity (Putnam 2000). As stated by Lunt and Livingstone (1992: 149):

> Because money allows the anonymous exchange of goods without dependency ties, it erodes traditional dependency ties within communities, and so market relations tend to take over communities and undermine existing cultural ties.

In recent geographical scholarship this erosion of dependency ties has been a focus of work on mobilities. One in ten UK households move every year and our lives are increasingly dispersed both geographically and across different social networks (Cass et al. 2005; Holdsworth 2013). This is particularly the case for the middle classes, who are more likely to follow education and employment opportunities across the UK and beyond (Boterman 2012). For the middle classes, then, "mobility undermines connections to family, friends, community and locality" (Holdsworth 2013: 144) with busy, mobile lives sustained through a spatially and figuratively wide social network of weak ties, less rooted in locality (Vincent et al. 2008).

In terms of consumer needs, one item that has traditionally been passed through kin and social networks in the community is children's clothing. Gregson and Crewe (1998) talk about the 'moral economy' of second-hand children's wear, referencing the obligations felt by parents to pass on and reuse. Such items are often considered 'nearly new' in any case as children grow out of them before the item has worn out (Gregson and Crewe 1998; Waight 2014). This chapter looks at what has become of the traditional 'hand-me-down' economy in the UK at a time of heightened mobility, coupled with global financial and ecological instability. A 'hand-me-down' is a garment or other item that has been handed down after been used and discarded by another. The chapter explores the moral economy of childrenswear using the case study of nearly new sales (NNSs) to access a sample of middle-class mothers. These NNSs are organised nationally by branches of the UK's largest parenting charity as a fund-raising activity and service to support new and expectant parents as they buy and sell second-hand/used children's clothes, toys and equipment. Throughout this chapter I situate NNSs as a systematisation of local hand-me-down economies, a way of drawing together otherwise disparate community exchange networks into a locally grounded form.

Whilst the erosion of traditional dependency ties within communities may be seen to limit such community economies, this chapter explores the way in which parents make use of diverse economies to continue to benefit from children's hand-me-downs. The hypermobility of the middle classes has not had a detrimental affect on their ability to benefit from second-hand economies of childrenswear, but rather altered their consumption practices so that online platforms and NNSs have become the key routes for such provisioning (Waight 2014). Apart from the example of Freecycle, which only offers the exchange of goods without monetary exchange, these new systematised forms of hand-me-down economies, including NNSs, do tend to operate with monetary exchange thus differentiating them from traditional hand-me-down economies.

Although second-hand economies can be key in times of economic crisis, multiple notions of 'crisis' are evident in this chapter as taken from a broader research project on second-hand consumption and middle-class mothering (Waight 2014). NNSs are not just a cheaper and more sustainable way of clothing children during challenging economic and ecological times, but, as will be seen later in the chapter, the sharing economy of the NNS also creates a social field in which new and expectant parents can share parenting knowledge and experiences with like-minded others as a way of managing the sense of isolation, anxiety and indeed crisis, entwined with such a pivotal change in the lifecourse.

If we consider second-hand economies more broadly, the cultural and materials turns in geography have led to a significant increase in scholarship on such alternative, informal, or inconspicuous second-hand consumption sites since the early 1990s. Studies of British charity shops (Chattoe, 2000; Gregson et al. 2000; Horne and Maddrell 2002), car boot sales (Gregson et al. 2013), retro or vintage stores (Gregson et al. 2001), nearly new sales (Clarke 2000) and US garage sales or thrift stores (Harrmann 2004; Medvedev 2012) demonstrated that by studying these diverse sites of consumption we can explore the intimacies of the mundane by reflecting on class, identity and the multiple ethics of consumer practice. By their very nature forms of second-hand consumption vary greatly, from the precarious bric-a-brac stand at the side of the road to the exclusive vintage boutique. Although we have seen an increasing formalisation of charity shops in the UK[2], second-hand retail sites are generally considered informal, exempt from many of the conventions influencing regulated shopping sites (Horne and Maddrell 2002; Gregson et al. 1997). And whilst charity shops have remained a key feature of UK-based research on second-hand shopping, childrenswear rarely makes it to these shops because they tend to be passed through private systems of exchange instead (Clarke 2000; Horne and Maddrell 2002).

Previous studies, including my own on motherly consumption, have found consumers cite common risks associated with buying second-hand/ used goods, these being that items are inscribed with an unknown material biography and may be harbouring contaminants, be unsafe or unfit for purpose (Gregson and Crewe 2003; Horne and Maddrell 2002; Waight 2015). Despite these 'risks', second-hand consumption is not a practice restricted to the financially or socially excluded. Indeed, individuals choose to consume second-hand goods for a wide range of reasons (Arnould and Bardhi 2005; Gregson and Crewe 2003; Horne and Maddrell 2002). These may be political, social, economic, hedonist or moral, but cost-saving or thrift has been found to be the most prevalent (Guiot and Roux 2010; Harrmann 2004). Investigations of motherly second-hand consumption are surprisingly few considering the regularity of finding children's clothing and other goods moving through diverse second-hand economies. A notable exception to this is Clarke's (2000) study on NNSs. Although the NNSs used as the focus of Clarke's study are not the same NNSs used in my own research, I revisit many of the themes she explores regarding motherly consumption but in a different socio-economic climate.

Clarke (2000) was one of the first to study the gendered nature of motherly consumption and note that it cannot be regarded as a subjective, singular practice but as shaped by a complex web of social norms, expectations, anxieties and desires. Work involved in caring for a child and including consumption practice is one way in which women 'do' mothering. Cook (2008) describes this motherly consumption as 'co-consuming' as women consume on behalf of another, negotiating and prioritising the needs of both her child and herself. Similarly, consumption has been identified for its crucial role in enabling the transition to first-time motherhood, constructing an identity of mother and child through the material before the child is even born (Layne 2000; Layne et al. 2004; Prothero 2002).

A parallel to my own research can be seen in the work of Ogle et al. (2013) on second-hand maternity clothing. Like childrenswear, maternity dress is often consumed second-hand and shared through informal economies because it is only needed and used for a short space of time. This, the authors found, incites a desire to reuse rather than waste, a feeling that continues through to the consumption of baby and children's clothing (Clarke 2000; Gregson and Crewe 1998). The women in Ogle et al.'s (2013) study are torn between the desire to be thrifty and the desire to limit disruption to their self-identity. This disruption comes from the various ambivalences they face in dressing their pregnant selves and the limited availability of choice in their second-hand maternity dress, which may be passed on to them from family and friends.

As expectant women become new parents, the negotiations and rationalisations they have had to manage in dressing their pregnant selves become focused on caring for and dressing the child. The risks of consuming second-hand goods (in terms of hygiene, safety and socially constructed stigma) come to the fore, as mothers negotiate the myriad responsibilities of parenthood and want to shelter their child from harm (Kehily and Martens 2014). Although goods handed down from kin may be more familiar, second-hand items purchased from a charity shop, car boot sale, or NNS comes with a more precarious and opaque past. When consuming second-hand baby goods, mothers have been found to exact a number of strategies to mitigate this risk, including hygiene rituals and complying with institutionalised safety advice (Waight 2015).

Nearly new sales as a case study

Despite the perceived risk, one in five parents purchased extra second-hand goods for their children between 2008 and 2012 as a result of the global economic recession of 2008 (Mintel 2012). The rest of this chapter focuses on the ways in which middle-class mothers diversify traditional hand-me-down consumption patterns and find ways to expand their opportunities to acquire used childrenswear both through NNSs and extended social networks. As stated, NNSs run by a national UK parenting charity were used as a case study and route to explore motherly consumption practice. Mothers were chosen as the focus of study, as they remain primary caregivers in the home and manage the consumption, washing and disposal of clothing in the household (Holloway 2010; Waight 2015). Thirty interviews were conducted with mothers in early 2013 across three regions of the UK: Gosport and Winchester in the South and Birmingham in the Midlands. Alongside the interviews ran a broader ethnographic study where I conducted participant observation at 15 NNSs over the course of 18 months.

Generally the NNSs run by this particular charity are held biannually across the UK through local branches and situated in schools, church halls or leisure centres for just a couple of hours. Organised and staffed entirely by volunteers, the sales allow parents[3] to buy and sell second-hand or otherwise used baby and children's clothes, toys and equipment, along with maternity clothing. Sales are either table-top or ticketed. Table-top sales required a seller to purchase a pitch (table) and sell their own goods, while ticketed allowed sellers to drop off their wares which are then sorted by volunteers and ordered more akin to a conventional retail site. Both routes included a donation to the charity, and sales superseding this went in the seller's pocket.

In an age of increased geographic mobility for the middle classes, the sales offer a useful, organised method for the trade of used children's goods within the local community, albeit within a monetary exchange system. Whilst the NNSs provided a point for accessing interviewees, many of the mothers used the sales as one of a range of channels to acquire second-hand goods which were also discussed during interviews. Interviewees were recruited by conducting a short sampling questionnaire as buyers entered NNSs in the three case study regions. Interviewees varied in age range from '20 to 24' to '40+' with nearly half aged '30 to 34'. Two were first-time expectant mothers, the others all being mothers of one or two children up to the age of 10.

Two thirds of the participants were educated to degree level or higher, significantly greater than the UK national average of 38 per cent graduate attainment for working age adults (ONS 2013). All interviewees were white British, apart from one participant, who was Turkish. It should be said that the parenting charity associated with the sales offers other parenting services known to attract a middle-class demographic such as antenatal classes and coffee mornings. The classed nature of the charity is deep-rooted and partly based on the paid-for nature of many of their services (Waight 2014). Parenting practices in general are commonly considered to be shaped by class, along with the geographical boundaries in which people live (Holloway 2010; Holloway and Pimlott-Wilson 2014). I therefore view the NNSs accessed for this research as a middle-class phenomenon, shaped by middle-class values and mobilities.

Second-hand economies at times of 'crisis'

Even individuals choosing to avoid second-hand economies for their own clothing are likely to be more amenable to receiving second-hand or 'hand-me-down' clothing for their children (Waight 2014). Most of the middle-class mothers I interviewed had both received and passed on such items. As the following quote shows, however, the social or kin ties linking these economies do not have to be close. Hilary used the NNSs to supplement a regular delivery of girl's clothing from a distant relative:

> I've had a steady stream of the stuff because she passes it on to her sister, who then passes it on to basically her father-in-law – my father-in-law – this little one's granddad, and he then arrives down with it. In some ways it's a bit like going to a sale but I don't get any choice. I open up the boxes when they arrive and there's this heap of clothes, but her mother-in-law bought a lot of the stuff in Next and Monsoon. All good quality stuff but I couldn't have bought it at full price anyway. So we're gaining from it all. It makes sense, and also I don't worry about it if something gets damaged.
> (Hilary: mother to one, civil servant, co-habiting, aged 40)

Hilary is the epitome of the mobile middle-class as she moved south for her husband's job, away from family and close friends. As far as I could tell the two women above had never met. Rather, the clothes parcels are the only (fairly) regular link between them. It would probably be easier for the owner of the clothes to donate them to a charity shop (or throw them away) but instead she keeps hold of them to pass them to her sister who in turn can pass them down the chain to someone who she knows can make use of them. The clothes thus link the women, and their families, together. It could be seen as an example both of not wanting the goods to be wasted (perhaps Monsoon[4] is too good for the charity shop), and an act of kindness, in helping a distant relative in a similar position.

Hilary demonstrates that children's clothing can still be handed-down through networks but that these networks are not necessarily locally grounded. Of clothing that was handed-down, such items predominantly went to friends and relatives rather than neighbours. At other times the NNSs were described as being particularly helpful for new parents who lacked the social network needed to benefit from the hand-me-down economy either because they lived far from friends and family, or they were the first in their peer group to become a parent. In this case the nearly new sales filled a gap when there was no access to the informal hand-me-down economies (that others may take for granted) by re-localising these second-hand economies.

A key cultural difference however, between socially networked hand-me-down economies and NNSs is the inherent risk inscribed by the 'unknown'. Unless it is a table-top sale (where buyers can at least speak to the sellers), buyers at nearly new sales have no idea where their second-hand purchase have come from and who has been using it. This does not mean that attendance to the sale is entirely random, however. Like any social event, participation is enabled and structured by strong social networks (Trotter 1999). Indeed, half of all those attending the sales nationally had been previously involved in the parenting charity, many others were friends of those who were.

Mothers choose nearly new sales over other forms of second-hand consumption in order to minimise the risks invoked by second-hand goods because they are engaging as part of a homophilous group. We could view this as an example of 'embedded behaviour', the idea that many human behaviours are not conducted alone but rather are the result of interactions with other agents (Trotter 1999: 15).

This shared social field, I argue, enables the sales to offer a 'safer' alternative to the likes of charity shops or car boot sales, which are oft considered 'dirty' or at least riskier due to the sense of the unknown (Gregson and Crewe 2003; Horne and Maddrell 2002). Another benefit of the sales over both informal hand-me-down economies and charity shops is the breadth of choice available and efficiency incurred by having a dedicated space to buy second-hand childrenswear. This perceived convenience factor will be discussed later when I explore the tension of thrift juxtaposed with excess.

In addition to shopping, the NNSs offer a social space for parental bonding and learning. The intimacy invoked by the baby items for sale allow parents to use these items to negotiate the complexities of parenting as a point of reference for discussion and to reflect on their own identity, values and practices (Waight 2015). The addition of the material as an object of interest and common intermediary further facilitates bonding amongst attendees who are not previously connected. This is particularly true in the case of the volunteers, for whom the shared experience of sorting and organising goods provides a basis for conversation as discussion shifts from what they are selling/hope to buy, to broader conversations about their family, home and career.

We could situate the concept of second-handedness as undesirable by drawing on the notions of risk, dirt and hygiene yet some mothers viewed the fact that an item had been used by another as a recommendation that it was in fact, useful. This was described by Maggie:

> If it's at the sale it's like someone else is saying "this is good, I've used this, this has worked". So that's better than buying blindly off the Internet if you know someone else has had good use out of it.
>
> (Maggie: married, 30–34, full time mum)

Literature to date focuses on the fact that second-hand goods have been disposed of by another, so for that person they are *useless*. Maggie's discussion shows that it could be seen as a recommendation that it is in fact, *useful*. As such she is putting implicit trust in the association to a group of people, whilst in actuality she may not know where that item has come from. She would not be able to draw on this homophilous association at charity shops or car boot sales, for example, two places considered further along the disposal hierarchy than NNSs and thus more likely to offer *useless* goods.

NNSs are dynamic economies with the same group of people often selling and buying. Buyers consider all kinds of issues when faced with a potential purchase. These may be related to need, value for money and quality. Sometimes though, mothers demonstrated broader awareness of the second-hand economy and before making a purchase weighed up the potential resale value as well as use-value. As a first-time mother, Kate (quoted below) has yet to dispose of any baby goods but describes her intention to sell goods on once she no longer needs them:

> I haven't sold anything at the sales yet myself but I think if you buy brand names they will always sell on again if I want to sell them, which I will I think.
>
> (Kate: mother to one, retail manager, married, aged 25–29)

In this quote, Kate does not refer to the direct use-value of the goods at all (unless you consider her reference to quality), but rather focuses purely on the commodity value. This is a strategy used by other mothers in order to justify the expense of consumption and manage the financial burden of parenthood. Brand names are considered to hold their value because they are good quality and retain a symbolic value tied up in certain covetable labels.

Selling is a laborious process though and seems barely worth it for the money alone (at least for the middle-class group). The mothers described how they prepared the items for sale; washing, ironing, pricing and generally divesting them of their previous biography so that they were ready for a new owner. This is a chore that has to be fitted in around existing roles and responsibilities, as this mother explained:

> One motivation has been the money however I regard it as a very ineffective way to raise money because it's a huge amount of work to raise a small amount of money. So it's irrational that I sell at the sales and I'm glad I'm now at the point where I don't feel obliged to. I used to feel like I ought to.
> (Karen: mother to two girls, 'homemaker', lives alone, aged 40+)

Karen's concern that she ought to participate in the sales as a seller links to the ethical and social obligations found to underpin the middle-class mother's participation in the sale. A desire to support the charity and their peer group encouraged selling, buying and volunteering. In arguing that the sales are an inefficient way to make money, or to produce economic capital, Karen is suggesting that the sales are part of an altogether different economy. Rather than considering the nearly new sales in purely economic terms, they can be conceptualised as a moral economy built on the mutual reciprocity of the community in giving and taking from the sale.

Karen was a keen environmentalist so also felt a moral duty to ensure any of her used items did not go to waste. However, it would have been easier for her to give these items to her local charity shop, or to other community members through the Freecycle group she moderated. Her obligation then is social. She spoke, as many other mothers did, about the desire to give back to the sale; the charity itself through the fundraising potential, and the parents who frequented them. The sale relies on this sense of reciprocity in order to be a success; otherwise it may lead to a disparity with more buyers than sellers. In this sense the sale semi-formalises the traditional hand-me-down culture, creating an efficient space for local parents to pass around second-hand goods as part of an informal economy to which they belong.

Moralities of thrift

The previous section described the way in which NNSs link local parenting networks and facilitate an expanded economy of neighbourly second-hand exchange. There is a tension, however, between whether this constitutes frugality, thrift, or is simply an opportunity for overconsumption. Part of the sale's success is realising that twenty-first-century parents desire a degree of choice, partly due to the increased pressures on time, and partly due to the marketisation of childhood (Martens 2010). It was certainly the case at the NNSs that buyers left with bags full of items, many of which are spontaneous purchases or duplicates of items they already had.

Indeed interviewees spoke about buying extra clothes for playing in the garden or attending nursery (unsuitable places for 'best dress'), extra games and puzzles for further stimulation (building on the child's cultural capital) and extra equipment to keep at the grandparents' house. One participant discussed the need for multiple pairs of wellington boots:

> If they go to nursery they need a pair at nursery and then you never remember to bring them home, so you need another pair for home, you might have another pair at granny's house too so you end up with three pairs of wellies in the same size and they wear them for half an hour to splash in a puddle and then not again for a few weeks.
>
> (Amanda: mother to two, special needs teacher married, aged 40+)

Amanda describes how the NNSs allow for her to buy extra goods in order to make everyday life easier. She is not what Williams and Windebank (2002) would call an 'excluded consumer'. The ability to own such extras is not a luxury available to everyone and could be construed as part of the modern day economy of convenience. In such case, when goods are little used, it is deemed foolish to buy items full price because children grow out of things so quickly and second-hand items still have plenty of use-value. This could be why many customers cite cost-saving as their primary reason for purchasing second-hand goods as they are saving money on the cost price of individual items. Looking at their consumption practices as a whole, however, they are purchasing more than they need in order to clothe and care for the child, so it could still be suggested that in some instances they are spending more money than they may need to.

It could be argued that the NNSs are not reaching those most in need of cheap, second-hand childrenswear but rather servicing the 'false needs' of the middle-class (Marcuse 1964). That said, there are multiple iterations of need and for mothers trying to do the right thing by their families, it is difficult to define what constitutes true need when social and cultural obligations are so complex (Evans 2011; Hall 2015). In addition, studies by Gillies (2007) and Ponsford (2011; 2014) on working-class and/or young mothers suggest that these 'excluded consumers' may not want to participate in such economies and are socially excluded even from these alternative spaces of second-hand consumption.

Ponsford (2014) argues that the ability of young mothers to provide for their children while managing on a low income provided an important basis of self-worth. In experiencing the anxiety of being, and be seen to be, a good mother, materiality is the main route through which mothers can display their competence publicly. Ponsford (2011: 541) clarifies:

> Consumption emerges as an important site for oppositional strategies through which the young women who took part in this study seek to re-image themselves as respectable carers and deflect negative associations of poverty away from their children.

These young women desperately tried to remain within known exchange networks, either informal (friends, family) or in purchasing items brand new.

Second-hand goods from charity shops or similar were simply not acceptable, seen as a marked sign of poverty and bound by negative connotations of being teased during their own childhood (Ponsford 2014). This trait was evidenced in a younger expectant mother I managed to interview who had attended one NNS to date and clearly had an issue with buying second-hand clothes, although had attended the sale to have a look around and buy small, token items (such as a pregnancy book). She said:

> When you have this little person you want everything to be new but you can't have everything new.
>
> (Faye: expectant mother, shop assistant, co-habiting, aged 25–29)

Faye had gained from hand-me-down clothing from close friends and family, whom she still lived near in her hometown of Gosport. For her, she felt comforted by the notion of knowing where these items had come from. In contrast, the practice of thrift was a source of pride for the more middle-class mothers I spoke to. Whilst still anxious to be a good mother, these mothers do not place such high regard on displaying good mothering through the child's dress.

Other interviewees recognised the environmental benefits of using second-hand goods. This was described by Karen, who we met earlier in the chapter: "I just like to not consume more than is necessary." Karen was unusual in citing this as her primary reason for buying second-hand baby goods but nevertheless environmental notions did surface in a number of interviews. In many cases this was not related to environmental concerns, but rather a general sense that the items themselves will 'go to waste' if they are not reused when they still have useful life left in them. There was also a sense that other children should have the chance to use an item, if it had been useful to the participants' own children, and/or gave them pleasure. This correlates with the work of Gregson and Crewe (2003: 198) when they explain:

> Reuse then, was not – as we had imagined it to be – a politicised practice. Rather it was constructed more as a conservation practice, where preserving and/or extending the lives of things has come to matter rather more than thinking about the connections of such practices to the conditions of commodity production.

Miller (1999: 132) states, "thrift has been found to represent the central ritual in the transformation of shopping from spending to saving". This suggests that consumers still desire to shop, but that the focus of their consumption is to spend as little money as possible in order to procure the things they desire. Thrift is categorised by social competition, something Miller (1987) documents as far away as Trinidad, describing "the rivalry between female relatives wanting to demonstrate their skills by buying the same goods cheaper than someone else". This form of competition transpired through my own research with shoppers queuing long before the sale started in order to get ahead of the crowd and snag the best items. This allowed mothers to 'keep up with the Joneses' without spending large amounts of extra money, although money is nevertheless being spent and is therefore different to non-financial hand-me-down economies.

These observations directly correlate with Miller's (1999: 137) early ethnography on family consumption. He says:

> There seems very little evidence to suggest that in most cases thrift is actually a means to save money. In many cases it is equally the justification for spending more money.

Thrift is central to household management as a way of justifying and moderating consumption. Where money is saved in one place, it is spent elsewhere. Thrift involves having knowledge of markets, demonstrated at the nearly new sales by the mothers who researched the going-price of toys, clothes and equipment both new and used, online and at the sales. Thrift therefore requires an element of skill and is a way in which women 'do mothering'. As a skill, it can be learnt and improved upon, shown clearly in the way participants spoke about the strategies they enacted at the sales, developed over repeated visits and through drawing on their social and cultural capital. Indeed, it is the mobilisation of these forms of capital that enable success within the field of the nearly new sale and why social class plays a fundamental role in structuring forms of attendance.

Concluding remarks

By considering the NNS as a diverse economy, they are modelled as a route for semi-formalising the traditional culture of hand-me-downs in order to fit the contemporary middle-class lifestyle in an era of boundless spatial mobility. As the sales attract a homophilous group, the oft-perceived precarious act of second-hand consumption is diverted away from the unknown and pulled back into an arena of localised shared social networks. The material then, provides a route to bond otherwise disparate community ties; a practice described by Clarke (2000) as 'mother swapping' due to the sharing of experience, information and expertise attached to the physical act of sharing used clothes. Access to this network is shaped by class, as indeed is need, as working-class parents are more likely to live close to and rely on kin and social ties. The NNS then can be viewed as a way for middle-class parents to manage the 'crisis' of parental responsibility, perhaps living far away from their close friends and family.

Work on diverse, alternative, non-capitalist economies is growing but more consideration is required to understand how local second-hand economies fit within these. Theories on alternative economies have surfaced since the cultural turn, including feminist post-capitalist critiques (Gibson-Graham 1996), moral sharing economies (Gold 2004) and more-than-capitalist economic practice (Fraser 2014). Second-hand exchange networks play a key role in these economies, encouraging sharing, sustainability, thrift and a social bonding and as such should be seen as a key route for future research. The notion of whether NNSs facilitate cost-savings and sustainable consumption in turbulent economic or ecological times is up for debate. But by structuring the discussion around these narratives, mothers have demonstrated that the sales and second-hand consumption more generally do support their consumer needs as middle-class mothers in an ever-commercialised world where parenting practices are often up for scrutiny.

Notes

1   I am grateful to the ESRC and NCT for co-sponsoring this research through the Doctoral RIBEN scheme and would like to thank Dr Kate Boyer and Dr Nick Clarke for aiding the development of ideas in this chapter.
2   Charity shops can be found on most UK high streets and rely on donations of second-hand goods from the public to fundraise for the charity's causes, as well as selling a small range of new goods. They are predominantly run on volunteer labour and benefit from business rate reductions.
3   It is not only parents and expectant parents who attend and benefit from the sales. Other buyers include grandparents and even commercial traders.
4   Monsoon is a mid-market high street clothing store in the UK known for their evening wear and embellished accessories.

References

Arnould, E. J. and Bardhi, F. (2005) 'Thrift shopping: combining utilitarian thrift and hedonic treat benefits' *Journal of Consumer Behaviour* 4(4): 223–233.

Boterman, W. R. (2012) 'Residential mobility of urban middle classes in the field of parenthood' *Environment and Planning* A 44(10): 2397–2412.

Cass, N., Shove, E. and Urry, J. (2005) 'Social exclusion, mobility and access' *The Sociological Review* 53(3): 539–555.

Chattoe, E. (2000) 'Charity shops as second-hand markets' *International Journal of Nonprofit and Voluntary Sector Marketing* 5(2): 153–160.

Clarke, A. (2000) '"Mother swapping": the trafficking of nearly new children's wear' in Jackson, P., Lowe, M., Miller, D. and Mort, F. [eds.] *Commercial Cultures, Economies, Practices and Spaces*. Oxford: Berg, 85–100.

Cook, D. T. (2008) 'The missing child in consumption theory' *Journal of Consumer Culture* 8(2): 219–243.

Evans, D. (2011) 'Thrifty, green or frugal: reflections on sustainable consumption in a changing economic climate' *Geoforum* 42(5): 550–557.

Fraser, N. (2014) *Behind Marx's 'Hidden Abode': Towards an Expanded Conception of Capitalism*. Invited lecture: Centre for Citizenship, Globalisation and Governance. University of Southampton.

Gibson-Graham, J.K. (1996) *The End of Capitalism (As We Knew It): A Feminist Critique of Political Economy*. Duluth: University of Minnesota Press.

Gillies, V. (2007) *Marginalised Mothers: Exploring Working Class Experiences of Parenting*. Oxford: Routledge.

Gold, L. (2004) *The Sharing Economy: Solidarity Networks Transforming Globalisation*. Aldershot: Ashgate.

Gregson, N., Brooks K. and Crewe, L. (2001) 'Bjorn again? Rethinking 70s revivalism through the appropriation of 70s clothing' *Fashion Theory*, 5(1): 3–28.

Gregson, N., Brooks K. and Crewe, L. (2000) 'Narratives of Consumption and the Body in the Space of the Charity Shop' in Jackson, P., Lowe, M., Miller, D. and Mort, F. [eds.] *Commercial Cultures, Economies, Practices and Spaces*. Oxford: Berg *Commercial Cultures, Economies, Practices and Spaces*. Oxford: Berg, 101–123.

Gregson, N., Crewe, L. & Longstaff, B. (1997) 'Excluded spaces of regulation: car-boot sales as an enterprise culture out of control?' *Environment and Planning A* 29: 1717–1737.

Gregson, N. and Crewe, L. (1998) 'Dusting down second hand rose: Gendered identities and the world of second-hand goods in the space of the car boot sale' *Gender, Place & Culture* 5(1): 77–100.

Gregson, N. and Crewe, L. (2003) *Second-Hand Cultures*. Oxford: Berg.

Gregson, N. and Crang, M., Laws J, Fleetwood T, and Holmes H (2013) 'Moving up the waste hierarchy: Car boot sales, reuse exchange and the challenges of consumer culture to waste prevention' *Resources, Conservation and Recycling*, 77: 97–107.

Guiot, D. and Roux, D. (2010) 'A second-hand shopper's motivation scale: antecedents, consequences, and implications for retailers', *Journal of Retailing*, 86(4): 355–371.

Hall, S.M. (2015) 'Everyday ethics of consumption in the austere city' *Geography Compass* 9(3): 140–151.

Harrmann, G. (2004) 'Haggling spoken here: gender, class and style in US garage sale bargaining' *The Journal of Popular Culture* 38(1): 55–81.

Holdsworth, C. (2013) *Family and Intimate Mobilities*. London: Palgrave Macmillan.

Holloway, S. L. (2010) 'Local childcare cultures: moral geographies of mothering and the social organisation of pre-school education', *Gender, Place and Culture*, 5(1): 29–53.

Holloway, S. L. and Pimlott-Wilson, H. (2014) '"Any advice is welcome isn't it?" Neoliberal parenting education, local mothering cultures and social class' *Environment and Planning A* 46(1): 94–111.

Horne, S. and Maddrell. A. (2002) *Charity Shops: Retailing, Consumption and Society*. London: Routledge.

Hovland, R. and Wolburg, M. (2010) *Advertising, Society, and Consumer Culture*. Abingdon: Routledge

Kehily, M. and Martens, L. (2014) 'Selling infant safety: entanglements of childhood preciousness, vulnerability and unpredictability' *Young Consumers*, 15 (3): 239–250.

Layne, L.L. (2000) 'Baby things as fetishes: memorial goods, simulacra, and the "real-ness" problem of pregnancy loss' in Ragone, H. and Twine, F.H. [eds.] *Ideologies and Technologies of Motherhood*. London: Routledge.

Layne, L. L., Taylor, J. S. and Wozniak, D. F. (2004) *Consuming Motherhood*. London: Rutgers University Press, 111–138.

Lunt, K. and Livingstone, S. (1992) *Mass Consumption and Personal Identity*. London: Open University Press.

Marcuse, H. (1964) *One-Dimensional Man: Studies in the Ideology of Advanced Industrial Society*. Boston: Beacon.

Martens L. (2010) 'The cute, the spectacle and the practical: Narratives of new parents and babies at The Baby Show' in Tingstad, V. and Buckingham, D. [eds.] *Childhood and Consumer Culture*. Palgrave MacMillan, 146–160.

Medvedev, K. (2012) 'It is a garage sale at Savers everyday: An ethnography of the Savers thrift department store in Minneapolis' in Giorcelli, C. and Rabinowitz, P. [eds.] *Exchanging Clothes: Habits of Being II*. London: University of Minnesota Press, 230–254.

Miller, D. (1987) *Material Culture and Mass Consumption*. Oxford: Blackwell.

Miller, D. (1999) *A Theory of Shopping*. Cambridge: Polity Press.

Mintel (2012) *Baby and Nursery Equipment January 2012*. London: Mintel Group.

Ogle, J. P., Tyner, K. E. and Schofield-Tomschin, S. (2013) 'The role of maternity dress consumption in shaping the self and identity during the liminal transition of pregnancy' *Journal of Consumer Culture* 13(2): 119–139.

ONS (2013) *Graduates in the UK Labour Market*. London: Office for National Statistics.

Prothero, A. (2002) 'Consuming motherhood: An introspective journey on consuming to be a good mother' *Gender and Consumer Behaviour* 6: 211–226.

Ponsford, R. (2011) 'Consumption, resilience and respectability amongst young mothers in Bristol' *Journal of Youth Studies*, 14(5): 541–560.

Ponsford, R. (2014) '"I don't really care about me, as long as he gets everything he needs": young women becoming mothers in consumer culture' *Young Consumers*, 15(3): 251–262.

Putnam, R. (2000) *Bowling Alone: The Collapse and Revival of American Community* London: Simon & Schuster.

Trotter, R. T. (1999) 'Friends, relatives, and relevant others: conducting ethnographic network studies' in Schensul, J.J., LeCompte, M.D., Trotter, R.T., Cromley, E.K. and Singer, M. [eds.] *Mapping Social Networks, Spatial Data and Hidden Populations*. London: Sage, 1–49.

Vincent, C., Braun, A. and Ball, S. (2008) 'Childcare and social class: caring for young children in the UK' *Critical Social Policy*, 28(1): 5–26.

Waight, E. (2014) *The Social, Cultural and Economic Role of NCT Nearly New Sales: Second-hand Consumption and Middle-class Mothering*, Unpublished PhD thesis, University of Southampton.

Waight, E. (2015) 'Buying for Baby: How Middle-Class Mothers Negotiate Risk with Second-Hand Goods' in Casey, E. and Taylor, Y. [eds.] *Everyday Life and Intimacies of Consumption*, London: Palgrave Macmillan, 197–215.

Williams, C. and Windebank, J. (2002) 'The excluded consumer: A neglected aspect of social exclusion?' *Policy and Politics* 30(4): 501–513.

8 Franchising the disenfranchised?

The paradoxical spaces of food banks

Nicola Livingstone

Across the United Kingdom today the experience of food is uneven, inconsistent and chaotic. Food has never been a universal experience, enjoyed by all, nor a common ground experienced equally, but rather access to food reflects an ongoing relation of poverty and inequality. Such relations demonstrate ongoing crises in our society; crises of food, hunger, welfare and alienation, but also crises in the corresponding responses, considering how (in)effective these responses may prove to be.

Responses typically emerge from charities and individuals, from our apparent 'moral conscience' and a desire to help others in whatever way possible. Motivations to both donate food and time in response to the crises of hunger today are mediated through contemporary spaces of food aid, specifically through the development of food banks that provide emergency, short term food parcels to an ever-growing number of people. The rapidity with which these spaces have emerged is prodigious, indicating not only the severity of the crisis for those who are hungry, but illustrating the need for a comprehensive response from both the state and the charitable sector across the UK. Food banks in 2015 are becoming familiar and normalised, evolving into charitable enterprises and social franchises. But through food banking charities, by sharing and gifting food, are we franchising the very people who are disenfranchised? And if so, to what end?

The very notion of 'charity' is generally accepted in society today as an ideal moral response to the various forms of ongoing contemporary crises locally and worldwide, as an opportunity to 'make things better' in an effective and straightforward way – through giving. In this way, charity appears in many forms, often as positive individual, community or state action, across the spectrum from local to global. Yet charity perpetuates crisis-ridden, fragile and destructive capitalism. Charity is diverse and unique to a particular cause, yet it is limited in effecting transformative social change as it has become an inherent form of capitalism. One space which offers insight into this charitable paradox is the food bank. Food banks are 'relational ... internally complex' (Massey 2004: 5) spaces, representative of social practices and crises. Although it can be argued that the charitable giving of food has been a feature of society for centuries and is not a modern concept, the beginning of this century has seen the development of food banks as a new, alternative form of charity in response to the increase in hunger and food poverty. This chapter considers the space of the food bank in the UK today, by linking the context of their development to the influence of the state, austerity and welfare reforms with the specific, day to day experiences of food redistribution. It considers relations of both the evolving system of food banking generally and more particularly, the operation of food bank outlets in a critique from the left.

Food banks are an interesting concept, offering people the opportunity to donate and volunteer, to proactively engage with their local communities, to feed and to nourish. But what are the social relations driving the evolution of food banks across the UK? What can the space of the food bank tell us about our social form and our everyday experiences of, and responses to, capitalist crises? Antagonisms in food banking become apparent when the politics of the welfare state are considered and the government's detached position examined, when the direct effects of such detachment are manifest in the way people live in the UK today. It becomes clear that the redistribution of food indicates an increasingly unequal society. This chapter considers the evolution of food banking in the UK and is an initial conceptualisation of their spatiality through three distinct but interconnected narratives:

1 The first narrative begins by offering context on the development of food banking and government response in the UK, informed by literature which reflects the food banking experience internationally.
2 The second narrative unpacks the form of charity itself and sets a wider conceptual perspective, grounded in the left.
3 The third interprets the social relations which create the space of the food bank in UK by interweaving the conceptual perspective into theorising both the state response from a broader perspective (i.e. the system of food banking) and the more specific methods of operation adopted by food banks.

Perspectives on food banking

The charitable provision of food aid can be viewed as a typical feature of society, rooted in altruistic motivations, which has been ongoing in myriad ways for centuries. However, the manner in which food is redistributed and provided has shifted and continues to alter in line with the fluidity and dynamics of capitalist society, reflecting interconnections between the state form and social relations. This section of the chapter considers the intertwined narrative of food aid and government, considering the ongoing evolution of food banking and the relations of the state in the UK and across the world.

The vanguard response to hunger and food poverty in the UK today is through food banking. However, food banks and banking in the UK are a relatively recent phenomenon, emerging in the last 15 years, and relevant literature is in its infancy. However, food banking is significantly entrenched and embedded in the social form of other nations, such as Canada (since the early 1980s) and the USA (since the late 1960s). Warshawsky details the key role food banking plays in "neoliberal urban governance, as they control the conceptualisation of hunger, management of poverty and organisation of food distribution systems" (2010: 763) that "the state has legitimised … as a central approach to reduce food security" (2010: 772).

The network of food banks operating in America today function more like a business providing a service, as distinct non-governmental organisations, reliant on donations and corporate support. However, in Australia, where food banking is continuing to expand, state funding is often directed in support of the systems being implemented (Booth and Whelan 2014). Similarly, food banks have "become an integral part of contemporary Canadian society" (Theriault and Yadlowski 2000: 206), institutionalised through the Canadian Association of Food Banks (CAFB) and operating at a national scale in partnership with corporate retailers, or 'sponsors', such as Heinz and Campbell Soup. The food banking networks in North America are well established and entrenched today as charity, which reflects "the breakdown of the social safety net and the commodification of social assistance" (Riches 2002: 648). Indeed, food poverty in the first world globally has become increasingly prevalent as recent years have seen "the steady rise, institutionalisation, corporatisation and globalisation of charitable food banking in selected rich food secure countries, attested to by the growth of national food bank organisations" (De Schutter 2014: 3). The second edition of Riches and Silvasti's collection 'First World Hunger Revisited' (2014) has seen food charity considered in twelve countries, compared to the five represented in the first edition (1997), indicating significant shifts in hunger and corresponding charitable food aid provision.

Although the manifestation of the food banking system varies across the countries considered, the neoliberal state response to the expansion of food banking in the so-called first world is consistent, representing detachment and deniability of responsibility in relation to social welfare and food provision (Livingstone 2015; Dowler 2014). Reflecting on the situation in Canada, Riches suggests that food banking "enable[s] governments to look the other way and neglect food poverty and nutritional health and well-being" (2002: 648). Food banking has not been an integral element within a wider process of eradicating poverty, the emergency response has become normalised and relations of poverty are ongoing and consistently experienced. Indeed, there has been backlash from food bank volunteers, for example the 'Freedom 90' Union of Food Bank and Emergency Meal Program Volunteers in Ontario has created a charter which drives towards the eradication of food banks and therefore poverty, reflecting volunteer disillusionment with the inadequacies of the Canadian state to effect sustainable improvements in inequalities. The union want the government to act to eradicate the need for food banking; as volunteers they want to be unnecessary rather than relied upon to fulfil the state's duties. Their dissent and disappointment is palpable, even though it has been suggested that the very existence of food banks enables government withdrawal (Poppendieck 1998). Now, more than ever, we must seriously examine the role of food banking, which requires that we no longer praise its growth as a sign of our generosity and charity, but instead recognise it as a symbol of our society's failure to hold government accountable for hunger, food insecurity and poverty.

(Winne 2009: 184)

Food security is a human rights issue, one which theoretically, should be addressed predominantly by the government. However, considering the development of food banking internationally, it is apparent that the UK is following the governmental precedent set by Canada and the USA.

In the UK, the Department for Environment, Food and Rural Affairs (Defra) defines food security as "consumers having access at all times to sufficient, safe and nutritious food for an active and healthy lifestyle at affordable prices" (2008: 2), but for a significant number of people across the UK this is out of reach, even if the responsibility for food security rests with the state. All published evidence points to the UK becoming increasingly food insecure, demonstrating connections between hunger, food poverty and the evolution of food aid services (Cooper et al. 2014; Cooper and Dumpleton 2013; Lambie-Mumford et al. 2014; Sosenko et al. 2013). In response to this, food banking is becoming prolific, through a variety of operational structures and distribution policies, as well as different degrees of formality in relation to user access. Food bank charities typically provide users with the equivalent of three days' worth of food in response to an emergency or immediate crisis, and the majority food is donated to them by the public. The amount of food received is indicative of the number of people for whom food is required, and it is generally non-perishable, dried and often tinned. Food bank charities exist across a spectrum of formality, from the structured, businesslike procedures of the Trussell Trust as a more formal provider, to local independently run initiatives. Degrees of formality in this case reflect the varying approaches taken by food providers regarding how each assess the potential need of the users and how regularly such users can access food parcels over a particular time period. For some food banks referrals are needed in order to collect food, but for others this isn't necessary.

The Trussell Trust, a 'social franchise' (Lambie 2011: 9), was established in 2004 and today has a network of over 440 food banks across the UK. Churches and religious organisations become affiliated with The Trussell Trust and through their best practice guidelines set up local food banks. The Trussell Trust is the most visible and recognisable provider of food aid in the UK today and has proved key when tracking the increase of food parcel distribution. The reported figures of growth in food parcel access are consistently accelerating, as the following key statistics demonstrate:

- Between three key providers of emergency food aid (The Trussell Trust, FareShare and FoodCycle) over 20.2 million meals were distributed in 2013–14 (Cooper et al. 2014).
- The year 2010–11 saw Trussell Trust affiliated food banks distribute 61,468 emergency food parcels. By 2013–14 the equivalent figure was

913,138 parcels (The Trussell Trust 2014) and by 2014–15 had risen to 1,084,604 (The Trussell Trust 2015).

- In 2014–15, over 396,000 of the parcels distributed were received for children (The Trussell Trust 2015).
- The number of people obtaining food aid increased 54% year on year in 2013–14 (Cooper et al. 2014).
- On average, food bank users received two food parcels a year (The Trussell Trust 2015).

However, although these figures paint a disheartening picture of the situation in relation to the growth of food poverty today, only a limited number of larger charities actively monitor and collate information relating to their food parcel distribution and user access. Many independent charities and associations provide ad hoc food parcels across the country, through food banks, soup kitchens and drop-in centres. Less is known about these providers, therefore it is difficult to quantify or even estimate the volume of food redistributed through these channels. It is likely that in reality there is significantly more food being redistributed through more informal food banks and alternative providers than is recognised in the data above (Lambie-Mumford et al. 2014; Sosenko et al. 2013). Across the UK there is a "lack of systematically collected data on drivers of need" (Lambie-Mumford and Dowler 2014: 1421), but evidence which does exist has been consistently dismissed by recent Conservative-led governments

The approach of recent UK governments since the 2008 financial crisis to the growth of food aid has been to casually fail to respond to the ongoing crises of hunger, fail to address the relations of poverty and fail to acknowledge the role its relations play in perpetuating the daily struggle experienced in food banking. Food bank charities, as an extension of the welfare state are performing the government's remit relating to ensuring food security. Food banks are becoming institutionalised as a function of the capitalist state. The present neoliberal government has made concerted efforts to earnestly refute any suggestion that there are links between welfare policies and the growth of food banking in the UK, stating consistently that there is "no robust evidence" (Downing et al. 2014: 9) to connect reforms with food poverty. Conversely, Wells and Caraher report that "the growth in food banking in the UK is contextualised by a squeeze on food and fuel spending … and a programme of welfare reform by the UK coalition [government]" (2014: 1427) – a direct link to government policies in a period of austerity and rising costs. The Trussell Trust reported in 2013–14 that the three primary reasons driving people to use their food banks were benefit delays (30.9%), low income (20.3%) and benefit changes (16.9%) (2015).

Further evidence has been collated which links welfare cuts (such as the introduction of the bedroom tax) with increased food bank use (Cooper et al. 2014; Sosenko et al. 2013) and the All-Party Parliamentary Group (APPG) Inquiry in hunger and food aid published recommendations on the best approach to address food poverty in their 'Feeding Britain' report (Forsey,

APPG Report 2014a). A substantial amount of evidence gathered for this report emphasises the effects of austerity measures, welfare reform, sanctions, and benefit delays among food bank users (Forsey 2014b). Research by Loopstra et al. (2015: 2) notes that "each 1% cut in spending on central welfare benefits was associated with a 0.16% rise in food parcel distribution" by Trussell Trust food banks. In addition to the links with welfare reforms, food poverty due to austerity and deprivation is evident in the labour market, where zero-hour contracts are now commonplace, and many people who are employed in low-income jobs experience food crisis (Sosenko et al. 2013). Given 2015 was an election year, it is unlikely that any decisive action will be taken in response to either the APPG report or the ongoing food crises; however, it is ironic that food banking is politicised in campaigns, as it was during the Scottish Independence debate in 2014 (MacNab 2014). Such politicisation is effective only if it ameliorates the situation of those experiencing food poverty and reflects a drive towards action, rather than merely being adopted as a tool for political gain. Unfortunately, this is the current situation in the UK. Today, the UK "government's resistance to acknowledging structural contributions to household food insecurity, to monitoring their effects or to addressing causes, is a clear dereliction of duty to implement the human right to food" (Dowler 2014: 175) and an impasse of charitable action and state inaction has been reached.

The "wicked problem" (Booth and Whelan, 2014: 1400) of food insecurity is experiencing a desperate renaissance, one which is being exacerbated and dismissed by the current government, as food banking responds in their stead. Considering the commodification of food provision as a social franchise, the detached illusions of the neoliberal government and the ongoing drive towards food bank charities becoming an extension of the welfare state, it seems likely that the social form of food aid is moving towards a similar experience to that of North America. As Marx said with reference to Hegel's assertion that history repeats itself, "the first time as tragedy, the second time as farce" (Marx 1973b: 146), the social relations of charitable food banking are moving towards becoming yet another farce of capitalism's crises. Why is the UK not learning from what has gone before?

Capitalist charity

There is no shortage of accessible research into the charitable and third sectors. A wide and varied spectrum of research exists, examining myriad perspectives, from faith-based research projects (Bassous 2015; Johnsen 2014), effective management and governance in non-profit organisations (Pallotta 2008; Parsons and Broadbridge 2004), the function and purpose of charity retailing (Livingstone 2011; Gregson et al. 2002), to patterns of donor behaviour and motivations for giving (Breeze 2013; Michel and Rieunier 2012). There has, however been minimal interpretation of the form of contemporary charity and the relations which it mediates in line with the spaces it creates.

This chapter is moving towards addressing this lacuna through interrogating the system of food banking and the operational space of the food bank, to unsettle the preconceived assumptions of charity and how we give, through a critique grounded in a polemic from the left – in this narrative the conceptual scene is set.

Open Marxism is a relational approach which emerged in the 1970s as an alternative discourse, moving away from the enforced categorisations of structural Marxism, to a process of thinking which is "dynamically open" (Bonefeld 1987: 36), as ongoing and incomplete. Through interpretation of ongoing processes, open Marxism moves towards a narrative of 'form'. Form can be understood as a "mode of existence of the contradictory movement in which social existence consists" (Bonefeld et al. 1992a: xv) and illustrates the interconnected relations inherent in society. Form recognises the intricacies of social reproduction and struggles as free from classification, metanarratives and totalising discourse. In adopting open Marxism and interrogating the 'mode of existence' in society, the approach is grounded in capitalism's "negation … [and] this negativity is expressed through the category of form" (Holloway 1993: 18). Charity is a social form of capitalism, which operates in order to negate and move past the outcomes of capitalism, but which also continues to simultaneously create capitalism. Therefore charitable spaces of food banks and the system of food banking are both antagonistic and contradictory – paradoxical spaces. In order to augment understanding of food banks and food banking as part of the social form of charity in the UK, the idea of 'charity' itself must first be interpreted from an open Marxist[1] perspective.

Capitalist relations rupture and fragment, yet we constantly reproduce capitalism. We are the authors of our own fate, but not under conditions of our own choosing. As such "it is not the *unity* of living … which requires explanation … but rather the *separation* … a separation which is completely posited only in the relation of wage-labour and capital" (Marx 1973a: 489). The ongoing realisation of the "value-form, whose fully developed shape is the money-form" (Marx 1983: 19), drives the vast process of commodification in society where our expended labour power finds expression "not as direct social relations between individuals at work, but as what they really are, material relations between persons and social relations between things" (1983: 78). In this case, it is the question of separation from access to food and money resulting in spatial relations represented through operational food banks. Our existence is mediated and socially conditioned; we are all separated, but in a way which appears to be unified. But it is this precarious unity which represents the fragile façade of capitalism that continually needs to reconstitute relations of power and money, thus exposing its vulnerability. The experience of separation-in-unity is oppressive, dehumanising and limiting, and it is something which we must struggle against (Holloway 2002) in order to transcend the instabilities and uncertainties perpetuated by capitalism.

Charity is a form of this struggle even though it has become an inherent part of this precarious capitalist society, becoming a commodity and a fetishised idea, representative of the very material relations between people that Marx discusses. The spaces of food banks created by the form of charity reflect relations of power and capitalist inequalities, which stimulate a proactive response. The experience of precarity permeates the system of food banking – from the fragility of capitalism itself to relations of precarity experienced by those accessing food, a precarity of hunger, of labour, of money, of uncertainty and insecurity. Waite's understanding of the concept of precarity "explicitly incorporates the political and institutional context in which the *production* of precarity occurs" (2009: 421). In this case, precarity is represented through the production of the charitable spaces of the food bank and the food banking system in capitalism through which relations of separation are manifest.

Charity is a paradox, an antagonistic discourse riddled with contradictions and struggles, even though it is presented as hopeful, progressive and inherently positive. Charity is an indication of sharing and giving, a benevolent act which presupposes some benefit to others, but typically such donations are in the form of money or commodities. Charity, therefore, is antagonistically determined by the capitalist market economy, the very repercussions of which charity seeks to remedy. Money may be the social form of capitalism, manifest through the wage-labour relationship, but it is also the social form of charity and essential for its continued existence. On the one hand, the act of giving, contributing or donating time, money or commodities in some way in the pursuit of a cause which actively improves and positively contributes to the lives of others is an inherently altruistic action. However, charity is a limited response, rather than transformative action, as it is charity that is directly mediated by capitalism (which perpetuates inequality) (see Livingstone 2013). This is what makes the consideration of charity so complex and intriguing, as it is at once reflective of human nature, an indelible moral imperative, a desire to help. However, by helping are we merely appeasing our own social conscience? Do we think about the consequences of our giving and whether the act of charity itself is for ourselves, or because society expects it of us, or indeed what the outcomes of our charity is in the longer term?

By directing our giving through established charities we are inter-passive (Pfaller 2003), happy in the assumption that the charity will act appropriately with donations. Our struggle for change is displaced through charitable channels, for both those who donate and those who receive charity, as any changes in the social form are mediated by capitalism. However, by contributing to charities, altruism is apparent (even if it is interpassive); there is a moral social force at work, a "care for distant strangers, others with whom one has no personal connection" (Sack, 2003: 29). Such relations find expression through food banks, forming "new modes of spatial relationship[s] ... constituted through institutionally mediated practices of generosity" (Barnett and Land, 2007: 1073). Our experience of charity is representative of mediated relations of giving, generosity and morality, but also of capitalism, spatiality and social form. Via charity, capitalism's inherent crisis-ridden tendencies are somewhat regulated and appeased.

Our interactions and relationships are mediated by capitalist relations, reflected in how we utilise our labour power, spend our wages, create commodities and donate to charities. Charity today is an ideal to be consumed, which strives towards unattainable utopian concepts such as equality for all, and the eradication of poverty and hunger. However, it cannot be said that charity is without purpose or indeed positive outcomes. For those who receive and benefit from the action of charity, the contradiction lies in the fact that the benefit is restricted, as it is one which reinforces the perpetuation of alienation, of poverty, of inequality. As capitalist society encourages the creation of wealth, consequently it produces and exacerbates relations of greed, class, poverty and charity. It is through these relations that food banks have emerged, as a space of charity and therefore of paradox. The following section further breaks down these relations in the case of food banks and the system of food banking from the perspectives of the state, the operations of food banks and the recipients of food, as a complex and antagonistic space.

Relations of food banking – franchising the disenfranchised?

Food banks are becoming a common feature of the urban landscape across the UK, a feature which is representative not only of the social form of charity and detached state relations, but also of the spaces themselves. This section of the chapter seeks to uncover the specific actions which reproduce and create food banks, considering their methods of operation and user interactions, concentrating on drilling down to the "substance of key processes" (Katznelson 1992: 6) that form food banks.

Food is a commodity, something which "by its properties satisfies human wants of some sort or another. The nature of such wants, whether for instance they spring from the stomach or from fancy, makes no difference" (Marx 1983: 43); they are something to be consumed under capitalism. As we know today, however, the hunger springing from the stomach is being addressed and mediated by the system of food banking and the consequential operation of food bank charities. As discussed, food banks represent the detached relations of the state form, the consequences of welfare reform and the precarity of the labour market. Marx's material relations between people are reflected in the charitable redistribution of food. Such material relations form and are formed through the interaction of the systems in place, the users and the volunteers within the space of the food banks themselves, which represent experiences of poverty, dispossession and ongoing separation.

Food banks can adapt a formalised or informal system in redistributing the food they collect. The social franchise of The Trussell Trust is formal in their parcel distribution, because in order to collect food from one of their banks you must first be referred. Giving is conditional and contingent; with frontline professionals (such as social workers and doctors) judging if a voucher for food should be issued depending on individual circumstances. It is also unlikely that more than three parcels of food are distributed by The Trussell Trust to the same person over a period of 6 months (although discretion can be used). This is due to the emergency, short-term nature of The Trussell Trust food banks provision and is effectively a method employed to prevent dependency on them as a food aid provider. It is also prescriptive and criteria driven, harking back to Victorian style determination of the 'deserving' and 'undeserving poor'. Access is limited and restricted, as relations of poverty are managed by the food bank, as they reconstitute capitalist relations of alienation whilst becoming increasingly formalised into the extended welfare state.

Although access to food is limited and based on judging specific criteria, for many people three days' worth of food is a welcome respite (albeit a short-term and finite one), even if it does very little to actively alleviate everyday social relations of poverty. But accessing food banks are a stigmatised last resort for many, an act of desperation and indignity (Power 2014; Scottish Parliament 2014; Tarasuk and Beaton 1999). Van der Horst et al. discuss the emotional experiences of food bank users, noting feelings of shame and negativity; accessing emergency food aid "may be harmful to the self-esteem of receivers" (2014: 1506). Also, the giving of food may be a temporary, short-term benefit, but what happens at the end of the three days?

Food crises are generally a representative symptom of a deeper cause of poverty or challenging social relations and it is unlikely that such a crisis will be ameliorated due to three days of food. Those who need to access the food parcels are engaged in a pseudo-bureaucratic process which then determines if they qualify. Today, notions related to conditional giving, like judging 'worthiness' in society, are a method of operation for some food bank providers, even though "holding the poor responsible for their own fate undermines the anger that poverty and inequality provoke while removing the blame from the system that is responsible" (Jones and Novak 1999: 5). The moral question of giving is complex and antagonistic. Conditional giving further stigmatises the experience of food banks for users, provoking feelings of humiliation and failure, reconstituting material relations of class and poverty – reinforcing our separation and 'difference'. Indeed, Riches suggests that "the stigma associated with charitable food banking suggests it is not a normal channel of food distribution and is a socially unacceptable way to obtain food" (2002: 648).

Although food banks are becoming visible and familiar spaces across the urban landscape of the UK, the experience of the spaces themselves and the various systems in play reflect extreme variations in social relations. There are those for those whom accessing food aid is representative of ongoing experiences of social relations of poverty and deprivation. Conversely, those operating food banks and mediating these social relations do so in a way which provides temporary respite from crisis, but actively controls and manages access to their food and concomitantly reinforces separation. Therefore, the paradox of food aid charities is perpetuated.

In order to get a referral and access food via a Trussell Trust affiliated food bank, the crisis experience of hunger and poverty must fall within certain boundaries. In this respect The Trussell Trust is actively disengaging and distant from the apparently 'undeserving' who fail to meet specific criteria, namely those whose social relations are too chaotic to firstly successfully obtain a referral voucher and then get to the food bank to collect a parcel. Through their system, the Trussell Trust food banks manage the relations of poverty, but only for those who are deemed eligible.

However, there are food banks which provide food in an unconditional way, offering parcels to the same people on a regular basis (Sosenko et al. 2013). These food banks are typically independently run, not affiliated with a social franchise network and do not require referrals for accessing their parcels. Access is not conditional; the spaces are entirely open to anyone requiring food assistance. Relations of poverty are addressed differently in these spaces, but although giving is unconditional and therefore potentially a less stigmatised process of access, the underlying structural causes of poverty remain unaffected. Independent food banks may not be 'franchising the disenfranchised' and the experience of those accessing food is less prescriptive and bureaucratically bound, but as with franchised food aid providers the end result is the same: the gifting of food is an inherently antagonistic and contradictory struggle for those who access and distribute it, as a process subsumed into reproducing capitalism.

The state form consistently attempts to 'manage' the struggle of poverty in varied and fluid ways, which reconstitute the social form in terms of economic relations. The state itself is fragile as it enforces the precarious relations of labour power and the value form (wage labour and money relations). Each form of the state seeks to "impose its will not only upon its opponents but upon the anarchical flux, change and uncertainty to which capitalist modernity is always prone ... struggling to impose its will upon a fluid and spatially open process of capital circulation" (Harvey 1989: 108). The state is ensnared in the reproduction of capitalist relations and mediates the social form of existence through our separation; it is "limited and shaped by the fact that it exists as just one node in a web of social relations" (Holloway 2002: 13), which it is consistently trying to control.

Shifts in the labour market, such as increased employment levels, access to easy credit and improved state welfare – support previously contributed to the mediation of antagonisms in the social form, therefore ensuring challenges to the capitalist form – were 'controlled'. However, the post-war welfare state is being slowly dismantled and reformed by neoliberalism; the labour market is becoming increasingly precarious through zero-hour contracts; the repercussions of the financial crises and the resulting austerity measures implemented demonstrate that the mediation of antagonisms represents a false displacement, revealing the insecurities and alienation of our social form. How the state form operates is directly related to the systems in place relating to food banking, influencing and controlling the role of charities in the UK. By refusing to address and accept the food poverty experienced across the UK today the state form has become detached, but this detachment has resulted in a response through food banks and food aid providers, who are effectively performing the state's welfare role through charity. In this respect, relations of capitalism are being reformed and fundamental social transformation evaded, as food banks are operating in a way which can only fail to effect radical change under capitalism.

Will food crises continue?

It is unlikely that we will ever see a society without relations of charity, sharing and giving – relations which attempt to overcome the daily crises experienced by a multitude of people throughout the UK: crises of hunger, of poverty and, as a result of these, crises of food. Through three connected narratives, this chapter has explored how politics and the capitalist state form perpetuates these crises, while actively distancing itself from an effective welfare response, accepting that charities act in their stead. The practices of food banks and the systems of food banking in place indicate that the UK will soon follow the trend of other 'first world' economies, such as the US and Canada. The practices of the state and the lack of response would imply that these crises are indeed here to stay, although the form is likely to change. Food banks are an increasing presence on the urban landscape – both a force for progress, a moral response to denial of the right to food for all and an effective recourse in the short term to those experiencing crises.

However, although food banks cannot eradicate hunger through provision of emergency parcels and are limited as spaces of neoliberalism today, the space of the food bank is an implicit social presence, where there are indelible opportunities to move past the current situation by continuing to struggle towards negating capitalist relations. Whether or not this struggle is possible – considering the antagonistic spatial relations food banks represent, as extensions of the welfare state, as capitalist charity, as conditional and unconditional providers, as spaces of volunteers and users – there are a mass of complexities but also opportunities.

Food banks are currently in limbo, somewhere between the extremes of becoming pure functions of the state form and spaces of radical change. In order to move beyond the paradox of food banking and actively transform social relations, to ensure that the disenfranchised do not become indefinitely franchised, there must be a drive to recognise food banking charities both as forms of capitalism that can become unsettled and ruptured, and as spaces which can move towards something alternative, something less chaotic, less uneven, increasingly equal and universal. Only time will tell what form these alternatives may take; the paradoxical spaces of food banks and the systems they adopt in line with state relations must be exposed and confronted in order to progress towards a more just and equitable society.

Note

1　For more on open Marxism see Bonefeld, Gunn & Psychopedis (eds.) (1992a & 1992b), Bonefeld, Gunn, Holloway & Psychopedis (eds.) (1995), Holloway (2010, 2002), Bonefeld (2003).

References

Barnett, C. & Land, D. (2007) 'Geographies of generosity: Beyond the "moral turn"' *Geoforum*, 38: 1065–1075.

Bassous, M. (2015) 'What are the factors that affect worker motivation in faith-based non-profit organisations?' *Voluntas*, 26(1): 355–381.

Bonefeld, W. (2003) [ed.] *Revolutionary Writing: Common Sense Essays in Post-Political Politics*. New York: Autonomedia.

Bonefeld, W. (1987) 'Open Marxism' *Common Sense*, 1: 34–38.

Bonefeld, W., Gunn, R., Holloway, J. and Psychopedis, K. (1995) [eds.] *Open Marxism Volume III: Emancipating Marx*. London: Pluto Press.

Bonefeld, W., Gunn, R. & Psychopedis, K. (1992a) [eds.] *Open Marxism Volume II: Theory and Practice*. London: Pluto Press.

Bonefeld, W., Gunn, R. & Psychopedis, K. (1992b) [eds.] *Open Marxism Volume I: Dialectics and History*. London: Pluto Press.

Booth, S. and Whelan, J. (2014) 'Hungry for change: The food banking industry in Australia' *British Food Journal*, 116(9): 1392–1404.

Breeze, B. (2013) 'How donors choose charities: The role of personal taste and experiences in giving decisions' *Voluntary Sector Review* 4(2): 165–183.

Cooper, N., Purcell, S. & Jackson, R. (2014) *Below the Breadline: The Relentless Rise of Food Poverty in Britain*. Church Action on Poverty, Oxfam and The Trussell Trust.

Cooper, N. & Dumpleton, S. (2013) *Walking the Breadline: The Scandal of Food Poverty in 21st Century Britain*. Church Action on Poverty and Oxfam.

Defra (2008) 'Ensuring the UK's Food Security in a Changing World' Discussion paper, July 2008.

De Schutter, O. (2014) 'Foreword', in Riches, G. and Silvasti, T. [eds.] *First World Hunger Revisited: Food Charity or the Right to Food?* 2nd Edition, London: Palgrave Macmillan.

Dowler, E. (2014) 'Food Banks & Food Justice in Austerity Britain', in Riches, G. & Silvasti, T. [eds.] *First World Hunger Revisited: Food Charity or the Right to Food?* 2nd Edition, London: Palgrave Macmillan.

Downing, E., Kennedy, S. & Fell, M. (2014) *Food Banks and Food Poverty*. House of Commons Library SN06657 (09/04/2014).

Forsey, A. (2014a) *Feeding Britain: A Strategy for Zero Hunger in England, Wales, Scotland and Northern Ireland*. The report of the All-Party Parliamentary Inquiry into Hunger in the United Kingdom. London: The Children's Society.

Forsey, A. (2014b) *An Evidence Review for the All-Party Parliamentary Inquiry into Hunger in the United Kingdom*. London: The Children's Society.

Gregson, N., Crewe, L. & Brooks, L. (2002) 'Discourse, displacement and retail practice: Some points from the charity retail project' *Environment and Planning A*, 34(9): 1661–1683.

Harvey, D. (1989) *The Condition of Postmodernity*. Oxford: Basil Blackwell.

Holloway, J. (1993) 'The freeing of Marx' *Common Sense*, 14: 172–221.

Holloway, J. (2002) *Change the World without Taking Power*. London: Pluto Press.

Holloway, J. (2010) *Crack Capitalism*. London and New York: Pluto.

Johnsen, S. (2014) 'Where's the "faith" in "faith-based" organisations? The evolution and practice of faith-based homelessness services in the UK' *Journal of Social Policy*, 43(2): 413–430.

Jones, C. & Novak, T. (1999) *Poverty, Welfare and the Disciplinary State*. London: Routledge.

Katznelson, I. (1992) *Marxism and the City*. Oxford: Oxford University Press.

Lambie, H. (2011) *The Trussell Trust Foodbank Network: Exploring the Growth of Foodbanks Across the UK*. Coventry University, Coventry.

Lambie-Mumford, H., Crossley, D., Jensen, E., Verbeke, M. & Dowler, E. (2014) *Household Food Security in the UK: A Review of Food Aid*. Food Ethics Council & the University of Warwick.

Lambie-Mumford, H. & Dowler, E. (2014) 'Rising use of "food aid" in the United Kingdom' *British Food Journal* 116(9): 1418–1425.

Livingstone, N. (2011) 'The changing structure of charity retailers in Edinburgh's built environment' *Local Economy* 26(2): 122–133.

Livingstone, N. (2013) 'Capital's charity' *Capital and Class* 37(3): 347–353.

Livingstone, N. (2015) 'The Hunger Games: Food poverty and politics in the UK' *Capital & Class* 39(2): 188–195.

Loopstra, R., Reeves, A., Taylor-Robinson, D., Barr, B., McKee, M. & Stuckler, D. (2015) 'Austerity, sanctions, and the rise of food banks in the UK' *British Medical Journal*, 360: 1775.

MacNab, S. (2014) 'Independence "could bring end to food banks"' *The Scotsman*, 11th August.

Marx, K. (1973a) *Grundrisse*. Harmondsworth: Penguin.

Marx, K. (1973b) 'The Eighteenth Brumaire of Louis Bonaparte' in Fernbach, D. [ed.] *Surveys from Exile*. Harmondsworth: Penguin.

Marx, K. (1983) *Capital: Volume One*. London: Lawrence & Wishart.

Massey, D. (2004) 'Geographies of responsibility' *Geografiska Annaler*, 86(1): 5–18.

Michel, G. & Rieunier, S. (2012) 'Nonprofit brand image and typicality influences on charitable giving' *Journal of Business Research* 65(5): 701–707.

Pallotta, D. (2008) *Uncharitable: How Restraints on Nonprofits Undermine their Potential*. Medford: Tufts University Press.

Parsons, E. & Broadbridge, A. (2004) 'Managing change in nonprofit organisations' *Voluntas*, 15(3): 227–243.

Pfaller, R. (2003) 'Little gestures of disappearance: Interpassivity and the theory of ritual' *Journal of European Psychoanalysis* 16 (Winter–Spring).

Poppendieck, J. (1998) *Sweet Charity? Emergency Food and the End of Entitlement*. New York: Penguin Putnam.

Power, A. (2014) 'Hunger pains: Rise of the food bank' *LSE Connect*, Winter: 14–15.

Riches, G. (2002) 'Food banks and food security: Welfare reform, human rights and social policy. Lessons from Canada?' *Social Policy & Administration* 36(6): 648–663.

Riches, G. and Silvasti, T. [eds.] (2014) *First World Hunger Revisited, Food Charity or the Right to Food?* 2nd Edition. London: Palgrave Macmillan.

Sack, R. (2003) *A Geographical Guide to the Real and the Good*. New York: Routledge.

Scottish Parliament, The (2014) *Food Banks and Welfare Reform*. Welfare Reform Committee, 2nd Report, 2013 (session 4). Edinburgh: The Scottish Parliament.

Sosenko, F., Livingstone, N. & Fitzpatrick, S. (2013) *Overview of Food Aid Provision in Scotland*. Edinburgh: Scottish Government Social Research.

Tarasuk, V.S. & Beaton, G.H. (1999) 'Women's dietary intakes in the context of household food insecurity' *The Journal of Nutrition* (129(3): 672–679.

The Trussell Trust (2014) 'Latest foodbank figures top 900,000: Life has got worse not better for poorest in 2013/14, and this is just the tip of the iceberg' *The Trussell Trust Online*. Retrieved from: www.trusselltrust.org/foodbank-figures-top-900000

The Trussell Trust (2015) 'Foodbank stats' *The Trussell Trust Online*. Retrieved from: www.trusselltrust.org/stats

Theriault, L. & Yadlowski, L. (2000) 'Revisiting the food bank issues in Canada' *Canadian Social Work Review* 17(2): 205–223.

Van Der Horst, H., Pascucci, S. & Bol, W. (2014) 'The "dark side" of food banks? Exploring emotional responses of food bank receivers in the Netherlands' *British Food Journal* 116(9): 1506–1520.

Waite, L. (2009) 'A place and space for a critical geography of precarity?' *Geography Compass* 3(1): 412–433.

Warshawsky, D. N. (2010) 'New power relations served here: The growth of food banking in Chicago' *Geoforum* 41: 763–775.

Wells, R. and Caraher, M. (2014) 'UK print media coverage of the food bank phenomenon: from food welfare to food charity?' *British Food Journal* 116(9): 1426-1445.

Winne, M. (2009) *Closing the Food Gap: Resetting the Table in the Land of Plenty.*, Boston: Beacon Press.

9 Shared moments of sociality

Embedded sharing within peer-to-peer hospitality platforms

Katharina Hellwig, Russell Belk and Felicitas Morhart

As a hoped-for response to the hyperconsumption hangover of many developed nations, the "New Sharing Economy" was welcomed by numerous advocates and many consumers. Referring to a plethora of technologically mediated peer-to-peer exchanges, the term was hyped by Rachel Botsman and Roo Rogers (2010) in their book *What's Mine Is Yours: The Rise of Collaborative Consumption*. Therein, access and experience instead of ownership and sharing, barter and lending instead of buying were advocated as possible ways out of an economic, social and environmental crisis of unsustainable overconsumption. And *Time* magazine even suggested the Sharing Economy to be one of "10 ideas that will change the world" (Walsh 2011). But lately the "New Sharing Economy" finds itself in a crisis as it faces growing criticism: it is accused of fuelling unsustainable consumption behaviour (e.g. by increasing emissions through cheap access to cars and travel destinations like in car-sharing and CouchSurfing, Schor and Thompson 2014), rampant neoliberalism, and marginally legal business practices that support tax fraud and undermine workers' rights and social security (Cagle 2014; Morozov 2013).

Oftentimes, the business practices of many prominent "sharing businesses" have little to do with the romantic ideal of sharing as joint (psychological) ownership, prosocial intentions and the absence of expectations of reciprocity (Belk 2007; 2010). ZipCar, for example, has been found to display negative reciprocities and a Big Brother governance model instead of stimulating feelings of community (Bardhi and Eckhardt 2012). Similarly the taxi service Uber is accused of exploiting participating drivers and ruining wages in the taxi business (Giesler 2014). The hospitality industry has in many cities and regions started to actively fight for stronger legal interventions, regulations, and taxation directed at peer-to-peer hospitality platforms like Airbnb in order to protect them from such new competitors.

Given the dominance of economics in treatments of business it is not surprising that much of the existing research focuses precisely on the redistribution of idle capacity and thus on purely economic efficiency within a system labelled sharing. Given this focus on the "economic" side of the Sharing Economy, many of the findings of such studies revolve, unsurprisingly, around how participants perpetuate a traditional capitalist mindset by presumably maximizing their utilities under the guise of a socially romantic label – a practice that has sometimes been called "sharewashing". However, if a socially romantic aspect within material sharing systems is to be found, it is not advisable to focus solely on economically efficient behaviours, but on the opposite: on economically "inefficient" behaviours, namely participants' spending time and congeniality with each other even though the redistribution of physical resources would not require it. That is, just as business generally has been found to be socially embedded rather than hyper-rational and impersonal (Granovetter 1985), peer-to-peer platforms are especially prone to social embeddedness. Rather than staying as anonymous guests in a large hotel or motel chain, participants choose to stay with someone whom they can get to know. Likewise, the ride-sharing service BlaBlaCar allows participants to share rides with someone who will engage them in conversation.

Among the plethora of peer-to-peer service offerings, two popular cases in the new Sharing Economy appear particularly well suited for investigating the sociality of shared moments: the hospitality platforms CouchSurfing and Airbnb. Social interaction is an essential part of the non-profit CouchSurfing experience and while many for-profit Airbnb hosts temporarily rent their apartments without their presence, there are also many who more personally accommodate guests by sharing not only space, but also time and at least some conversation, interaction, and social moments with each guest (Ikkala and Lampinen 2015). Mostly referred to as "encounters", the notion of shared moments has found attention in literature on services (see, e.g., Arnould and Price 1993; Czepiel 1990; Solomon et al. 1985) and hospitality (Bell 2007; 2012; Bialski 2012a; Di Domenico and Lynch 2007; Lynch and MacWhannell 2000), but also plays an important role in humanistic psychology (Friedman 1976; Rachman 1975). In line with these literature streams, we define shared moments as encounters of at least two people that are co-present in terms of temporality and spatiality (see Bell 2007). In a hospitality setting like the present, the spatial dimension of the shared moment is particularly noteworthy because, once the guest departs, the social roles of host and guest that are implied by hospitality are abolished.

With a focus on the social ideology of sharing, we examined such shared moments within one market-based (i.e., involving monetary exchange; e.g., Airbnb) versus one non-market-based (i.e., not involving monetary exchange; e.g., CouchSurfing,) sharing system in order to understand how the notion of sociality is produced and shaped through each system's market-based or non-market-based sharing ideology.

Sharing and the "new sharing economy": sharing as mode of consumption

Sharing can be seen as one of the most basic forms of human social behaviour – its existence and relevance as a form of distribution in human societies can be traced back several hundred thousand years (Price 1975). In his work on sharing as a mode of consumption, Belk (2007) defines sharing as "the act and process of distributing what is ours to others for their use and/or the act and process of receiving or taking something from others for our use" (p. 126). Another definition conceptualises sharing as "nonreciprocal pro-social behavior" (Benkler 2004). In contradistinction to gift-giving and commodity exchange, Belk (2010; 2013) defines sharing as involving joint ownership (at least de facto) with prosocial intentions and as excluding direct expectations of reciprocity.

Considerable semantic confusion reigns the literature about sharing and peer-to-peer consumption, the latter being indifferently referred to by popular media as "sharing businesses" (Belk 2013). In this context, Belk (2013) introduces the labels "true sharing" and "pseudo sharing" to differentiate between actual sharing and commercially motivated forms of consumption such as short-term rentals or "access-based consumption". According to Belk's (2010) typology that identifies monetary payments and commercial interest as clear counter indicators of sharing, sharing takes place only in the absence of a market environment. Bardhi and Eckhardt (2012), for example, show that, despite being labelled car "sharing", participation in Zipcar largely resides in commercial and self-interested motives for participation, and hence comes closest to what Belk (2013) has labelled "pseudo-sharing". Ozanne and Ballantine's (2010) study of toy libraries and Jonsson's (2007) study of a small scale car sharing operation, where users pay membership fees and volunteer their services to the cooperative organisation rather than to a business organisation, in contrast offer models of non-commercial sharing organisations where social transactions are of key importance.

Against this background, we suggest that such reflections on the interface of sharing and a market environment, and especially the way they are applied in consumer research, lack an important consideration. All studies conducted thus far largely rely on the characteristics of sharing tangible and partible objects – and hence cover only a part of the meaning spectrum that is intuitively and ubiquitously associated with the term of sharing. Although the sharing of experiences, ideas, or knowledge is acknowledged in several articles (Albinsson and Yasanthi 2012; Belk 2010; Chen 2009), scholarly discussions of sharing as an alternative mode of consumption remain very closely tied to the characteristics of sharing material resources like cars, mobile phone plans, or toys (Bardhi and Eckhart 2012; Lamberton and Rose 2012; Ozanne and Ballantine 2010). In contrast, Vaughan's (1997) feminist critique of exchange emphasises the importance of the non-material aspect of sharing. Her model of sharing is the conversation – not as an exchange of words with obligatory turn-taking, but as a joint process of co-construction. The conversation is not something to be owned, but a mutually shared possession.

Given that many peer-to-peer consumption activities of the Sharing Economy involve shared moments as 'side effects' (e.g. ride-sharing, apartment sharing, shared meals), it is ever more surprising that the scholarly discussion of sharing theory remains so closely tied to the characteristics of sharing material resources. This might be due to the fact that much of this work has been conducted in the locus of consumer research. We suggest that Vaughan's (1997) metaphor of sharing as conversation is a viable approach to think about the relevance of sharing experiences, moments, conversations, and emotions that goes beyond the view of sharing as a mere consumer behaviour.

Concretely, we propose that the focus on sharing material objects that dominates the theoretical and empirical work on sharing neglects the particularities of social resources such as love and affection, status, or information, that are well known from research on social relationships (Foa 1971; Foa and Foa 1975), which constitute an essential part of the concept of sharing. The present work aims to extend this view by explicitly looking at the sociality of shared moments.

The literature on embeddedness (e.g., Carrier 1995; Granovetter 1985) suggests that economic assumptions of impersonal business transactions are quite wrong and that most business dealings are at least partly personal and social in nature. Inasmuch as this work occurred before the rise of e-mail and the Internet, these embedded transactions, like the networks of "friends" on Facebook and business contacts on LinkedIn, may ironically be less intimately embedded than previously. But to an even greater degree, C2C (consumer to consumer) interactions as with the platforms studied here, are apt to be highly social in nature, despite the premises of Becker (2005) that all human interaction involves rational economic exchange, even those between family members. As Burgoyne (1990) and Zelizer (2005) find, human relations, even when they involve money, are essentially social, although borderline cases sometimes do cause confusion when they mix considerations of love and marketplace exchange. Here too, updating these findings for an Internet age is called for. There is some evidence that the boundaries between social and economic exchanges have become fuzzier (e.g. Scaraboto 2015). Especially in the case of the so-called sharing economy and peer-to-peer sharing, the combination of money and hospitality may well blur the distinctions between personal social interaction and commercial business dealings.

On one hand, as robot service personnel become more common in the hospitality industry, hotels may become more like Japanese "love hotels" where the guest enters a single car garage, inserts a credit card, and moves inside to a hotel room without ever encountering any service provider (Basil 2008). But as Sobh, Belk, and Wilson (2013) find in the context of Arab hospitality, the high end B2C "hospitality industry" in the Middle East often moves in the opposite direction to make commercial hospitality seem more personal in nature. By addressing guests by name, remembering and catering to their individual preferences, and providing free services like dates, Arab coffee, and limousine service, they often blur the line between expectations of commercial and social hospitality. This is also the case in prior borderline cases like seasonal guest houses, traditional bed and breakfast establishments, and lodging houses (e.g., Di Domenico and Lynch 2007; Lynch and MacWhannell 2000). And Germann Molz (2004; 2007) notes the expectation-defying paradox of free lodging in CouchSurfing and other non-monetised C2C hosting organisations.

The study

The present study is part of a multi-method and multi-sited collection of qualitative data over a 3-year period that was aimed at exploring peer-to-peer hospitality platforms with regard to their recent developments, the role of the provided infrastructure for shaping the social interaction among guests and hosts, and the nature of social moments. Our methods include qualitative in-depth interviews, participant observation and the analysis of online content such as member profiles, forum discussions, newspaper articles, and social media posts.

This chapter draws on participant observation and 14 in-depth interviews that were conducted with Airbnb hosts renting out rooms while they are present (4), CouchSurfing hosts (who are necessarily present) (5), and individuals who host on both platforms (5) in Europe and the Americas. All of the interviewees except for one Airbnb host also had experiences as guest travelling with the respective platform(s). The interviewees were recruited via the respective platforms or in local CouchSurfing group meetings. We used a purposive sample of participants with diverse socio-economic, educational and cultural backgrounds, ranging from 21 to 36 years of age. Six were female. Their engagement with the respective platforms varied from "newbies", who had hosted or travelled only a couple of times via CouchSurfing or Airbnb, to experienced users with several years of active experience.

The interviews were conducted between October 2012 and November 2015 and lasted from 30 to 150 minutes. All interviews except for one via Skype were conducted face-to-face in coffee shops, respondents' apartments, and the researchers' office, and all except for one were captured on digital audio files and transcribed. The interview guideline comprised broad questions about the participants' motivations for participating in CouchSurfing or Airbnb, their hosting experiences, and the relationships with their guests and hosts. Both framing and probing questions encouraged participants to provide detailed narratives about their participation in CouchSurfing or Airbnb and their encounters with others using the platform. We interpreted our data by means of a hermeneutic approach (Thompson 1997) and used our field notes and comparisons with web-content (i.e., participants' online profiles and contributions on discussion boards) as sources for triangulation regarding attitudes and behaviours reported in the interviews (Mays and Pope 1995).

Findings

CouchSurfing and Airbnb – two distinct business models of peer-to-peer hospitality

At first glance, the business ideas of the two poster children for the peer-to-peer hospitality sector appear to be very similar: In both cases, an online platform brings together hosts who offer a short-term accommodation in form of a couch, a room in a home, or a full apartment or house and travellers who are looking for accommodations. Both were founded upon the idea of offering domestic space to strangers – but while CouchSurfing was born out of the idea of asking hosts whether they could kindly provide a free couch or spare bed to stay, Airbnb was explicitly founded to offer accommodations that are somewhere between CouchSurfing and hotels in order to turn idle space into money. But upon closer inspection, both operate quite differently. We highlight two major differences:

1) Money versus No-money: The first obvious but important distinction is that Airbnb involves the payment of money, while the exchange of money or comparable material value is an articulated taboo in CouchSurfing whose official mission is to connect travellers with locals offering a free place to stay (CouchSurfing 2014). CouchSurfing hosts offer free shelter and oftentimes food and entertainment to strangers whom they have never met and might never meet again after their face-to-face encounter. A direct reciprocation of the visit is not expected and happens only occasionally. It is, moreover, common and accepted for a member of the CouchSurfing community to exclusively surf and never host another member, and vice versa (albeit less common in practice) (Lauterbach et al. 2009). This is not to say that there is no indirect hospitality by "paying it forward" or more subtle exchanges of conversation, household chores, and talents. While direct tit-for-tat reciprocity is quite uncommon, many CouchSurfers acknowledge the benefits that they have from meeting others via the hospitality platform. Karl, a 20-year-old CouchSurfing host from France, for example, states:

> Thinking rationally, CouchSurfing gives you a lot of profit just not the material ones. You get a lot of benefits from knowing other people, enjoying the pleasure of talking, of learning, of finding out about different ideas, different languages.

This sort of exchange is described later in the results. The accommodation with Airbnb, in contrast, is explicitly provided in exchange for monetary value (paid online to the platform via credit card). Airbnb hosts list pictures and descriptions of their place, its availability, and prices and those seeking a room reserve more or less as they might if they were making a hotel reservation. Since its founding, Airbnb has experienced an increasing professionalisation over the course of which the commercial aspect of the business model for hosts became ever more salient, entailing a number of legal clashes with landlords, tourism boards, and government officials over unregistered and unregulated business practices, untaxed incomes, and rising rental prices (Huet 2014). In CouchSurfing, by contrast, users share their homes and their time with strangers, without any money involved, even after a controversy about its incorporation in 2010–2011.

2) Core Product and Added Value: The materiality of the hospitality experience is at the core of the value proposition of Airbnb – when booking a listing via the platform the central part of the agreement is the exchange of

money for a room at a certain location. Prices with Airbnb vary according to the attractiveness, size, season, and location of the listed property, while any personal description of the individual who is offering the place is a marginal consideration. Accordingly, hosts on this platform typically emphasise the uniqueness and attractiveness of their space, and usually provide only a short description including their name, age, profession and sometimes their interests.

This is in line with our finding that even Airbnb hosts who are present at the same time as their guests, say that they do not particularly care about guests' personal descriptions and merely reject potential guests if they appear scary, complicated, or inconsiderate. When asked whether she ever rejects Airbnb requests because she feels uncomfortable with the person requesting, Cecilia, a 29-year-old Airbnb host from France, for example, explains:

CECILIA: Yeah, I have actually, a few times. When old men write me … especially with no information on their site and just short messages like, "Is it available from tomorrow?", then I'll be like, "Hmm, no. Sorry." [chuckles]
INTERVIEWER: How many times did you reject people?
CECILIA: Rejected some because I was not feeling right about them? Maybe five times out of 20, thereabouts.

Some of the female hosts also indicated that they prefer hosting other females of approximately their age but all agreed that they seldom purposefully select others according to shared interests or favourable personality traits.

This is in stark contrast to the modus operandi of CouchSurfing, where we found, in line with prior research, that personal encounters and social relatedness are central components of the overall experience (Bialski 2012b; Germann Molz 2012; 2014). However, rather than establishing enduring social relationships, what is of interest to CouchSurfers is closer to Simmel's (1949) notion of sociability, which he defines as a play form of social interaction that can be an end in itself with intrinsically rewarding properties for the individual (Bialski 2012b). CouchSurfing users mutually choose their hosts and guests according to the attractiveness of the individual's profile and the personal information that is provided by the CouchSurfing site, and through the reputational references by former CouchSurfing partners (Lauterbach et al. 2009). Rather than booking accommodation, the CouchSurfing users that we interviewed and observed explicitly chose a particular individual according to perceived prospects of such intrinsically valuable social interaction:

It's about people looking to meet other people, new other people, different people, and learning, exchanging about the different experiences, different cultures, different centres of interest. Not about going to someone and just sleeping, it's about spending time together and exchanging non-material things. That's the important thing in that project.

(Claude, CouchSurfing host, 29, Luxemburg)

Participants felt considerable pride when talking about some of their most interesting and unique CouchSurfing partners and seemed to collect experiences as with CouchSurfers who studied at Harvard, were professional triathletes or successful entrepreneurs, or who came in their own plane to attend a MENSA meeting for intellectually gifted individuals. The CouchSurfing website provides a rich set of tools that aims at "[bringing] out the essence of people", as one of the founders of CouchSurfing puts it in an interview with Bialski (2012b). Its design facilitates selecting individuals and encourages users to present a comprehensive and insightful overview of themselves: apart from the obvious personal description, users are asked to write about their personal philosophy, the types of people they enjoy, things they would like to learn, things they can share and teach as well as examples of amazing things they have seen or done. CouchSurfing further encourages members to add as much personal information as possible and gives clear guidelines on how the selection procedure should work and which criteria might be most relevant.

In CouchSurfing, the absence of money and an active denial of materialities help build a normative frame that shifts the focus to the social aspects of the consumption act. Social interaction is a central part of the CouchSurfing experience, where it is taboo not to spend time with each other.

In Airbnb, by contrast, the core product of the peer-to-peer hospitality experience is the economic exchange of money for a room and location. However, there is still a "couch" (or even a room with a bed) as part of the CouchSurfing experiences, and in many cases there is social interaction within Airbnb stays. We find that those aspects of the peer-to-peer hospitality experience take the form of an "added value" that is not expected yet can enhance the value of the experience. In CouchSurfing, comforts beyond a simple place to sleep are not decisive factors for the choice of host, whereas they are usually appreciated. One informant, for example, remembers being delighted by the impressive penthouse of her CouchSurfing host in New York City:

> [My host] had a crazy penthouse at Port Authority. He agreed to host me for five days. Perfect. So lucky. Crazy perfect ... we had the most spectacular view on 50th floor, which is awesome for first time tourists.
>
> (Pia, 28, CouchSurfing host from Germany)

And in several instances in our data, CouchSurfers recall the pleasant surprise of having their own bed and room rather than just a couch to sleep on – the "upgrade to Business Class" in CouchSurfing terms, according to Lewis-Kraus (2013). In general however, accommodation in the sense of a nice apartment or house is a rather peripheral choice criterion among CouchSurfers, where surfers primarily choose hosts rather than places.

In Airbnb, sociability among guests and hosts is often found to be welcome and appreciated, a finding that is in line with other studies on sociability in peer-to-peer hospitality platforms (Ikkala and Lampinen 2015).

In contrast to CouchSurfing, however, we found social interaction to not be expected – even among the stay-at-home Airbnb hosts that we focused on in this study. Ida, a 30-year-old Norwegian Airbnb hostess, for example, talked about two of her guests, an Italian couple with whom she did not really connect (mainly due to language barriers). She usually rents out only one of the rooms in her apartment in Oslo and is remembered by one of the authors as a vividly outgoing and actively interaction-seeking hostess. Nevertheless, she willingly accepted the lack of communication with her Italian guests as a matter of fact and simply stayed with her boyfriend while they were in her apartment. Asked about her expectations for the interaction with her guests, she said:

IDA: I don't know if I had any expectations of making friends. I didn't have that with my Airbnb guests. Like, if someone called me or came around, then great, but I didn't expect – especially since they were a couple too – I didn't expect any kind of relationship with them.

INTERVIEWER: Maybe not a relationship, but just maybe a good talk or something?

IDA: Yeah. I definitely thought it would be easier to talk to them, but . . . but no, I wasn't disappointed in any way. It was just okay. I stayed at my boyfriend's place most nights and the day.

Such low expectations regarding interactions and social bonds with guests are rarely found among CouchSurfers. A lack of interaction, either due to the absence of the host or the guest, language barriers, or overly distinctive personalities and interests, were universally perceived as negatives by the informants who actively participated in CouchSurfing. Giovanni, a 26-year-old Italian medical student who hosts on both platforms, explained that to him, it is absolutely okay to hide the keys and leave a note with important information for an arriving Airbnb guest in case he cannot be around, but could not imagine doing the same with an arriving CouchSurfer, reflecting that not spending time with a CouchSurfing guest would be "very bad". This statement as well as numerous complaints made about uninterested or socially awkward guests who would arrive, drop their luggage, and leave without major social interaction exemplify the centrality of social interaction in CouchSurfing.

Table 9.1 summarises the main differences that can be observed between Airbnb and CouchSurfing with regard to the prevailing market model, as well as the core offer and the added value that shape the guest-host relationships in both peer-to-peer hospitality platforms.

According to these key observations, the CouchSurfing model would be fairly close to what Belk (2013) defined as "true sharing," whereas Airbnb is better characterised as businesslike "pseudo sharing," even among the amateurs on whom we focus. However, we found several accounts of disappointment among CouchSurfers in our data, indicating violations of their expectations of sociability and intrinsically rewarding sociability

Table 9.1 Major differences between CouchSurfing and Airbnb

	CouchSurfing	*Airbnb*
Market Model	No exchanges of money or things of material value	Money-based market exchanges
Core Offer	Sociability	Accommodation
Added Value	Nice "couch" (accommodation)	Sociability

(Simmel 1949). More specifically, it was found that CouchSurfing encounters in which no sociability occurs in terms of shared time and attention were perceived as disappointments or even as a breaches of implicit agreements. Marijn, a Dutch CouchSurfer, explained that she was hosted by a German girl in Munich, who picked her up at the train station and brought her to her house, where she offered her a room of her own to stay in but then left her alone for the next two days while the hostess spent time with her boyfriend:

> I thought that this was a bit strange. I had to stay at home all day, the weather was bad. And that girl never called again, I felt so lonely. I thought: "For me, this isn't CouchSurfing". I mean, it's cool what she is trying to do. She has the best intentions, but I felt so shit, so lonely. I thought ... I don't know what I should do. [...] Actually I left earlier to meet the other couple that was supposed to host me next. So I left that place and it was a really weird experience because of course that girl felt really bad – and she obviously did this with her best intentions – but this is not CouchSurfing.

Similar to Marijn's leaving earlier than she initially planned, CouchSurfing hosts told us that they could imagine throwing out guests who don't participate in social interaction, and some have done this. Not conforming to social expectations (both as guest and as a host) is hence seen as a legitimate reason to terminate the implicit agreement of staying with another person for a specific amount of time. These observations give reason to conclude that the social interaction in CouchSurfing can be characterised as what Belk (2010) and others (Price 1975; Woodburn 1998) define as "demand sharing." That is, it is something both hosts and guests feel is their right. The following section further examines the key differences of such feelings of entitlement and their importance for understanding the sociality of shared moments.

Shared moments of sociality

In the case of Airbnb, reciprocal claims are clearly integrated into the business model on the level of the material exchange of money versus accommodation. They are based on economic exchange and explicitly stated in the contractual agreement between host and guest. Hence, both have rights for mutual compliance (e.g. a clean apartment that looks like the Internet pictures, the monetary payment that both have agreed upon).

In CouchSurfing, by contrast, there is an implicit agreement for social engagement in which claims for mutual sociality are embedded. This is illustrated by the disappointment, anger and frustration that were expressed by the CouchSurfer informants in cases where such implicit agreements about the mutual expectations of time and attention broke down.

In Foa and Foa's (1971; 1975) terms, while the resource transacted in Airbnb is money, the key resource in CouchSurfing is the time and attention that is invested in the social engagement. In their circular model or resources, social currencies are anathema to monetary exchange because they are non-economic and particular in character whereas money is economic and universal (Foa and Foa 1975).

By non-economic we mean not only non-financial, but that nothing of economic value is exchanged. The exchange of otherwise autotelic time and attentiveness for money for example would turn the sociality into an economic product of inherently different character more like that with a waiter, concierge, personal butler, or a prostitute. Although money is not always the universal medium that economists maintain (Belk and Wallendorf 1990; Zelizer 2005), it offers an extrinsic rationale for the sociality of CouchSurfing and would ruin its autotelic character.

In Airbnb, the social interaction that may take place between guest and host is secondary and is certainly not a part of the agreement to exchange money for accommodation. Counter to our initial assumptions, interactions between those Airbnb hosts who remained in their homes and their guests did occur and added autotelic benefits external to the economic exchange, revealing the embeddedness of many market transactions (Granovetter 1985). This observation is supported by interviews with people like Ida, who frequently host on Airbnb. When we asked her about whether she somehow feels obliged to spend time with her guests while she is in her apartment, she stated:

IDA: I don't think I feel like I had to. Even though they've been alone, I've never felt like I had to. But sometimes, I've wanted to, like, "We're home. Come on – let's watch TV. I'll cook dinner ... Do you want something in the shop? Do you want to go for a walk?" ... But, I haven't felt like it was something I needed to do!

INTERVIEWER: Did you have the impression that some of your guests expected that?

IDA: No, not really. No, I didn't.

This points to the insight that, ironically, when it comes to sociality, Airbnb sometimes comes closest to the idea of "true sharing" without underlying expectations or obligations. However, in the case of CouchSurfing, sociality is an "expected benefit". There, interactions are obligations and entitlements that suggest demand sharing (Belk 2010; Price 1975; Woodburn 1998) of attention and time. Materially CouchSurfing is clearly closest to true sharing;

but non-materially such demand sharing is institutionalised and expected, even though it is often freely given and autotelic.

Many respondents who actively hosted on both platforms acknowledged sometimes perceiving the shared moments within CouchSurfing as demanding and energy-consuming, a finding that is in line with previous research on CouchSurfing (Bialski 2012a). Such intensive emotional involvement, paired with disappointment in cases where others do not show this same level of engagement, made several of these dual hosts to prefer hosting on Airbnb, where participation or denial of social interaction appeared to be more of a free choice. This finding holds for informants who were guests on both platforms as well.

We found that especially in CouchSurfing, the expected interactions were perceived as a burden when the time and the energy needed for being a caring partner were limited:

> So I guess as I grow older right now, I kind of enjoy Airbnb more, interacting with more serious people. [...] CouchSurfing is more about people maybe to have fun, have a good time and cultural exchange, and it's more exhausting. I have to show them around, I have to explain a lot of things about culture, and then I have to spend lots of time bringing them for sightseeing different places. But with Airbnb I don't have the obligation. I just provide them the place to stay and, if they want to, we can hang out, we can go for drinks, and I can show them around but I don't have to. I'm not obligated. But for CouchSurfing I kind of feel I'm obligated to show them around. So it's more involved for me.
>
> (Tim, CouchSurfing and Airbnb host, 27, New York City)

Like Tim above, several respondents indicated preferring Airbnb over CouchSurfing as they grow older because time and social energy became increasingly rare resources for them. In Airbnb, by contrast, social interaction remains a non-economic behaviour that is not subject to demands, like those of demand sharing (Belk 2010).

Concluding discussion

The aim of this chapter has been to explore how sociality in the sense of moments of social togetherness is produced and shaped through the respective prevailing (market or non-market based) sharing ideology. We find that hospitality is particularly prone to the phenomenon of social embeddedness (Granovetter 1985) because it relies on two major components – the component of materiality in the sense of concrete accommodations, and oftentimes food and drinks, and the nonmaterial component of social interaction between host and guest.

We suggest that the two investigated peer-to-peer hospitality platforms offer two substantially different approaches that put different weights on these two key components of hospitality, resulting in different peculiarities of social moments. As summarised in Table 9.1, the sociability aspect of hospitality is the core offer of CouchSurfing, where the actual accommodation takes the form of an added value. The opposite is true for Airbnb, where the accommodation aspect is central to the value proposition and sociability is not expected.

As such, these key resources that constitute the respective core offers of CouchSurfing and Airbnb are considerably different from each other and thus follow different logics. Drawing on Foa and Foa's (1975) circular representation of resources of interpersonal exchange helps to understand their distinctiveness. They suggest six key resources that they arranged in a circle along the dimensions of particularity and concreteness.

Those close to each other are exchangeable, those far from each other aren't. This implies for example that love and money are not exchangeable against each other, and neither are status and goods, or information and services. Sociability, the key resource that can be seen as the core product of CouchSurfing, can be placed between the resources of love, status, and services when it comes to the defining characteristics of particularity and concreteness. According to Foa and Foa's (1975) logic, it is thus not exchangeable against money or goods – which explains why the couch that is provided by the host cannot be reciprocated by the sociability of the guest; only money would suffice. In contrast, the expectations and claims made in CouchSurfing relate to time and attention from the respective partner and are outside of Foa and Foa's (1975) focus on exchange. This finding is in line with earlier studies on CouchSurfing – Bialski (2012a) for example describes conversations as a "vague and implicit" form of reciprocity. And Chen (2012) finds that the expectations that underlie the host-guest dyads in CouchSurfing to become especially visible in cases of different cultural understandings of hospitality; namely, whenever the expectations of the Taiwanese CouchSurfers in her study do not align with the practices, needs and desires of their Western hosts and guests. It is also clearly exemplified by the profound dissatisfaction of CouchSurfing guests like Marijn, who was provided with a full room to stay in but who lacked attention from her host. However, we do not find that CouchSurfers see this as a reciprocal exchange as much as an entitlement, as is the case with demand sharing. In Fiske's (1992) terms, CouchSurfing hence involves something closer to communal sharing.

In Airbnb, by contrast, the exchange is more obvious and more explicitly settled in the core offer: individuals exchange accommodation (a good with certain service elements) against money. It is closer to what Fiske (1992) terms market pricing. Sociability is not included in this equation and, being placed on the opposite site of the Foa (1971) circle, cannot be demanded by means of either money or goods.

We find that what changes the perception of sociability in both platforms is whether they are part of the core offer, or whether such social moments occur as 'added value' beyond the agreement. The sometime occurrences of social interactions in Airbnb are unsolicited and when they do take place they are not driven by reciprocal expectations. They are the extra embeddedness that Granovetter (1985) finds in other business transactions. In CouchSurfing, however, such social embeddedness is the *sine qua non* of the expectations of both hosts and guests. Here the failure of these moral norms cannot be compensated by the lavishness of material affordances; it is not a part of an exchange.

Whether the hospitality platforms themselves can be classified as sharing or not hence depends directly on the perspective that we want to take. The nonmonetary environment of CouchSurfing is clearly closer to what Belk (2010) has defined as prototypical sharing. Here the physical offering is the extra when it happens in the form of a lavish or private room. In Airbnb, by contrast, the accommodation is at the core of the transaction and sociality is the extra that is nice, but is not expected and cannot be 'demanded'. Ironically this very lack of feelings of entitlement to sociality in Airbnb makes this social aspect of it closer to true sharing when it does occur than in the case of CouchSurfing, where it is seen as an entitlement.

Coming back to the question how social moments are shaped by the prevailing environment, we can hence conclude that sociability comes closest to the ideal of prototypical sharing whenever it is perceived as autotelic. Our findings do however show that this is mostly (yet not exclusively) the case whenever moments of social togetherness are not overtly expected or induced by the system. Moreover, sociability seems to be perceived as particularly autotelic whenever time is perceived as something that is not in limited supply. As in the case of Ida, if a host was going to spend an evening at home watching TV anyway, it would not be a sacrifice to "spend" this time with her guest. However, as soon as her time became a scarce resource (e.g., she would need to finish a job), she would probably be less likely spend it with a guest. In this sense social time is more discretionary in Airbnb than in CouchSurfing.

While research on consumption practices in the so-called Sharing Economy mostly examines how existing material resources are redistributed among individuals, the present project looks at how shared experiences are also created and shaped through the respective prevailing context. This is the sort of social embeddedness that has previously been found in business transactions (e.g. Carrier 1995; Granovetter 1985; Miller 1986; 2002). This perspective sheds new light on the ongoing discussion on sharing that is developing in consumer research, and adds to understanding how the sociality of shared moments is shaped by the prevailing environment.

The consideration of shared moments was hitherto absent from the discussion of peer-to-peer exchange platforms. This omission might explain some of the confusion in literature and in practice as to which businesses in the 'New Sharing Economy' really qualify as 'true' sharing in the sense of Belk (2010) and hence hold up the promise of economically uninterested sociality between involved parties. As such, many of those 'sharing businesses' that fall short of shared moments of true sociality have probably led to the crisis that the New Sharing Economy nowadays faces. With this study, we hope to have contributed to a better definitional demarcation between sharing businesses creating mainly social value and those creating mainly economic value, the latter belonging to the traditional sphere of capitalist (market-based) business models.

References

Albinsson, P.A. and Yasanthi B.P. (2012) 'Alternative Marketplaces in the 21st Century: Building Community through Sharing Events' *Journal of Consumer Behaviour* 11(4): 303–315.

Arnould, E.J., and Price, L.L. (1993) 'River Magic: Extraordinary Experience and the Extended Service Encounter' *Journal of Consumer Research* 20(1): 24–45.

Bardhi, F. and Eckhardt, G.M. (2012) 'Access-Based Consumption: The Case of Car Sharing' *Journal of Consumer Research* 39(4): 881–898.

Basil, M. (2008) 'Japanese Love Hotels: Protecting Privacy for Private Encounters' *Advances in Consumer Research* 8: 505–510.

Becker, G. (2005) *A Treatise on the Family*, enlarged edition. Cambridge, MA: Harvard University Press.

Belk, R.W. (2007) 'Why Not Share rather than Own?' *The Annals of the American Academy of Political and Social Science* 611(1): 126–140.

Belk, R.W. (2010) 'Sharing' *Journal of Consumer Research* 36(5): 715–734.

Belk, R.W. (2013) 'Sharing versus Pseudo-Sharing in Web 2.0' *The Anthropologist* 4(2): 7–23.

Belk, R.W. and Wallendorf M. (1990) 'The Sacred Meanings of Money' *Journal of Economic Psychology* 11(1): 35–67.

Bell, D. (2007) 'Moments of Hospitality' in Germann Molz, J. and Gibson, S. [eds.] *Mobilising Hospitality: The Ethics of Social Relations in a Mobile World.* Aldershot: Ashgate, 29–46.

Bell, D. (2012) 'Hospitality Is Society' *Hospitality & Society* 1(2): 137–152.

Benkler, Y. (2004) 'Sharing Nicely: On Shareable Goods and the Emergence of Sharing as a Modality of Economic Production' *Yale Law Journal* 114(2): 273–358.

Bialski, P. (2012a) 'Technologies of Hospitality: How Planned Encounters Develop between Strangers' *Hospitality & Society* 1(3): 245–260.

Bialski, P. (2012b) *Becoming Intimately Mobile.* Frankfurt: Peter Lang GmbH, Internationaler Verlag der Wissenschaften.

Botsman, R. and Rogers, R. (2010) *What's Mine Is Yours: The Rise of Collaborative Consumption.* New York, NY: HarperCollins.

Burgoyne, C. B. (1990) 'Money in Marriage: How Patterns of Allocation Both Reflect and Conceal Power' *The Sociological Review* 38(4): 634–665.

Cagle, S. (2014) 'The Case Against Sharing' *Medium.* https://medium.com/the-nib/the-case-against-sharing-9ea5ba3d216d.

Carrier, J. (1995) 'Maussian Occidentalism: Gift and Commodity Systems' in Carrier, J. [ed.] *Occidentalism: Images of the West.* Oxford: Clarendon Press, 85–108.

Chen, D-J. (2012) 'Global Concept, Local Practice: Taiwanese Experience of CouchSurfing' *Hospitality & Society* 1(3): 279–297.

Chen, Y. (2009) 'Possession and Access: Consumer Desires and Value Perceptions Regarding Contemporary Art Collection and Exhibit Visits' *Journal of Consumer Research* 35(6): 925–940.

CouchSurfing (2014) 'About CouchSurfing' https://www.couchsurfing.org/n/about.

Czepiel, J. A. (1990) 'Service Encounters and Service Relationships: Implications for Research' *Journal of Business Research* 20(1): 13–21.

Di Domenico, M.L. and Lynch, P. (2007) 'Commercial Home Enterprises: Identity, Space and Setting' in Lashley, C., Lynch P. and Morrison, A. [eds.] *Hospitality: A Social Lens*. Oxford: Elsevier, 117–128.

Fiske, A. P. (1992) 'The Four Elementary Forms of Sociality: Framework for a Unified Theory of Social Relations' *Psychological Review* 99(4): 689–723.

Foa, U.G. (1971) 'Interpersonal and Economic Resources' *Science* 171(3969): 345–351.

Foa, U.G. and Foa E.B. (1975) 'Resource Theory of Social Exchange' in Thibaut, J.W., Spence, J.T. and Carson R.C. [eds.] *Contemporary Topics in Social Psychology*. Morristown, NJ: General Learning Press, 99–131.

Friedman, M. (1976) 'Aiming at the Self: The Paradox of Encounter and the Human Potential Movement' *Journal of Humanistic Psychology* 16(2): 5–34.

Germann Molz, J. (2004) 'Playing Online and between the Lines: Round-the-World Websites as Virtual Places to Play' in Sheller, M. and Urry, J. [eds.] *Tourism Mobilities: Places to Play, Places in Play*. London: Routledge, 169–180.

Germann Molz, J. (2007) 'Cosmopolitans on the Couch: Mobile Hospitality and the Internet' in Germann Molz, J. and Gibson, S. [eds.] *Mobilizing Hospitality: The Ethics of Social Relations in a Mobile World*. Aldershot: Ashgate, 65–83.

Germann Molz, J. (2012) 'CouchSurfing and Network Hospitality: "It's Not Just about the Furniture"' *Hospitality & Society* 1(3): 215–225.

Germann Molz, J. (2014) 'Collaborative Surveillance and Technologies of Trust: Online Reputation Systems in the "New" Sharing Economy' in Jansson A. and Christensen, M. [eds.] *Media, Surveillance and Identity: A Social Perspective*. New York: Peter Lang, 127–144.

Giesler, M. (2014) 'Building a Sharing Economy: The Case of Uber' *Markus Giesler – Official Homepage*. September 18. Retrieved from: http://www.markus-giesler.com/markus-gieslers-blog/2014/9/18/building-a-sharing-economy-the-case-of-uber

Granovetter, M. (1985) 'Economic Action and Social Structure: The Problem of Embeddedness' *American Journal of Sociology* 91(3): 481–510.

Huet, E. (2014) 'New York Slams Airbnb, Says Most of Its Rentals Are Illegal' *Forbes*. October 16. Retrieved from: http://www.forbes.com/sites/ellenhuet/2014/10/16/new-york-slams-airbnb-says-most-of-its-rentals-are-illegal/.

Ikkala, T., and Lampinen A. (2015) 'Monetising Network Hospitality: Hospitality and Sociability in the Context of Airbnb' In *CSCW '15 Proceedings of the ACM 2015 Conference on Computer Supported Cooperative Work*. New York, NY, USA.

Jonsson, P. (2007) 'A Tale of a Car Sharing Organization (CSO) Monster' in Brembeck H. and Ekstrom K.M. and Morck M. [eds.] *Little Monsters: (De)coupling Assemblages of Consumption*. Transaction Publishers: New Brunswick. Berlin: LIT Verlag, 149–64.

Lamberton, C.P. and Rose, R.L. (2012) 'When Is Ours Better Than Mine? A Framework for Understanding and Altering Participation in Commercial Sharing Systems' *Journal of Marketing* 76(4): 109–25.

Lauterbach, D., Truong, H., Shah, T. and Adamic, L. (2009) 'Surfing a Web of Trust: Reputation and Reciprocity on CouchSurfing.com' *Proceedings of the International Conference on Computational Science & Engineering* 4: 346–353.

Lewis-Kraus, G. (2013) 'Su Casa Es Mi Casa' *T Magazine*. http://tmagazine.blogs.nytimes.com/2013/05/05/su-casa-es-mi-casa/

Lynch, P. A., and MacWhannell, D. (2000) 'Home and Commercial Hospitality' in Lashley, C. and Morrison, A. [eds.] *In Search of Hospitality: Theoretical Perspectives and Debates*. Oxford: Butterworth-Heinemann, 100–117.

Mays, N., and Pope, C. (1995) 'Rigour and Qualitative Research' *British Medical Journal* 311(6997): 109–112.

Miller, D. (1986) 'Exchange and Alienation in the "Jajmani" System' *Journal of Anthropological Research 42(4)*: 535–556.

Miller, D. (2002) 'Turning Callon the Right Way up' *Economy & Society* 31(2): 218– 233.

Morozov, E. (2013) 'The "Sharing Economy" Undermines Workers' Rights' *Financial Times*, October 14. Retrieved from: http://www.ft.com/cms/s/0/92c3021c-34c2-11e3-8148-00144feab7de.html#axzz3OySZ7svi

Ozanne, L. K., and Ballantine, P. W. (2010) 'Sharing as a Form of Anti-Consumption? An Examination of Toy Library Users' *Journal of Consumer Behaviour* 9(6): 485–948.

Price, J. A. (1975) 'Sharing: The Integration of Intimate Economies' *Anthropologica* 71(1): 3–27.

Rachman, A. W. (1975) 'The Humanistic Encounter' *Psychotherapy: Theory, Research & Practice* 12(3): 249–254.

Scaraboto, D. (2015) 'Selling, Sharing, and Everything in Between: The Hybrid Economies of Collaborative Networks' *Journal of Consumer Research*.

Schor, J. B. and Thompson, C. M. (2014) *Sustainable Lifestyles and the Quest for Plenitude: Case Studies of the New Economy*. New Haven, CT: Yale University Press.

Simmel, G. (1949) 'The Sociology of Sociability' *American Journal of Sociology* 55(3): 254–61.

Sobh, R., Belk, R.W. and Wilson, J.A.J. (2013) 'Islamic Arab Hospitality and Multiculturalism' *Marketing Theory* 13(4): 443–463.

Solomon, M.R., Surprenant, C., Czepiel, J.A. and Gutman, E.J. (1985) 'A Role Theory Perspective on Dyadic Interactions: The Service Encounter' *Journal of Marketing* 49(1): 99–111.

Thompson, C.J. (1997) 'Interpreting Consumers: A Hermeneutical Framework for Deriving Marketing Insights from the Texts of Consumers' Consumption Stories' *Journal of Marketing Research* 34(4): 438–455.

Vaughan, G. (1997) 'For-Giving: A Feminist Critique of Exchange' *Austin: Plain View*.

Walsh, B. (2011) '10 Ideas That Will Change the World' *Time*. http://www.time.com/time/specials/packages/article/0,28804,2059521_2059717_2059710,00.html.

Woodburn, J. (1998) 'Sharing Is Not a Form of Exchange: An Analysis of Property-Sharing in Immediate-Return Hunter–gatherer Societies' in Hann, C.M. [ed.] *Property Relations: Renewing the Anthropological Tradition*. Cambridge: Cambridge University Press, 48–63.

Zelizer, V. (2005) *The Purchase of Intimacy*. Princeton, NJ: Princeton University Press.

Part III

Alternative sharingscapes

This third section – bringing with it the rich and textured understandings of sharing economies in crises discussed so far – turns to consider how sharing economies may offer examples of and the possibility for alternative forms of social and economic formation. Evoking the notion of 'caringscapes' – a term used to acknowledge the spatial and temporal nature of care both in everyday life and across the lifecourse (see Chapters 2 and 4 in this collection) – we too are concerned with the shifting terrains of sharing economies in a crisis-ridden future. We therefore see fit to describe these possibilities as 'alternative sharingscapes', not only restricted to lived and remembered experiences, but also to imaginings and future generations, including beyond anthropocentric time scales.

Furthermore, and as the chapters herein confirm, alternative sharingscapes encompass not only various forms of socio-economic exchange and reciprocity, but also various ways of living and working, alongside or apart from others. Much like previous sections, the sharing of material goods such as home and land sit alongside more ephemeral sharings like skills and stories. Importantly, the sharing of these material and immaterial entities, and the possibilities and tensions that can surface, remind us of how sharing economies, in their multiple forms, are entrenched also in political concepts of citizenship, value, identity, and of course the economy. In times of crisis, we argue, considerations of power, place and position are further exposed.

10 Swimming against the tide

Collaborative housing and practices of sharing

Lucy Sargisson

Introduction

> We've moved house 4 times in the last 6 years and every time the rent goes up. It's crazy. We're just sick of being ripped off for shoddy accommodation. We want to live somewhere where we feel secure, integrated and connected to the people around us, a place where there's an ethos.
>
> (Prospective cohousing group member, UK, 10/6/2015)
>
> I'm lonely and I'm bored. I may be old, but I'm not ready to roll over and die. I want to live in a community where I feel that I'm making a contribution, being useful and being valued. I want to feel safe and I want to feel useful.
>
> (Cohousing group member, UK, 11/6/2015)

We live in a time of growing social and economic inequality which, for many people, is associated with a complicated and multifaceted crisis of housing. Taking this crisis as its springboard, this chapter introduces a movement which attempts to create qualitatively different and better homes, neighbourhoods and communities. The movement is known as 'collaborative housing', or 'cohousing', and the quotations above come from members of this movement. Cohousing predates the current crises and began in Scandinavia during the 1960s. It was largely ignored in the UK until the 1990s, since when a handful of groups have successfully struggled against the tides of planning, building and financing rules to establish living models of collaborative housing. It has never been a particularly radical movement, does not offer a panacea for capitalist crises, and will not solve the housing crisis, or economic inequality. Instead, it offers an alternative that operates within the existing economic/social system: it seeks to facilitate high quality of life in ecologically sustainable homes and vibrantly interactive neighbourhoods, designed following a cooperative ethos. It does this within the dominant system, creating neighbourhoods in which, members say, a significantly better quality of life is possible.

I will suggest that cohousing offers a viable alternative housing model based on ideas about sharing, which is of particular relevance in the current socio-economic context of neoliberalism. Cohousing communities are resident-designed and resident-managed, governed by locally made rules and agreements. Their ethos privileges sharing, collaboration and quality of life, rather than competition, individualism and materialism. Cohousing is critical of the status quo, but not oppositional to it. These communities are living experiments, swimming against the tide inside the multilayered context of a capitalist financial economy, a housing market firmly geared towards individual profit and gain, and towns and cities in which most homes are designed, built, owned and occupied along different norms.

This chapter will draw on existing research[1], while building on first-hand primary research. Key sources include official statistical reports and datasets[2], textual analysis of the websites and other public facing documents produced by over 50 cohousing communities, including the results of a 2010 survey of the websites of US cohousing communities (see Sargisson 2012), ethnographic interviews and fieldwork with cohousing groups in the UK, USA and New Zealand[3]. The chapter begins with a brief contextualising discussion of the housing crisis in the UK[4] before moving on to introduce cohousing and to examine some of the ways in which it seeks to facilitate a qualitatively different way of life inside the broader system of capitalism. This section of the chapter is analytically structured around ideas and practices of 'sharing', a concept that informs cohousing narratives in complex ways.

Housing crisis

Recent research from non-governmental organisations (Shelter 2015a), academic institutions (e.g. Centre for Analysis of Social Exclusion at the London School of Economics) and individual scholars (e.g. Dorling 2015), persuasively establishes the case that the UK is experiencing a housing crisis and that this forms part of a wider set of related socioeconomic crises. This situation is not unique to Britain, it is apparent in other market driven economies, but I focus on the UK in this chapter because there are local variables. Home ownership is a cultural norm in the UK and this fact shapes both experiences of the housing crisis and the significance of the cohousing alternative. This crisis presents several different aspects, including a slowdown in property sales, rising levels of homelessness, rising levels of private rentals, decreasing levels of public rentals, rising rent prices and falling or stagnant prices of house prices (outside London). The situation is complicated, and I will attempt to illustrate some of the complexity by focusing on declining house sales and the state of the rental sector, both of which contribute to the social malaise identified by the cohousing movement.

The headline statistics on house sales from the UK Land Registry (May 2015) stated, 'The number of property transactions has decreased over the last year. From December 2013 to March 2014 there was an average of 69,282 sales per month. In the same months a year later, the figure was 61,789' (Land Registry 2015). The July 2015 campaigns by the organisation 'Shelter' identified the following housing-related concerns:

• Home ownership is slipping out of reach: On average, house prices are now almost seven times people's incomes. ... In the last decade, home ownership fell for the first time since Census records began (2015b).

• Housing costs are hugely expensive. Now that the economy is struggling, people are finding it harder to meet their monthly repayments. – 28,900 homes were repossessed across the UK in 2013 (2015c).
• More families are renting from private landlords: There are now more than 9 million renters in private rented accommodation (2015d), including almost 1.3 million families with children.
• Levels of homelessness are rising. The number of homeless households has risen to more than 60,000 a year (2015e).

These factors have varying impacts on different social-economic and demographic groups. For example, particular impacts have been observed on young people, known as 'generation rent' (Walker 2010). Young, often highly educated people are living with parents well into their 30s, or renting, usually in the private sector. The Office for National Statistics 2014–15 English Housing Survey summarises the situation thus:

> In 2004–5, 24% of those aged 25–34 lived in the private rented sector. By 2014–15 this had increased to 46%. Over the same period, the proportion of 25–34-year-olds buying with a mortgage decreased from 54% to 34%. In other words, younger households aged 25–34 are more likely to be renting privately than buying their own home, a continuation of a trend first identified in 2012–13.
>
> (ONS 2015: 1)

A second significantly affected group is families with children, which also has overlaps with 'generation rent'. The same ONS study reported,

> Over the last 10 years, the proportion of households in the private rented sector with dependent children increased from 30% in 2004–05 to 37% in 2014–15. With considerable growth in the overall number of private renters over this period, this seven percentage point increase equates to about 912,000 more households with children in the private rented sector.

The report also showed that (45%) of households buying with a mortgage had children compared with just 7% of outright owners, while around a third of private (36%) and social (33%) renters had children. The fact that these groups rent in the private sector is significant for their quality of life. Private rental housing stock was shown in the English Housing Survey of 2014–15 to be less frequently maintained, less well insulated, damper and less efficiently heated than social housing (ONS 2015: 4; 35). Rents are also higher in the private sector. In 2014–15, the average (mean) rent (excluding services but including Housing Benefit) for households in the private sector was £179 per week in the private rented sector, compared with £99 in the social sector (ONS 2015: 3). Tenures tend to be less stable in the private sector. For childless young renters, multiple occupancy is the norm, often involving one bedsit or bedroom in a 'shared house' (ONS 2015: 13). The actual amount of 'shared' space in multiple occupancy private rentals is minimal, owing to the fact that landlords often maximise the income potential of their property by renting former lounge/dining-rooms as bedrooms. Shared space is often limited to a lobby, kitchen and bathroom. The picture generated by the data is one in which a significant proportion of the younger population and families with children are trapped in the private rental sector, which does not offer security, stability or high quality of life.

Danny Dorling (2015) has argued, persuasively, that poor-quality or badly maintained housing stock, cheaply designed new housing developments, and increased income inequality all contribute to a context of urban decay, social isolation and disconnected communities (cf. Tunstall 2015). Significant numbers of young people and families move home frequently, seeking stability and decent homes, while older people feel isolated in their homes and unsafe on the streets. Older people (aged 65+) are more likely to be owner-occupiers than renters (ONS 2013) . This gives them greater stability, but older people face particular challenges. AgeUK has produced studies that indicate isolation, and loneliness to be significant threats to elder well-being. For example, in April 2014, over 1 million older people said they always or often feel lonely and 49% of over 65-year-olds reported that television or pets are their main form of company (2016a: 23; cf. ND; 2016b). A 2011 qualitative study of 1,000 randomly selected older people concluded that

> quality of life in old age is driven by psychological and social factors, rather than objective indicators, such as home ownership, income or education. ... The survey results highlight the importance to older people of living in a neighbourly and safe area, and of having good local facilities to promote friendly and helpful relationships with other people. They also emphasise the value of participating in social or voluntary activities as a way of 'keeping busy' – and to stop people 'worrying', 'feeling alone', or 'dwelling on the past'.

The context is bleak, but some people are seeking alternatives that address all the issues raised in this summary. They are doing so through collaborative housing[5].

Cohousing

Cohousing is a form of intentional community, which is to say a group of people who have decided to live together (in neighbourhoods) for a common purpose, other than familial ties or tradition. Cohousing communities are generally distinguished from other forms of intentional community (such as ecovillages, income-sharing communes and housing co-ops) through a set of shared core features (FIC 2015). For example, in her 1991 study, Dorit Fromm listed the following defining features: common facilities, private dwellings, resident-structured routines, resident management, design for social contact, resident participation in development process and pragmatic social objectives (Fromm 1991: 7–8). In his study of 2004, Martin Field identifies a similar cluster: 'designing for intentional neighbourhoods, the minimum provision of private and common facilities, size and scale to support community dynamics, and residents' control and management' (2004: 10). And cohousing architects McCamant and Durrett name the following: 'a balance of privacy and community, a safe and supportive environment for children, a practical and spontaneous lifestyle, intergenerational neighbourhoods, environmentally sensitive design emphasizing pedestrian access and optimizing open space, neighborhood design, and private homes supplemented by extensive common facilities' (ND: no pagination). These lists typically generate a picture of resident-run domestic housing schemes that combine a number of social and physical features designed to facilitate social interaction. Significantly, for a discussion of alternatives in a housing crisis, cohousing does not require its members to share a worldview or ideology. It is a form of intentional community which requires some shared values, but cohousing works with a light ideological touch. This makes it widely transferable.

National cohousing associations exist in Northern Europe (Britain[6], Denmark[7], Sweden[8] and Holland[9]), North America (United States[10] and Canada[11]), and the Antipodes (New Zealand[12] and Australia[13]). The movement is described as having two 'waves' (Williams 2005). The first focused on mainland Europe where it grew steadily from the 1960s–90s. The second started in the USA, where it grew exponentially following the 1988 publication by two American architects of the book *Cohousing: A Contemporary Approach to Housing Ourselves* (McCamant and Durrett 1988). This second wave has seen the emergence of cohousing communities in Britain, New Zealand and Australia. The first and second waves differ in important ways. In Scandinavia, for example, cohousing communities almost always combine rented and privately owned homes and some are all-rented. In North America, almost all are owner-occupied. In Scandinavia, some cohousing communities are state-financed (forming part of state social housing policy). This is not the case in North America, where cohousing communities are privately financed.

In what follows, I will examine three areas in which significant sharing can be observed to occur in cohousing communities. The first relates to shared intentions. The second and third are the 'practical' applications of intent: physical and social features that facilitate sharing. My examples will come from second wave cohousing, which is pertinent to the UK housing crisis.

Sharing

Shared intentions

Members of cohousing communities are critical of modern housing arrangements. This statement from the UK Cohousing Network in 2008 is typical:

> Modern life means neighbours often don't recognise each other and day-to-day collaboration is minimal. Research has shown that 65% of people have nobody with whom they can co-operate in their daily lives

and 84% don't have close relationships with their neighbours. One in three people live alone, rising to 44% of older women. When people are asked what concerns them most about the area they live, they highlight crime and antisocial behavior, dirty streets, neglected open spaces, lighting and lack of facilities for young people.

(UK Cohousing Network 2013: 3)

Cohousing is designed to facilitate positive alternatives. In 2016 the same organisation stated the following:

Cohousing communities are created and run by their residents. Each household has a self-contained, private home but residents come together to manage their community and share activities. Cohousing is a way of combating the alienation and isolation many experience today, recreating the neighbourly support of the past. This can happen anywhere, in your street or starting a new community using empty homes or building new.

(UK Cohousing Network 2016a: no pagination)

In place of isolation, then, cohousing desires connection, in place of alienation it imagines neighbourly relationships and participation. These are forms of political sharing: members become collectively responsible co-managers and active local citizens of a shared local environment (Firth 2011). Research commonly indicates that the diverse cohousing community members feel a strong sense of group belonging and commitment and that this form of housing generates high levels of citizenship and wider community participation (see Chatterton 2013; Design Coalition 1992; Widener 2010)[14].

Individual community descriptors of cohousing often evoke these notions of active participation and shared responsibility, linked to the need to balance shared (community-focused) and private activities. The following statements are from Springhill and Lancaster cohousing, which were Britain's oldest and newest cohousing communities at the time of writing:

We believe that people need community and privacy. Cohousing is a way for people to live together so that they can have as much community and privacy as they want. The concept is simple and immediately comprehensible. It is the way forward for human beings to live together in a safe, independent and caring neighbourhood. It is a revolution that is beginning now. We will no longer just choose a new house when we move, we will join a new community.

(Springhill Cohousing 2014: no pagination)

Cohousing is a housing development that balances the advantages of home ownership with the benefits of shared common facilities and connections with your neighbours. These co-operative neighbourhoods are designed to encourage both social contact and individual space, and are organised, planned and managed by the residents themselves.

(Lancaster Cohousing 2016: no pagination)

Similar ideas resonate through American community statements:

> Cohousing communities balance the traditional advantages of home ownership with the benefits of shared common facilities and ongoing connections with your neighbours. It attempts to overcome the alienation of modern subdivisions in which no one knows their neighbours, and there is no sense of community. ... We believe that today's neighbourhoods have in large part served to isolate people from one another and encourage alienation from ourselves and our communities.
>
> (Sonora Cohousing Community ND: no pagination)

These statements articulate a shared social criticism and an intention to create alternatives. Cohousing members want better neighbourhoods and wider access to a good community life.

Shared space: Ownership and organisation

> There is a crisis in affordable housing in this country. House prices are still much higher than average earnings. In 2010 the house price to income ratio in the UK was 4.44 (average annual household earnings £57,996 and average house prices £251,634). LILAC is responding to this situation through adopting a 'mutual home ownership scheme' (MHOS). An MHOS is a new way of owning a stake in the housing market. It is designed to bring the bottom rung of the property ladder back within reach of households on modest incomes in areas where they are priced out of the housing market. It is designed to remain permanently affordable for future generations. Members of the society are the residents who live in the homes it provides. The society and not the individuals obtain the mortgage and so borrowing is cheaper.
>
> (LILAC 2014: no pagination)

Cohousers argue that housing is currently organised and distributed amongst local populations in ways that separate people, reinforcing social isolation. Part of the cohousing alternative is shared ownership, which binds people together. A range of different models exist for shared ownership in cohousing and the extract above illustrates a financially radical one. Other groups adapt condominium or co-operative models (Chatterton 2013; Design Coalition 1992; Widener 2010). Typically, all households collectively own (usually by freehold) the land on which the community sits, while householders hold long (999-year) leases on their homes. This is not a universal model but it is common (UK Cohousing Network 2016b). Setting aside the intricacies of the individual ownership models, one core feature of all cohousing communities is shared ownership and use of some community space. This communal space varies according to the size, needs and nature of each group but usually includes land/gardens and a 'common house', which will be considered in turn.

Cohousing sites are designed to maximise social interaction outdoors, whilst maximising household privacy:

> The design of our site is intended to build community life. It is based around the Danish co-housing model: mixing people's needs for their own space in private homes with shared facilities and encouraging social interaction.
> (LILAC ND: no pagination)

Cohousing sites are almost always car-free and parking is located on the street edges of the site. Paths meander through shared gardens to each home, taking residents past the common house and each other's homes. Typically, kitchen windows will face this public space, which might contain a play area for children, swimming pool, seats, gardens, orchards, and/or a 'village green'. This lays the basis for daily informal encounters with neighbours; a design for conviviality which underpins daily social sharing. The layout affects the feel of the space: residents share ownership of outdoor space which can be seen from inside their homes. It also permits casual surveillance of this space by all neighbours. Privacy is typically provided by small personal outdoor areas (patios or small gardens) which lie outside the more private areas of each home, such as the lounge or main bedroom. The actual site design varies from group to group but careful spatial design always underpins the sharing activities that occur in cohousing[15]. A 2005 urban planning study (of two cases in California) revealed regular formal and informal interactions in common spaces as key to the success of this model (Williams 2005). Visits to cohousing communities reveal different patterns of usage in the collectively owned gardens but most combine shared and individual areas. The former are maintained through the labour pool, of which more below.

All cohousing communities have a collectively owned 'community building' or 'common house' and the design of common houses is an art in itself (Kim 2006). In most cases, it will contain mailboxes, large kitchen and dining room. The location of mailboxes in the common house means that most residents will visit the space at least once a day, again maximising opportunities for casual daily interactions with neighbours. Often, the common house will contain guest bedrooms, 'Our homes have a small footprint, why would we heat empty rooms in each home, when we can share the use of community guest rooms?' (Lancaster Cohousing resident, 20/6/2014). Most contain flexible spaces that can be used for meetings, parties, workshops and other gatherings. Often a large area can be screened for multiple use. Some groups emphasize the need for a quiet room in which to practice meditation, yoga or prayer. Others want their social space to be open to the wider community, with glass walls that can be opened wide. Each group shapes the shared space to fit its own ethos and goals, as can be seen from the following examples:

> Our ... community hall is used often, for meetings, shared meals 2–3 times a week, parties, workshops, rehearsals, slide shows, concerts,

and meetings. We know our neighbors and help each other out in many ways.

(Rosewind Cohousing ND)

The Common House is the focal point of the community. At its heart is a shared kitchen and eating area where we share regular communal meals. The eating area is flexibly designed, so it is also a place where people can come for coffee, or to read, relax and chat round the wood-burning stove. Just across the pedestrian street is a foodstore, laundry and a playroom for the children.

(Lancaster Cohousing ND)

Food plays an important role in LILAC. In the Common House we have a shared kitchen and a pantry that we stock up regularly with food bought on bulk which of course reduces our food bills. We believe it's important to try and keep the food for our shared meals affordable and sustainable. We meet twice a week to eat together in the Common House: the time we spend relaxing over our meals, or working together to produce them creates spaces to talk and share and build the links that help sustain our community.

(LILAC ND)

It is significant that these facilities are owned by the group and also that the first generation of residents have participated in their design. They provide the foundations for what Helen Jarvis (2011) has called 'the infrastructures of daily life'. Working in collaboration with specialist architects, prospective residents share the design process and their collective ownership of the land permits them to shape it together.

The shared shaping of physical space is an important part of the cohousing experience. 'As much as constructing walls, Lilac builds community' (Chatterton 2015). The challenges are significant and often involve compromises and trade-offs, choices and clashes over expectations, priorities and budgets. Internal conflict is one challenge. Another is the inflexibility of dominant planning and funding models. Because cohousing is still at the pioneering stage, with just eighteen established groups in the UK (UK Cohousing Network 2016c), the model is unfamiliar to rule-bound planning and building authorities. Each group encounters significant hurdles with the planners, funders, developers, and local officials. One group, Older Women's Cohousing (OWCH) has collaborated to develop cohousing with a housing association in London. Their site was due for completion in June 2016, but they worked for 18 years to realise this dream[16]. Members have expressed concerns that they might die of old age before seeing the first brick laid.

Shared social processes: ownership and design

Collective governance involves rules, processes and codes of conduct. It is important for cohousing that these rules are made by the group because these are self-governing communities. In interview, members often stress the importance of community meetings, although these can involve steep learning curves: in order to co-govern, members need to learn to discuss, disagree, decide and act together. For many members, this is their first experience of both shared ownership and community governance and these meetings require time, patience, skill and commitment (see Baborska-Narozny et al. 2014). Social design for community is necessary because shared ownership and increased interaction with neighbours do not automatically produce harmonious communities. Each community member has their own stories of conflict inside their group. Misunderstandings, unrealistic expectations, unclear communication, and value clashes all trigger conflict and/or ill-feeling. Conflict occurs, but the cohousing model anticipates this with community agreements and codes about appropriate behaviour, activities and processes, each of which is designed to facilitate 'a better community' (e.g. Earthsong Eco-Neighbourhood ND; OWCH 2011). These are important because they create internal and enforceable rules. Members speak of this in terms of empowerment: their rules and guidelines enable people to co-exist, co-operate and co-govern inside these spaces. They are empowering because they are effective and because residents have collectively designed them (usually with professional facilitation). They form an important part of the 'sharing economy' that exists inside cohousing communities. I will consider just two illustrative examples which shape 'sharing behaviour': labour and possession pooling.

Joining a cohousing group means entering into a collective commitment to share tasks and responsibilities and this involves making a labour commitment: to give work to the community, without remuneration. The labour commitment is a formal and contractual undertaking, forming part of the tenancy/ownership contract. It normally involves certain hours-per-month from each adult member. The nature of work varies, such as babysitting, preparing a community meal, gardening, book-keeping, taking older members shopping, dealing with visitor enquiries and machine or building maintenance. This work is divorced from income or financial return. In this model, service is cast in terms of both individual utility and the common good.

> Imagine coming home from work exhausted, too tired to cook ... then you catch a whiff of red chilli baking in the community house and you remember, you've signed up for the meal tonight with your community! Since it's not your turn to cook or clean up, all you have to do is sit down next to your neighbours and enjoy a delicious organic meal.
>
> (Elliott 2015: no pagination)

In interview, members spoke about the satisfaction of working together, the social benefits and also (with some surprise) of the relationship between input and return: contributing a just few hours a month and receiving a disproportionate return such as twice-weekly meals in the common house, a weekly supply of fresh produce from the gardens and having their children collected from school each day. Working together brings people together: 'I just love the company of the youngsters. One of them comes to read with me after school each day and this is part of my labour commitment' (Cohousing member, UK, 10/12/2014).

Possession pools represent economies of scale and collaboration and cohousing communities often 'pool' large budget items that require occasional use:

> I'm just baffled why every house in an ordinary street has to have their own set of everything: lawn mowers, power tools, etc.
>
> (Simon ND: no pagination)

Examples can be found in LILAC and Lancaster cohousing, two newly established communities. Both are committed to ecological sustainability and each has a car share system. Both have a tool pool (a large storage area packed with garden and DIY equipment). Both have communal laundries with multiple washing and drying machines. There is, members say, simply no need for everyone to own a separate car, lawn mower or clothes drier. Pooling ensures that everyone gets access to high quality, well maintained facilities, when they need them. Some communities have a community food store for basic provisions (such as dried goods) for which purchases are made in bulk and from which items can be purchased on an honesty-box basis. Lancaster has its own water turbine and bio-mass boiler for producing electricity. These things would not be affordable without the economies of scale that come with sharing costs. Each 'pool' requires organisation: a rota or booking system, maintenance or servicing and responsibility for this organisation forms part of the labour commitment discussed above. No system works flawlessly all the time, and sometimes the car is double-booked, or somebody fails to clean and return tools to the shed. But these examples of social design to facilitate sharing are created and managed by the residents of cohousing groups and this enables members to feel a sense of autonomy which reflects and enhances their commitment to the group.

Conclusions

On fieldtrips to cohousing communities over a period of 20 years, I have been consistently impressed by three related things. The first is how they feel; there are always people about, working in the gardens, sitting on the porch, chatting, working together, or preparing a meal in the community house. The levels of day-to-day interaction between neighbours is consistently high. Cohousing communities feel safe and neighbourly. The second concerns the quality of housing. Housing stock is of high ecological standard, whether it be rented or owner-occupied. Homes are usually small but well designed, and they feel spatially adequate and high spec. They are warm in winter and cool in summer. The third concerns residents' levels of resilience, commitment and determination. Creating alternative housing models is difficult. Maintaining them requires constant interpersonal, individual and collective work. I have stressed the positive aspects of sharing for the sake of brevity in this short chapter but the negatives present real and everyday challenges and cannot be disregarded.

Notwithstanding the challenges, cohousing is a viable way of life for its participants, for whom it offers a better alternative to the three modes of tenure that dominate the UK housing arena. Cohousing can combine these: most combine owner-occupation with some private rentals and the OWCH group in London is pioneering a social housing model. What makes cohousing different is the cocktail of sharing indicated in this chapter. The sharing ethos of this model combines collective and private ownership, collaborative design of space and governance, day-to-day self-management and a series of social practices and processes that facilitate cooperation. It is an effective cocktail that does produce vibrant, participatory neighbourhoods. Cohousing is not going to completely change the world, and that is not its intention. But it does seek to provide local communities in which empowered residents develop complex social skills and regularly participate in their local community. Cohousing exists despite the norms of the housing market, mortgagers, planning authorities and local government. They swim against multiple tides. They offer a key lesson: that alternatives are possible, albeit incredibly difficult, within the existing system of capitalism and within the current housing context.

Notes

1 Cohousing is under-researched within my own field of political studies. Detailed research exists on the architectural aspects of these communities and some excellent scholarship has emerged from the disciplines of geography and urban studies See Chatterton (2013; 2015), Jarvis (2011; 2013) and Williams (2005).
2 Such as the UK government's Office of National Statistics, Homes and Communities Office and the European Union Statistical Office (Eurostat).
3 These regions were selected for two reasons: firstly, their property tenure systems, which are both comparable *and* culturally dominated by private ownership and owner-occupation and secondly, because they constitute the 'second wave' of cohousing development.
4 I am focusing on the UK owing to the space constraints of this chapter, but the housing crisis is not specific to the UK. A 2015 study' identified an EU "housing trap" as follows: expensive rental sector, prohibitive house prices, and insufficient social housing (Housing Europe 2015: no pagination).
5 Cohousing is just one form of intentional community that addresses these issues, others include housing co-operatives, communally owned properties, and ecovillages. However, cohousing is the largest growing *and* most transferable to a wider population.
6 The UK Cohousing Network http://www.cohousing.org.uk/
7 Approximately 1% of the Danish population live in cohousing (roughly 50,000 people.) Boflesskab i Danmark. http://www.xn--bofllesskab-c9a.dk/
8 Kollektivhus Nu, Swedish National CoHousing Association http://www.kollektivhus.nu/
9 Landelijke Vereniging Centraal Wonen http://www.lvcw.nl/
10 The Cohousing Association of the United States listed 95 completed communities in 2009 and roughly three times as many in the forming or building stages. http://www.cohousing.org/directory.

11 The Canadian Housing Network listed nine completed communities in 2009. http://www.cohousing.ca/summary.htm
12 New Zealand National Cohousing Association http://www.converge.org.nz/evcnz/
13 Australian National Cohousing Association http://home.vicnet.net.au/~cohouse/
14 This finding is common to practitioner, advocate and independent academic research. For examples of each, see The UK Cohousing Association http://www.cohousing.org, Meltzer (2005), Field (2004), and Poley and Stephenson (2007, cited with author permission).
15 See here for examples: Earthsong 'Resources': http://www.earthsong.org.nz/resources.html, LILAC 'Site Design': http://www.lilac.coop/about-lilac/site-design.html, Architype 'SpringHill Site Layout': http://www.architype.co.uk/project/springhill-co-housing/.
16 See http://www.owch.org.uk/. For details of the multiple challenges of developing senior cohousing in the UK see Maria Brenton 'Senior Cohousing' https://www.youtube.com/watch?v=Kt4RQ5U63q4

References

AgeUK (ND) *Loneliness and Isolation Evidence Review*. London: AgeUK.
AgeUK (2016a) Later Life in the United Kingdom. Retrieved from: www.ageuk.org.uk/Documents/EN-GB/Factsheets/Later_Life_UK_factsheet.pdf?dtrk=true [Accessed 11 July 2016]
AgeUK (2016b) Risk of Loneliness in England, 2016. Retrieved from: http://data.ageuk.org.uk/loneliness-maps/england-2016/ [Accessed 11 July 2016]
Baborska-Narozny, M., Stevenson, F. and Chatterton, P. (2014) 'A Social Learning Tool – Barriers and Opportunities for Collective Occupant Learning in Low Carbon Housing' *Energy Procedia* 62: 492–501.
Chatterton, P. (2013) 'Towards an Agenda for Post-carbon Cities: Lessons from Lilac, the UK's First Ecological, Affordable Cohousing Community' *International Journal of Urban and Regional Research* 37: 1654–1674.
Chatterton, P. (2015) *Low Impact Living: A Field Guide to Ecological, Affordable Community Living*. London: Earthscan Routledge.
Design Coalition (1992) *Ownership Options for Affordable Cohousing*. Madison, WI: Design Coalition.
Dorling, D. (2015) *All That Is Solid: How the Great Housing Disaster Defines Our Times and What We Can Do About It*. London: Penguin.
Earthsong Eco-Neighbourhood (ND) Our Communication Agreements. Retrieved from: http://www.earthsong.org.nz/docs/Communication%20Agreements.pdf [Accessed 11 July 2016]
Elliot, E. (2015) Cohousing: Community at Its Best. Retrieved from: https://www.youtube.com/watch?v=ef9azOeuCPY [Accessed 11 July 2016]
FIC (Federation for Intentional Communities) (2015) Welcome to FIC. Retrieved from: http://www.ic.org/ [Accessed 1 July 2015]
Field, M. (2004) *Thinking About Cohousing: The Creation of Intentional Neighbourhoods*. London: Edge of Time.
Firth, R. (2011) *Utopian Politics: Citizenship and Practice*. London: Routledge.
Fromm, D. (1991) *Collaborative Communities: Cohousing, Central Living and Other New Forms of Housing*. Oxford: Wiley.
Housing Europe (2015) *The State of Housing in the EU: A Housing Europe Review*. Brussels: Housing Europe.
Jarvis, H. (2011) 'Saving Space, Sharing Time: Integrated Infrastructures of Daily Life in Cohousing' *Environment and Planning A* 43(3): 560–577.

Jarvis, H. (2013) 'Progressive Nostalgia in Novel Living Arrangements: A Counterpoint to Neo-traditional New Urbanism?' *Urban Studies* 50(11): 2349–2370.

Kim, G.H. (2006) *Designing the Common House*. Seattle: Schemata Workshop.

Lancaster Cohousing (2016) What Is Cohousing? [Online] Available from: http://lancastercohousing.org.uk/About [Accessed 4 April 2016]

Lancaster Cohousing (ND) Common House. Retrieved from: http://www.lancastercohousing.org.uk/Project/CommonHouse [Accessed 4 April 2016]

Land Registry (2015) UK House Price Index – May 2015. Retrieved from: https://www.gov.uk/government/collections/uk-house-price-index-reports [Accessed 1 July 2015]

LILAC (ND) Community. Retrieved from: http://www.lilac.coop/concept/community.html [Accessed 4 April 2016]

LILAC (2014) Affordable. Retrieved from: http://www.lilac.coop/concept/affordable.html [Accessed 4 April 2016]

McCamant, K. and Durrett, C. (1988) *Cohousing: A Contemporary Approach to Housing Ourselves*. Berkley, CA: Ten Speed Press.

McCamant and Durrett Architects (ND) Homepage. Retrieved from: http://www.mccamant-durrett.com/characteristics.cfm [Accessed 1 June 2015]

Meltzer, G. (2005) *Sustainable Community: Learning from the Cohousing Model*. Victoria, BC: Trafford.

Office for National Statistics (ONS) (2013) *What Does the 2011 Census Tell Us About Older People?* Retrieved from: http://webarchive.nationalarchives.gov.uk/20160105160709/http:/www.ons.gov.uk/ons/rel/census/2011-census-analysis/what-does-the-2011-census-tell-us-about-older-people-/what-does-the-2011-census-tell-us-about-older-people-short-story.html#tab-Housing-tenure [Accessed 11 July 2016]

Office for National Statistics (ONS) (2015) *English Housing Survey Headline Report, 2014–15*. London: TSO.

OWCH (Older Women's Cohousing) (2011) Conflict Resolution Policy. [Online] Available from: http://www.owch.org.uk/s/CONFLICT-POLICY.pdf [Accessed 11 July 2016].

Poley, L. and Stephenson, M. (2007) 'Community and the Habits of Democratic Citizenship: An Investigation into Civic Engagement, Social Capital and Democratic Capacity-Building in U.S. Cohousing Neighbourhoods'. *103rd annual meeting of the American Political Science Association*. Chicago, Illinois, August 30–September 2.

Rosewind Cohousing (ND) Rosewind Cohousing. Retrieved from: http://www.cohousing.org/directory/view/2046 [Accessed 11 July 2016]

Sargisson, L. (2012) 'Second-Wave Cohousing: A Modern Utopia?' *Utopian Studies* 23(1): pp. 28–56.

Shelter (2015a) What Is the Housing Crisis? Retrieved from: http://england.shelter.org.uk/campaigns_/why_we_campaign/the_housing_crisis/what_is_the_housing_crisis [Accessed 11 July 2016]

Shelter (2015b) *Census: Mapping a Decade of Housing Change*. Retrieved from: http://england.shelter.org.uk/campaigns_/why_we_campaign/the_housing_crisis/census [Accessed 11 July 2016]

Shelter (2015c) Repossessions and Arrears. Retrieved from: http://england.shelter.org.uk/campaigns_/why_we_campaign/housing_facts_and_figures/subsection?section=repossession_arrears [Accessed 11 July 2016]

Shelter (2015d) Improving Private Renting. Retrieved from: http://england.shelter.org.uk/campaigns/why_we_campaign/improving_private_renting [Accessed 1 June 2015]

Shelter (2015e) Homeless Households. Retrieved from: http://england.shelter.org.uk/campaigns_/why_we_campaign/housing_facts_and_figures/subsection?section=homeless_households [Accessed 11 July 2016]

Simon (ND) Our Members – Simon. Retrieved from: https://mandorlacoho.wordpress.com/simon-2/ [Accessed 11 July 2016]

Sonora Cohousing (ND) *About Us*. Retrieved from: http://sonoracoho.com/about_us [Accessed 4 April 2016]

Springhill Cohousing (2014) *What Is Cohousing?* Retrieved from: http://www.therightplace.net/coco/public/index.html [Accessed 6 April 2016]

Tunstall R (2015) 'The Coalition's Record on Housing: Policy, Spending and Outcomes 2010–2015' *Social Policy in a Cold Climate* – Working Paper 18. London: London School of Economics.

UK Cohousing Network (2013) *Annual Report*. No location: UK Cohousing Network.

UK Cohousing Network (2016a) *Cohousing in a Nutshell*. Retrieved from: http://cohousing.org.uk/cohousing-nutshell [Accessed 11 July 2016].

UK Cohousing Network (2016b) Resources: Legal and Tenure. Retrieved from: http://cohousing.org.uk/resources-bookshelf?field_stage_tid=37 [Accessed 11 July 2016]

UK Cohousing Network (2016c) sCohousing Groups Directory. Retrieved from: http://cohousing.org.uk/groups [Accessed 11 July 2016]

Walker T (2010) 'No Place Like Home: The Generation Who Can't Afford to Buy' *The Independent*, Tuesday 16 March.

Widener MN (2010) 'Cohousing: Joining Affordable, Sustainable and Collaboratively-Governed, Single Family Neighbourhoods' *Real Estate Law Journal* 39: 113.

Williams J (2005) 'Designing Neighbourhoods for Social Interaction: The Case of Cohousing' *Journal of Urban Design* 10(2): 195–227.

11 Just enough to survive

Economic citizenship in the context of Indigenous land claims

Nicole Gombay

In Canada the 'taxpayer' has become ubiquitous in the country's public discourse, and is used both by the state and by citizens to justify or repudiate particular courses of action. It reveals a great deal about how both individuals and collectivities are constructed, and thus come to construct, their relations not only to one another but also to institutions that exist to represent and ensure their well-being and interests. It reflects a form of economic citizenship in which the forces that bind individuals to one another and to the state have become thoroughly defined in monetary terms.

Such constructions of citizenship suggest that capitalism is the essential mechanism through which people understand their relations to one another and to the state. As Marx points out in *Capital* (1983), capitalism is inherently crisis-prone. Despite this tendency, and despite the fact that capitalist production has repeatedly precipitated environmental crises whose ultimate expression can be found in a changing climate and the proposed geological era of the Anthropocene, for many, a capitalist framing of citizenship continues to be unquestionably axiomatic.

Although 'economic citizenship' sounds rather impressive, hiding behind this seemingly tidy expression are a number of interlocking questions about what we mean by citizenship, what we mean by economies, and what we understand to be the processes that structure the relations between the two. The taken-for-granted basis for discussions of economic citizenship in much of the literature essentially reflects a set of expectations about the nature of the individual, the collectivity, and the state, as well as the functioning of economic systems within which they operate that is grounded in Western European liberal ideals of personal freedom, individualism, and the market economy (cf. Kessler-Harris 2003; Turner 1986; White 2003; Woodiwiss 2002). Such literature naturalises and universalises this historically and culturally specific set of values. But for many Indigenous peoples, assumptions about the role of the individual, the nature of their ties to the collective, the meaning and role of state-like institutions, and the values underlying their economic conduct are grounded in altogether different sets of principles.

In the Canadian context, Indigenous peoples have become increasingly vocal in their opposition to capitalism-as-usual, stressing that its repercussions have not only been profoundly harmful to their well-being but also go hand-in-hand with environmental destruction. They can thus be *Idle No More* (cf. Kino-nda-niimi Collective 2014). Many are therefore calling for the need to practise sustainable forms of self-determination grounded in Indigenous values of sharing and reciprocity between human and nonhuman worlds (Corntassel and Bryce 2012; Coulthard 2014).

This chapter seeks, then, to examine the conjunction between Indigenous collectivities, their economic expression in the aftermath of land claims, and the sets of values that are at the root of Indigenous economies. It will explore debates about how citizenship has been configured in response to capitalist relations and assess the degree to which, in spite of these configurations, Indigenous peoples have been able to adopt forms of "insurgent citizenship" (Jeffrey et al. 2012: 1256), through which they have appropriated some aspects of citizenship whilst resisting others. Using Inuit as an example, it will interrogate whether the values that inform their economies actually shape how citizenship in their polities is expressed and performed. At root is the question of the extent to which Indigenous peoples are able to shape economic practices that reflect the sort of 'altermodernity' advanced by Hardt and Negri (2009: 106), whereby alternative models for conceiving of and enacting economies express Indigenous peoples' values and assertions that they should have "the right not 'to be who [they] are' but rather 'to become what [they] want'". The emphasis, then, is not on hearkening back to a frozen past, nor on being stuck in an unwished for present, but rather on shaping a desired future.

I have been grappling with these questions for some time. Since the early 1990s I have worked and done research with Inuit in Nunavut and Nunavik (Northern Quebec), two administrative regions of northern Canada with a total population in 2011 of 46,252, of whom approximately 85% were Inuit. These territories can be reached primarily only by air or, once the winter ice has melted, by sea. Their physical isolation and climatic conditions have meant that Inuit have historically been less affected by resource development and the permanent presence of settler colonial residents than Indigenous peoples in the southern Canada. As a result, and at the risk of oversimplifying their circumstances, the daily practices of northern Indigenous peoples tend to be more readily visible and convergent with customary values than is at first glance evident amongst many Indigenous peoples in southern Canada. But their state of relative independence from settler colonialism has progressively eroded since the latter half of the 20th century as vast hydroelectric, and mineral and hydrocarbon extraction schemes have moved northwards. To legitimise legally their access to these resources, since the mid-1970s federal, territorial, and provincial governments in Canada have negotiated and settled a series of comprehensive claims with the region's Indigenous peoples. These have given birth to a series of Indigenous corporations tasked with safeguarding the collective political, social, and economic interests of the 'beneficiaries' to these claims. Thus, for example, Makivik Corporation is responsible for representing the political interests of the Inuit of Nunavik, and for managing the moneys received when Inuit signed a land claim in 1975. Similar corporate structures have been designated in the USA, Aotearoa/New Zealand, and Australia (cf. Nehme and Juriansz 2012; Paulin 2007; Thornburg and Roberts 2012).

Given their mandate to represent the political, social, and economic interests of Indigenous collectivities, these institutions embody a marriage between new formations of citizenship for Indigenous peoples, and new collective economic practices that engage with national and international forces in the name and interests of these peoples. As such, in theory one might reasonably assume that they are manifestations of economic citizenship that articulate Indigenous peoples' values. The question is what they demonstrate in practice.

Some argue that these Indigenous corporations embody new forms of political and economic practice that allow Indigenous peoples to develop according to their particular values (Wilson and Alcantara 2012; Wuttunee 2004), whilst others argue that the capital and landholding institutions created subsequent to land claims, embody and impose inherent relations of imperialism that link treaties, resource extraction, and wider capitalist relations at the root of settler colonialism (Altamirano-Jiménez 2004; Kulchyski and Bernauer 2014). By such a reckoning, settler colonialism is structured by a logic of elimination that seeks to wrest lands and resources from the hands of Indigenous peoples and place them squarely in those of the settler colonial state (Wolfe 2006). As a consequence, the very terms of reference through which land claims have been conceived necessarily co-opt and absorb Indigenous peoples into the capitalist relations framing settler colonialism, thereby furthering the acquisition of Indigenous lands (Alfred 2005; Blackburn 2009; Cattelino 2010; Coulthard 2014; Meltzer 2013; Valdivia 2008). The founding of corporations and the particular framings of Indigenous peoples as 'citizens' within the context of land claims can thus be understood as setting structures in place that produce, enable, and reinforce ongoing processes of settler colonialism and Indigenous peoples' dispossession (cf. Brown 2014; Wolfe 2006).

It is in the context of such debates that I propose to consider how the institutions that have come into being subsequent to the signing of land claims have combined with socio-economic forces whose sources are both local and alien. What has this combination resulted in? How might Indigenous forms of economic citizenship present contemporary models for collective economic action grounded in ideas of sharing and reciprocity rather than purely that of isolated, self-interested individuals who are both the foundation and product of capitalist economies? My goal is to point toward larger theoretical concerns that merit consideration as we examine how Indigenous peoples' search for political sovereignty has been expressed via interlinked relations of citizenship and economic practice.

Citizenship and Indigenous peoples

The Oxford English Dictionary defines a citizen as, amongst its various meanings, one who is an inhabitant, occupant, or denizen (in contrast to an alien) of a given locality. One might split hairs and point out that a person who inhabits is different from one who occupies (Ingold 2007), and that the encounter between Indigenous peoples and colonisers is precisely about this distinction. One might equally ask who determines, and on what basis, who is a denizen and who is an alien? Again, Indigenous–settler colonial encounters are telling in this regard. In essence, however, discussions about citizenship are necessarily about relationships and the rules and entailing rights and responsibilities that govern those relationships. These rules are, to varying degrees, formally defined by institutions (which these days generally correlate to some version of the state). Generally, citizenship is both about relationships amongst individuals, which form collectivities, and between those individuals and the institutions that define and sanction the rules and obligations determining people's membership in collectivities. Although rarely stated clearly in the discussion on citizenship, ideally the relationship between citizen and 'state' ought to be two-way, i.e., just as citizens have rights and obligations vis-à-vis the state, so states should have rights and responsibilities vis-à-vis their citizens. In considering this dynamic, the question I wish to explore is the degree to which the rights and obligations of states to citizens reflect the socioeconomic values held by those citizens, with a particular emphasis on Indigenous peoples.

To contextualise this debate it is necessary to understand that there is an extensive literature that argues that in the terms of recognition granted by the state, which are then formalised through land claims, Indigenous peoples have been obliged to adopt institutions that are essentially not of their own making. Instead they impose on Indigenous peoples beliefs and behaviours inherent to the settler colonial state, thereby further subjugating and enmeshing them in the capitalist relations at the heart of that state (Alfred 2005; Altamirano-Jiménez 2004; Coulthard 2014; Kobayashi and de Leeuw 2010).

The literature discussing modern European notions of citizenship, underscores that a citizen is a full member of a political community that is enacted via legal and administrative rules and regulations on the basis of which an individual's civil, political, and social rights and responsibilities are determined vis-à-vis the community (cf. Kymlika and Norman 1994; Marshall 2009). Western notions of citizenship are closely linked to socio-economic transformations that occurred with the rise of capitalism, coupling liberal ideals of personal freedom and state defined and enforced rights. These occasioned the growth of autonomous, egocentric individuals and market economies based on contractual rather than communitarian social relations (Marshall 2009; Weber 1961). Since the end of the 20th century, the increasing neoliberal framings of citizenship that have dominated the ways states formulate their relations with citizens have intensified this dynamic with an accompanying emphasis on private care rather than public virtue (Oswin and Olund 2010; cf. Cheshire and Woods 2009; Mooers 2014). For Dean (2003: 27) the links between capitalism and citizenship have ultimately resulted in an "impossible partnership" that dehumanises people and depends on abstractions that cause economic actors to ignore their interdependence with one another and the natural world, and have ultimately provoked both social alienation and severe environmental degradation.

For Indigenous peoples in settler colonial states Western understandings of citizenship have been fundamentally problematic. As I shall discuss below, the rules and regulations that are at the root of their own understandings of 'citizenship' were not recognized, understood, or adopted by settler colonial states, whilst Indigenous polities were subordinated to edicts alien to their own. Although initially engaged in nation-to-nation diplomatic relations of alliance and protection, as the settler colonial state became more secure and sought to widen its territorial control, so its treatment of Indigenous peoples evolved into one of tutelage and trusteeship. The result was that Indigenous peoples were made wards of the state with such things as reservations and residential schools being amongst the outcomes of this relationship.

To overcome the perceived lack of capacity preventing Indigenous peoples from being full citizens, settler colonial states have attempted to reshape Indigenous peoples into economic actors with the skills, habits, and attitudes of 'responsible', individualised participants in the market. They should learn how to save money, act independently, and develop attitudes of care, cleanliness, and punctuality (cf. Altamirano-Jiménez 2004; Meltzer 2013). In short, they must emulate the comportment of Western labourers. But they are damned if they do and damned if they don't: where their commitment to the collective is reckoned to hold them back economically, they have been deemed to be morally flawed, and encouraged, for example, to divide their collective lands into individual allotments; and where judged to be too successful and 'Western' in appearance and/or behaviour, their treaty rights to hunt, fish, and gather, for example, have been called into question (cf. Cattelino 2010; Norrgard 2014).

A sense of concurrence with others, which is a fundamental component of any collectivity, exists only amongst individuals if they share categories of thought (Douglas 1986). Recognizing neither themselves nor the principles that govern the functioning of their societies in the constructions of citizenship of the settler colonial state, many Indigenous peoples have taken issue with the concept on the grounds that it is incompatible with their own conceptions of what such relations entail (Alfred 2005; Coulthard 2014; Porter 2005; Simpson 2014). For example, Johnson (2007), a Cree lawyer, describes how his ancestors, in signing a treaty in 1889, understood that they were adopting the colonisers as their cousins, and that each was charged with caring for the other. This reflects customary notions guiding Cree ideals of how to incorporate 'aliens' in their polities: one became kin, with all the requirements of trust and negotiation that such connections necessitate. In considering the notion of citizenship, then, we ought to consider how Indigenous peoples conceive of the individual in relation to the collectivity, for clearly this has implications not only for how they apprehend the ties that bind them, but also for how they behave as economic actors whereby certain behaviours are sanctioned and others are repudiated.

If, as Marshall states, "[c]itizenship is a status bestowed on those who are full members of a community" (2009: 149), then we need to think about how community is constituted for Indigenous peoples. Let us return again to the case of Inuit. Like the Cree, for Inuit the extended family is a crucial unit of the collectivity, but kinship relations are fluid, expansive, and subject to choice. So, for example, such relations can be built through systems of naming, through connections with, and understandings of the land and animals, or simply through elected connections of "fictive kinship" which customarily ensured that strangers have been integrated into Inuit communities (Nuttall 1992: 85; cf. Guemple 1976). This willingness to integrate individuals quickly into the collective is a distinguishing value for hunter-gatherers. As Ingold contends, "whereas for [Western society ...] every individual is an independent element of the aggregate collectivity, for [hunter-gatherers] the collectivity is present and active in the life of every individual" (1986; 24). Such behaviours reflect reciprocal bonds of solidarity. The question that arises is whether the values that inform the reciprocal bonds of hunter-gatherer communities continue to find expression in the context of associative bonds of solidarity foundational to the state-like institutions that have developed in the context of land claims.

Having considered one component of this concept of economic citizenship in so far as it relates to Indigenous peoples – even if in a back-to-front way – I wish now to turn to its other component.

Economies and Indigenous peoples

Economies involve "making, holding, using, sharing, exchanging, and accumulating valued things" (Gudeman 2001: 1). Economic practice thus focuses on the movement of value. Yet value does not inhere only in *things*. *Relationships* associated with the circulation of those things are also crucial in the composition of value. They serve not only to ensure the circulation of things, but more fundamentally, as the ground within which ideas about the value of those things take root, are nourished, grow, and are sustained. And these conditions vary.

In considering the ways in which Indigenous corporate institutions engage with economic processes, we need to understand that they are at once engaged with the values that inform market economies and with those generally foundational to Indigenous societies, which have variously been called sharing or gift economies (although the two are not synonymous, not only because the word 'sharing' has come increasingly to be used as an attractive substitute for 'renting', but also, as we shall see, because sharing economies have broader connotations than gift economies). So we are drawn into questions about the functioning of societies built on relationships of alienable and inalienable goods, about the degree to which the bonds that tie people to things and to one another might be objective or subjective, independent or interdependent, and about the extent to which, in the links between producer and consumer, the recipients of goods are passive consumers engaged in mercantile relationships or active participants engaged in the creation and maintenance of relationships.

Although there are debates about the degree to which it is achieved, sociality and the establishment and maintenance of relationships are central to the ideas of the gift. Distinctions between use and exchange values may partially help us to understand gift economies, but "bonding value" is what is really central to these economies (Godbout and Caillé 1998: 173). As objects, services, and acts are exchanged in gift economies, so people create and sustain bonding value whereby the relations between the individuals or collectivities concerned will be maintained in ongoing forms of exchange.

The term 'sharing' enlarges Mauss's formulation of the gift to include values and activities such as hospitality, land-people relations, and community self-awareness that encompass more than the mere exchange of goods and obligations (MacDonald 2000). Sharing is sustained by common expectations about correct social behaviour, which are grounded in moral imperatives associated with this behaviour. The nature of these imperatives varies according to different cultural beliefs, but generally they serve to establish and maintain relationships not only amongst people, but also between people and the larger environment. Taking the example of Inuit, the imperative to share is most strongly associated with food. Such sharing structures, and is structured by, a complex set of social relations that extend beyond humans to the animals who – and I use this pronoun intentionally – give themselves to hunters and fishers. Should the original gift offered by the animal not be respected by sharing with others thereafter, then people run the risk of the animals withholding themselves in the future (Gombay 2010). Value is thus created, extracted, maintained, and reproduced in the very act of sharing. Moreover, sharing can extend to other elements of the economy, such as money and equipment. The important point is that just as the structures that have customarily been part of Inuit 'citizenship' are essentially geared towards establishing and maintaining social relations, so too are their economic practices.

If a commitment to sharing is fundamental to many Indigenous economies, the question that arises repeatedly in the literature is the degree to which such values are maintained when they come into contact with market forces. Certainly this has been debated by academics who have argued, for example, that the individualizing relations of capitalism erode Indigenous peoples' commitments to the collectivity in the name of competition and profit, with the result that capitalism develops "by stealth" (Li 2014: 9; cf. Mitchell 1996). Others argue that Indigenous peoples develop their own brand of capitalism that reflects a commitment to the collective and discourages the private accumulation of wealth (Champagne 2010; Warriner 2007; Wuttunee 2004). In the case of Inuit, during interviews I have conducted over the years with individual entrepreneurs, they stressed that making money was a means to an end. As one person said, "I'm not a *business* business, you know. But more on relationship and helping out." His aim was not excessive profit.

> Because if I start to get a lot of money, then that's what I will be worried about, that's what I will be dealing with. And throwing aside a lot of

things. […] [I]t's not too good to be *too* business-minded […]. Just enough to survive.

These are not the values of *Homo economicus*. Another Inuk businessman talked about how the profits from his venture, went right back into the community. "That's why we developed this business, to provide work for our people." Hence in her study of Indigenous enterprises Wuttunnee (2004: 23) states, "Growth for its own sake is not valued. From an early age children are taught to 'think for yourself and act for others.'"

Yet is life really as tidy as we make it out to be? Perhaps. Perhaps not. If we return to the case of Nunavik, not all Inuit were convinced that the values advanced in the claim that brought Nunavik into being were desirable. In fact, some settlements refused to sign the claim. A resident of one of the 'dissident' communities explained his position in a poem involving a conversation between an old man and a boy. The man says, "My greed for the White man's wealth has turned me from my ancient way," causing his generation to give up their land in exchange for cash. "For I am vanquished by my present greed. My eyes I close to the accusing finger of my kin and say I had no other choice" (Tulugak and Murdoch 2007: 247). The boy responds,

> You who thought that all would share the wealth. Oh, you! Among the many reaching for your share but finding it was only for the few.
>
> (Tulugak and Murdoch 2007: 248)

So money causes people to forget their relations and forget the requirement to share. From the perspective of the dissident communities the land claim was the embodiment of this forgetting. As a member of one of the communities put it,

> I wish Inuit to be free again, with nobody dictating to them what to do, so that they might live in their own lands according to their own laws, and according to their own ways that are appropriate for their culture. That will be their only way to protect themselves against the regulations created and imposed by others.
>
> (Qumaq 2010: 136; my translation)

So we come to the question of whether this assessment of what the institutions founded as a result of land claims actually succeed in doing. Do they represent fundamental impositions on Indigenous peoples, inevitably giving rise to institutions based on money and 'greed,' causing them to close their eyes to their kin's accusing finger, or have they managed to develop institutions compatible with their moral codes? More particularly, are the institutions that have been developed to represent this new collectivity known as 'beneficiaries' actually managed to incorporate the values of sharing that underpin their socioeconomic systems? Have land claims corporations managed to express in action the sets of values and relationships that are central to Indigenous conceptions of economic citizenship?

Debating economic citizenship

The literature examining questions of economic citizenship generally assumes that people are operating within a framework of principles associated with a market economy. For example, Cheshire and Woods (2009: 115) understand economic citizenship to be the "required conduct of citizens in the sphere of the market as responsible and informed consumers, capable of managing their lives in an entrepreneurial and prudential manner." Others focus on how, in the context of capitalism, economic rights and obligations, and the structures that serve to ensure them, have contributed to the configuration of citizenship (Kessler-Harris 2003; Turner 1986; White 2003; Woodiwiss 2002). Generally wage labour and Western capitalist relations are assumed to be the norm.

Implicit in various analyses of economic citizenship, particularly in those that stress the effects of neoliberalism on the workings of economic citizenship, is an underlying portrayal of the "little man" up against a powerful nexus of state and capital (cf. Cheshire and Woods 2009; Jeffrey et al. 2012; Mooers 2014; Turner 1986). And in this relationship there is a dialectical struggle where, periodically, the little man wins. What I am interested in here is the degree to which these dialectical struggles – in so far as they involve Indigenous corporations – yield material relations in which sharing is a core value. In examining this question, let us again focus our attention on Inuit in Nunavik.

In a recent iteration of settler colonial occupation of Inuit territories, the government of Quebec formally launched its *Plan Nord* in 2011, with resource extraction and infrastructure development being central to its agenda. Indigenous leadership has complied with this initiative partnering with the government of Quebec in the Plan's elaboration. Yet these same leaders also appear to have qualms about the anticipated developments. At root are questions about the coexistence of market and sharing economies in the region.

In response to *Plan Nord*, Inuit developed *Plan Nunavik*, in which they underscore the need to promote development that enables Inuit to be active participants in the market economy whilst preserving their capacity to pursue a subsistence lifestyle. Thus on the one hand they note:

> Nunavik Inuit are no longer simple traditional harvesters of wildlife pursuing a nomadic existence. […] Today, the majority of Nunavik Inuit are part of the larger modern cash economy. [… So they] need employment and business opportunities.
>
> (Kativik Regional Government and Makivik Corporation, 2010: 357)

But on the other hand they recognise that their economy is founded on "values such as sharing, helping others in need and working collectively for the benefit of the community" (2010: 427), and they worry that the development projected under *Plan Nord*, "could have significant negative impacts on Nunavik Inuit culture, the traditional way of life and ultimately on Inuit identity" (2010: 434). Thus, *Plan Nunavik* contains various recommendations aimed at promoting Inuit participation in the market economy – for example, creating Inuit-owned mining companies – whilst also preserving Inuit values: for example, proposing that 50% of Nunavik's landmass be reserved for Inuit hunting and trapping.

The official institutions designated to play a leadership role for Inuit thus seem both amenable to extractive projects and protective of the interests of Indigenous economic practices that will be adversely affected by such projects. After releasing *Plan Nunavik*, Makivik consulted Inuit beneficiaries across the region. The consensus was that Inuit should determine the conditions under which development would be acceptable (Makivik Corporation et al. 2014). Moreover the Inuit of Nunavik have long been negotiating to gain increased self-government. In fact, in 2011, via popular referendum, they rejected the initial proposal for the Nunavik Regional Government, on the grounds that it did not sufficiently reflect or promote their cultural values, language, and identity (Papillon 2011). Consequently, during Makivik's Nunavik-wide process of community consultation about *Plan Nord*, published in a report called *Parnasimautik*, people expressed the desire to work towards a new autonomous governance structure in the region that would ensure that Inuit culture and practices – including economic ones – would be safeguarded (Makivik Corporation et al. 2014). Many Inuit residents of Nunavik wish to gain greater control over their region to develop according to principles that respect their own values. They feel that, as currently formulated, Nunavik's governance structures are not effectively meeting their expectations. Thus we return to this fundamental question asked by various critical Indigenous theorists: How might the institutions designated to promote and protect the (economic) interests of their Indigenous 'citizens' do so in ways that abrogate the capitalist, crisis-ridden relations that frame land claims, whilst pursuing futures in which notions of sharing foundational to their political economies are reinforced (Corntassel and Bryce 2012; Coulthard 2014)?

By way of a conclusion

In the murky daylight of December, in a village north of the 59th parallel, there is a knock at the door of the house where I am lodging. Opening it I find on the doorstep a box of frozen shrimp sent by Makivik Corporation as a Christmas present to the house of every beneficiary in Nunavik. They are produced by Unaaq Fisheries, one of Makivik's joint ventures. *Unaaq* is the Inuktitut word for 'harpoon'.

〜〜〜〜〜〜〜〜〜〜〜〜

It may be tempting to draw absolute conclusions: that Indigenous land claims corporations are finding new practices of economic citizenship based on Indigenous values; or, conversely, that they are failing to do so, and are instead, co-opted by settler colonial systems. But both would be unjust oversimplifications.

There is no clean division between sharing and markets, between tradition and modernity, between non-capitalist and capitalist economies. Such binaries ignore complex realities and impose idealised images on Indigenous peoples. Despite the structural limitations shaping the outcomes of land claims, Indigenous peoples develop economic responses that reflect the specificities of their own geographies, histories, cultural beliefs, and social practices. These evolve relationally reflecting entanglements between local and global economies. In producing a third space of sovereignty, Indigenous peoples have the possibility of refusing to adopt binary choices of assimilation or secession (Bruyneel 2007).

Inevitably the structures that have given rise to Indigenous land claims corporations are entangled with the settler colonial project. But to understand what Indigenous land claims corporations such as Makivik ideally attempt to accomplish, we would do well to apprehend that economies contain different, but related, transactional spheres, each with varying temporal and moral orders (cf. Kopytoff 1986; Parry and Bloch 1989). Economic processes contain transactions concerned both with the long-term social and cosmic order associated with the collectivity and the short-term order associated with individual competition. The latter is morally acceptable only to the degree that it is subordinate to, and not in competition with, the former. In fact, the short-term transactional sphere is often pursued as a means of yielding goods that maintain the long-term order.

As recipients and managers of funds received in exchange for signing land claims, Indigenous land claims corporations are creatures of the world of money and markets. They are therefore inevitably bound to short-term economic cycles. But their mandate to reflect their beneficiaries equally requires that they adhere to the principles informing the longer-term transactional orders that are at the root of Indigenous peoples' economies. In their ideal form, when the division between each sphere remains distinct, the values and principles informing the short-term economic order are used to promote and sustain the long-term order. When this supporting position is not clear, and the short-term is perceived to threaten the moral order of the longer-term sphere, contradictions and contestations arise.

In analysing the workings of Indigenous land claims corporations we need to be aware of this juggling act. We need to question the degree to which these corporations' involvement in short-term transactional orders are, indeed, reflective of, and subordinate to, the values underpinning the longer-term order. We need to consider how their moral basis is symbolically constructed and sustained. We need to think about how new regimes of value may be emerging. We need particularly to consider the degree to which the enmeshment of realms of value reinforce those undergirding long-term moral structures, so that perhaps in being "*business* business[es]" Indigenous land claims corporations *can* serve as a means of promoting the value that people require "just enough to survive". Clearly, in *Plan Nunavik*, Makivik is grappling with its responsibilities to engage with the market economy, but not to the detriment of its citizens' sharing economy. Clearly giving food at Christmas time is a symbolic material manifestation of its attempt to blend market and sharing economies.

Indigenous land claims corporations have the *potential* to express altermodernities in which the economic citizenship of Indigenous peoples might find expression, but as this chapter has shown, the means of doing so is debated, and requires carefully situated analysis. It is not a matter of one size fits all. In the case of Nunavik, the development projected for the region presents serious challenges to the social and environmental conditions that are intrinsic to the functioning of the sharing economy of Inuit. In light of the various debates I have considered in this chapter, it would be seeing the world through rose-tinted glasses to argue that corporations such as Makivik will succeed unwaveringly in creating a third space of sovereignty. *Plan Nunavik* and the broadly based discussions that happened in the region amongst Inuit, which resulted in *Parnasimautik*, suggest that both Indigenous 'citizens' and 'state' are determinedly debating how they might create this third space. As market economies continue to intersect with those predicated on sharing, the case of Indigenous economic citizenship underscores the need to consider the dynamics of interwoven realms of value and the need for overt discussions about the moral principles that bind people together as individuals, as collectivities, and as institutions of state.

References

Alfred, G. R. (2005) *Wasáse: Indigenous Pathways of Action and Freedom.* Peterborough, Ont. and Orchard Park, NY: Broadview Press.

Altamirano-Jiménez, I. (2004) 'North American First Peoples: Slipping up into Market Citizenship?' *Citizenship Studies*, 8: 349–365.

Blackburn, C. (2009) 'Differentiating Indigenous Citizenship: Seeking Mulitiplicity in Rights, Identity, and Sovereignty in Canada' *American Ethnologist*, 36: 68–78.

Brown, N. A. (2014) 'The Logic of Settler Accumulation in a Landscape of Perpetual Vanishing' *Settler Colonial Studies* 4: 1–26.

Bruyneel, K. (2007) *The Third Space of Sovereignty: The Postcolonial Politics of U.S.–Indigenous Relations.* Minneapolis, MN: University of Minnesota Press.

Cattelino, J.R. (2010) 'The Double Bind of American Indian Need-based Sovereignty' *Cultural Anthropology*, 25: 235–262.

Champagne, D. (2010) 'Tribal Capitalism and Native Capitalists: Multiple Pathways of Native Economy' in Hosmer B.C. [ed.] *Native Americans and the legacy of Harry S. Truman.* Kirksville: Truman State University Press, 308–329.

Cheshire, L. and Woods, M. (2009) 'Rural Citizenship and Governmentality' in Thrift, N. and Kitchin, R. [eds.] *International Encyclopedia of Human Geography.* Amsterdam: Elsevier, 114–118.

Corntassel, J. and Bryce, C. (2012) 'Practicing Sustainable Self-Determination: Indigenous Approaches to Cultural Restoration and Revitalisation' *The Brown Journal of World Affairs*, 18: 151–162.

Coulthard, G. S. (2014) *Red Skin, White Masks: Rejecting the Colonial Politics of Recognition.* Minneapolis: University of Minnesota Press.

Douglas, M. (1986) *How Institutions Think*. Syracuse, NY: Syracuse University Press.

Dean, K. (2003) *Capitalism and Citizenship: The Impossible Partnership*. London: New York, NY: Routledge.

Godbout, J. and Caillé, A. (1998). *The World of the Gift*. Montreal: McGill-Queen's University Press.

Gombay, N. (2010) 'Community, Obligation, and Food: Lessons from the Moral Geography of Inuit' *Geografiska Annaler B*, 92: 237–250.

Gudeman, S. (2001) *The Anthropology of Economy: Community, Market, and Culture*. Malden, MA and Oxford: Blackwell.

Guemple, L. (1976) 'The Institutional Flexibility of Inuit Social Life' in Freeman, M. [ed.] *Inuit Land Use and Occupancy Project: A Report (Vol. 2)*. Ottawa: Dept. of Indian and Northern Affairs, 181–186.

Hardt, M. and Negri, A. (2009) *Commonwealth*. Cambridge: Belknap Press of Harvard University Press.

Ingold, T. (1986) *The Appropriation of Nature*. Manchester: Manchester University Press.

Ingold, T. (2007) *Lines: A Brief History*. London and New York: Routledge.

Jeffrey, A., McFarlane, C. and Vasudevan, A (2012) 'Rethinking Enclosure: Space, Subjectivity and the Commons' *Antipode*, 44: 1247–1267.

Johnson, H. (2007). *Two Families: Treaties and Government*. Saskatoon: Purich Publishing.

Kativik Regional Government and Makivik Corporation. (2010) *Plan Nunavik*. Westmount, QC: Avataq Cultural Institute. Retrieved from: http://www.parnasi mautik.com/wp-content/uploads/2013/02/Plan_Nunavik_06_20.pdf. [Accessed 17 July 2015]

Kessler-Harris, A. (2003) 'In Pursuit of Economic Citizenship' *Social Politics: International Studies in Gender, State and Society*, 10: 157–175.

Kobayashi, A. and de Leeuw, S. (2010) 'Colonialism and the Tensioned Landscapes of Indigeneity' in Smith, S. J., Pain, R., Marston, S. A. and Jones, J. P. J. [eds.] *The SAGE Handbook of Social Geographies*. Los Angeles and London: SAGE, 118–139.

Kino-nda-niimi Collective (2014) *The Winter We Danced: Voices from the Past, the Future, and the Idle No More Movement*. Winnipeg: Arbeiter Ring Publishing.

Kopytoff, I. (1986) 'The Cultural Biography of Things: Commoditisation as Process' in Appadurai, A. [ed.] *The Social Life of Things: Commodities in Cultural Perspective*. Cambridge: Cambridge University Press, 64–91.

Kulchyski, P.K. and Bernauer, W. (2014) 'Modern Treaties, Extraction, and Imperialism in Canada's Indigenous North: Two Case Studies' *Studies in Political Economy*, 93: 3–23.

Kymlika, W. and Norman, W. (1994) 'Return of the Citizen: A Survey of Recent Work on Citizenship Theory' *Ethics*, 104: 352–381.

Li, T. (2014) *Land's End: Capitalist Relations on an Indigenous Frontier*. Durham: Duke University Press.

MacDonald, G. (2000) 'Economies and Personhood: Demand Sharing among the Wiradjuri of New South Wales' *The Social Economy of Sharing: Resource Allocation and Modern Hunter-Gatherers, Senri Ethnological Studies*, 53: 87–111.

Makivik Corporation et al. (2014) *Parnasimautik Consultation Report: On the Consultation Carried Out with Inuit of Nunavik in 2013*. Retrieved from: http://www .parnasimautik.com/wp-content/uploads/2014/12/Parnasimautik-consultation-report-v2014_12_15-eng_vf.pdf. Acessed 17 July 2015]

Marshall, T.H. (2009 [1950]) 'Citizenship and Social Class' in Manza, J. and Sauder, M. [eds.] *Inequality and Society*. New York: W.W. Norton, 148–154.

Marx, K. (1983) *Capital: Volume One*. London: Lawrence & Wishart.

Meltzer, J. (2013) '"Good citizenship" and the promotion of personal savings accounts in Peru' *Citizenship Studies*, 15: 641–652.

Mitchell, M. (1996) *From Talking Chiefs to a Native Corporate Élite: The Birth of Class and Nationalism among Canadian Inuit*. Montreal: McGill-Queen's University Press.

Mooers, C.P. (2014) *Imperial Subjects: Citizenship in an Age of Crisis and Empire*. New York: Bloomsbury Academic.

Nehme, M. and Juriansz, J. (2012) 'The Evolution of Indigenous Corporations: Where to Now?' *Adelaide Law Review*, 33: 101–135.

Norrgard, C. (2014) *Seasons of Change: Labor, Treaty Rights, and Ojibwe Nationhood*. Chapel Hill: University of North Carolina Press.

Nuttall, M. (1992) *Arctic Homeland: Kinship, Community and Development in Northwest Greenland*. London: Belhaven Press.

Oswin, N. and Olund, E. (2010) 'Governing Intimacy' *Environment and Planning D: Society and Space*, 28: 60–67.

Papillon, M. (2011) 'Le Référendum au Nunavik: un pas en arrière pour mieux avancer?' *Option Politiques/Policy Options*, 32: 10–14.

Parry, J. and Bloch, M. (1989) 'Introduction: Money and the Morality of Exchange' in Bloch, M. and Parry, J. [eds.] *Money and the Morality of Exchange*. Cambridge: Cambridge University Press, 1–32.

Paulin, C. (2007) 'Ngai Tahu: The New Zealand Success Story in Indigenous Entrepreneurship' in Daman, L.P. and Anderson, R.B. [eds.] *International Handbook of Research on Indigenous Entrepreneurship*. Cheltenham: Edward Elgar, 549–557.

Porter, R. O. (2005) 'Question 2: What Kind of Shared Citizenship Is Actually Possible in a World of Separate Nation-States? Two Rows, Two Peoples, Two Nations: The Meaning of Haudenosaunee Citizenship' *International Studies Review*, 7: 512–515.

Qumaq, T. (2010) *Je veux que les Inuit soient libres de nouveau: Autobiographie (1914–1993)*. Québec: Presses de l'Université du Québec.

Simpson, A. (2014) *Mohawk Interruptus: Political Life Across the Borders of Settler States*. Duke University Press.

Thornburg, S.W. and Roberts, R.W. (2012) '"Incorporating" American Colonialism: Accounting and the Alaska Native Claims Settlement Act' *Behavioral Research in Accounting* 24: 203–214.

Tulugak, A. and Murdoch, P. (2007) *A New Way of Sharing: A Personal History of the Cooperative Movement in Nunavik*. Baie-d'Urfé: Fédération des Coopératives du Nouveau-Québec.

Turner, B.S. (1986) *Citizenship and Capitalism: The Debate over Reformism*. London and Boston: Allen and Unwin.

Valdivia, G. (2008) 'Governing Relations Between People and Things: Citizenship, Territory, and the Political Economy of Petroleum in Ecuador' *Political Geography*, 27: 456–477.

Warriner, V. (2007) 'The Importance of Traditional Maori Values for Necessity and Opportunity: Maori Entrepreneurs – Iwi-based and Individually' in Dana, L.P. and Anderson, R.B. [eds.] *International handbook of research on indigenous entrepreneurship*. Cheltenham: Edward Elgar, 558–565.

Weber, M. (1961) *General Economic History*. Translated by Frank H. Knight. New York: Collier Books.

White, S.G. (2003) *The Civic Minimum: On the Rights and Obligations of Economic Citizenship*. Oxford: Oxford University Press.

Wilson, G. N. and Alcantara, C. (2012) 'Mixing Politics and Business in the Canadian Arctic: Inuit Corporate Governance in Nunavik and the Inuvialuit Settlement Region' *Canadian Journal of Political Science / Revue canadienne de science politique*, 45: 781–804.

Wolfe, P. (2006) 'Settler Colonialism and the Elimination of the Native' *Journal of Genocide Research*, 8: 387–409.

Woodiwiss, A. (2002) 'Economic Citizenship: Variations and the Threat of Globalisation' in Isin, E.F. and Turner, B.S. [eds.] *Handbook of Citizenship Studies*. London: SAGE, 53–68.

Wuttunee, W. A. (2004) *Living Rhythms: Lessons in Aboriginal Economic Resilience and Vision*. Montreal: McGill-Queen's University Press.

12 Crisis, capitalism, and the anarcho-geographies of community self-help

Richard White and Colin Williams

Introduction

> (T)hree decades of neoliberalism have failed to produce an economy that is not bubble-prone and that is capable of improving the living standards of most people in the world. Articulating an alternative to neoliberalism is therefore an urgent task.
>
> (Posey 2011: 299)

> (I)f we are to accept anarchism as the dismantling of unequal power relations and the pursuit of re-organizing the way we live in the world along more egalitarian, voluntary, altruistic, and cooperative lines, then it becomes necessary to appreciate anarchism as a geographical endeavor.
>
> (Springer 2013: 46)

One hundred years ago the anarchist geographer Peter Kropotkin (1998 [1912]: 197] wrote: "Such is the future – already possible, already realisable; such is the present – already condemned and about to disappear." These words act as both consolation and inspiration when held against our own epoch: a time of intersectional crisis (economic, political, social and environmental) which, as Shannon (2014) argues, may well result in the end of the world as we know it. We contend here that despite capitalism's uneven and variegated nature (Bruff and Hown 2012), crises do not exist beyond or outside it: they are – fundamentally – creatures of capitalism. In rejecting the oxymoronic notion of 'sustainable' capitalism, the chapter picks up the gauntlet laid down by Springer (2012: 136) when arguing:

> The point of our critiques should not be to temper neoliberalism with concessions and niceties, as capitalism of any sort is doomed to fail. The logics of creative destruction, uneven development and unlimited expansion – which stoke the fires of conflict and contradict the finite limitations of the earth – are capitalism's undoing regardless of the form it takes.

Certainly, there is no possibility of social, economic or environmental justice to be found in the toxic (economic) remedies administered by a neoliberal State.

Indeed the violent imposition of austerity, that "policy of cutting the state's budget to promote growth" (Blyth 2013: 2), as a response to the economic crisis will succeed only in entrenching and exacerbating inequality further. In such austere times, as Stephen Duncombe (1997: 6) observed,

> The powers[1] that be do not sustain their legitimacy by convincing people that the current system is The Answer. That fiction would be too difficult to sustain in the face of so much evidence to the contrary. What they must do, and what they have done very effectively, is convince the mass of people that *there is no alternative.*

But are we really to believe that is there no alternative to capitalism? Such is the success of the propaganda of capitalism realism that it seems a point-less exercise. Even if we could entertain thoughts about a "post-capitalist" or "post-state" world, so the metanarrative goes, we would be unable to envisage what this world would look like *in practice.* Indeed the crisis therefore affects as much our political and economic *imaginary* as much as it affects the mate-rial world 'out there'. Thus, any critique of capitalism – to stand the greatest chance of success – has to operate in these real and imagined spaces. We look to achieve this by provoking a collective re-thinking of "the economic", one that embraces an ontology of difference by recognising the centrality of other "non-capitalist" practices in our own lives.

The central aim of the chapter therefore is to draw critical attention toward the everyday material coping strategies employed at the household and com-munity level. Focusing on the UK in particular through Household Work Practice Survey findings, we deeply problematise the rhetoric that we live in an increasingly commodified world: an atomised sea of naked self-interest, where exchange with others is always calculated, mechanistic, abstract, self-interested, profiteering and quantifiable. Recognising the shallow penetration of capitalism in a deeper reading of economic exchange consequently opens up the future in new and important ways. This is particularly so for those who seek to move purposefully toward a truly "post-capitalist" society. To this end (rooted in the contemporary nature of community self-help) the chap-ters draw inspiration from anarchism – and anarcho geography – praxis in particular. In doing so we encourage greater spatial emancipation by calling for more prefigurative and direct forms of self-organisation, expressions of solidarity, mutual aid, and acts of reciprocity to be brought into being.

Anarchism and anarcho-geographies of community self-help

Anarchist thought and practice is as rich as it is diverse, and its essence escapes convenient definition. Perhaps, as Jun (2012: 116) argues,

> Anarchism is better understood as (a) universal condemnation of an opposition to all forms of closed, coercive authority (political, economi-cal, social, etc.) coupled with (b) universal affirmation and promotion of

freedom and equality in all spheres of human existence. Slight variations on and close approximations of these general themes abound in the anarchist literature.

In this way, perhaps the ongoing, open-ended *nature*(s) of anarchism is, as Dana Williams (2010: 249) argues, "about changing the unequal power relationships that exist in society." By seeking to solicit a closer understanding of anarchism by denoting its broad ambition, rather than unpacking it literally, has many advantages. Such a reading avoids the problem that Shukaitis (2009: 170) draws attention to:

> There is also a tendency in this dynamic to reduce anarchism to its linguistic instantiation that then further reduces it to only a specific kind of politics. In other words, we cannot reduce anarchism to the mere use of the word "anarchism," but rather might *highlight and propose social relations based on cooperation, self-determination, and negating hierarchical roles*. (italic added)

In the context of this chapter there are many advantages to think more explicitly of community self-help through an anarcho-geographic lens, particularly given the understanding that anarchist praxis is concerned with "the ways in which people organise themselves in any kind of human society" (Ward 1982: 4). In this way, Ward's reading of anarchism as being potentially rooted within everyday, local, and informal modes of organisation is consistent with the writings of Kropotkin, and the attention he paid toward mutual aid. For Kropotkin, mutual aid was means to greater ends: social justice, and freedom (see Brietbart 1981). As a social anarchist, Kropotkin maintained, "a firm belief in the capacity of people to organise their lives without structures of domination and subordination – to coordinate everything from a family to an economy on a cooperative participatory basis" (Brietbart 1981: 136). In this context anarchism, rooted in day to day life, has an inescapably *spatial* dimension: a key intersection that has been given greater recognition and visibility in response to the unfolding crises and acts of *archy* (see Ince 2012, 2014; White and Williams 2012a; 2012b; Springer 2014a; 2014b). In this respect the chapter reinforces Springer's (2013: 1607) reading of *anarchist geographies*,

> [w]hich are understood as kaleidoscopic spatialities that allow for multiple, non-hierarchical, and protean connections between autonomous entities, wherein solidarities, bonds, and affinities are voluntarily assembled in opposition to and free from the presence of sovereign violence, predetermined norms, and assigned categories of belonging.

It is to use anarchism both as a means to inspire social (and spatial) transformation and as an end: a free, just and compassionate world. In this respect the chapter also draws on the essence of Élisée Reclus, a man whose reputation as "the anarchist geographer par excellence" (Clark and Martin 2013: 52) was based on a life spent "writing *(graphein)* the history of the struggle to free the earth *(Gaia)* from domination *(archein)*" (ibid).

Rethinking capitalo-centric economy and economic representation

> The sociology of everyday communism is a potentially enormous field, but one which, owing to our peculiar ideological blinkers, we have been unable to write because we have been largely unable to see the object.
>
> (Graeber 2011: 208)

Asimakopolous's (2014: 85) important observation that "Economics is not the exclusive purview of any particular ideology nor synonymous with capitalism" is far removed from how "the economic" is typically approached, defined, governed, narrated, framed and represented. Mainstream readings of "the economic" are, in the words of Gibson-Graham (2006: 41) haunted by a *"capitalocentric"* imaginary; an imaginary which "involves situating capitalism at the centre of development narratives, thus tending to devalue or marginalise possibilities of noncapitalist development." In other words, it is a perspective that represents all economic activities in terms of their (subordinate) relationship to capitalism. This effectively promotes a particularly narrow, atomised, competitive, selfish, individualistic reading of exchange, one which views monetary transactions as always market-like and motivated by personal financial gain. This capitalist "realism", perpetuated and promoted effectively by the insidious argument – that There Is No Alternative (TINA) to capitalism – serves to reify "the market". This ensures that

> The market has become the model of social relations, exchange value the only value. Western governments have shown themselves weak and indecisive in responding to the environmental crisis, climate change and the threat to sustainable life on the planet, and have refused to address the issues in other than their own – market – terms.
>
> (Hall et al. 2013: 9)

Interpreted from a critical economic perspective, the mythologising of a market economy needs urgently unpacking because it "excludes participation from so much of human existence" (Buck 2009: 68). Happily, this anaemic reading of economic exchange has been convincingly contested by an increasingly diverse array of critical thinkers and disciplines in the last 20 years – and continues to gain further momentum in response to the ongoing financial and economic crisis. This has certainly been the case in anarchist readings of the crisis, and responses to it (e.g. Askimakopolous 2014; Buck 2009; Shannon et al. 2012; Shannon 2014; Ward 1982; White and Williams 2012b; 2014).

A widely accepted reading of the dominant economic trajectory of the Western world is that a great transformation has taken place in European

has seen society fundamentally shift toward a formal
.et economy (see Polanyi 2001 [1944]). Yet, when interpreted
,rical perspective, it becomes clear such a transformation is not
.d in reality. For example, Time Use Surveys (see ONS 2006), under-
over the last 40 years, emphasises the significant limits of capitalism
within so-called advanced capitalist societies. Focusing on the quantitative
findings emerging from the UK, France and the USA, for example, Burns et
al. (2004: 53) observed that "well over half of people's total work time is spent
engaging in unpaid work, and in some advanced economies, there appears to
be shift in the balance of work toward the non-market sphere." Appealing to
more qualitative and subjective evidence base, we would argue that the very
idea of living in a commodified society is also highly counter-intuitive.

To appreciate this, think carefully about the different forms of work and
organisation that *you* undertake individually or with the help and support of
others (for common examples, reflect on those tasks identified in Table 12.2).
Then think critically about the different spaces in which these encounters
occur: in particular, those embedded within the household and the local community. In the household work practice surveys, detailed below, discussion
around communities of self-help was typically focused on two typologies,
namely *self-provisioning*: "unpaid household work undertaken by household
members for themselves or for other members of the household" (Williams
and Windebank 2002: 232) and *mutual aid*, defined as "unpaid work done by
household members for members of households other than their own" (ibid).
What motivated you to engage in these practices (is it paid, or unpaid work)?
Could your participation be construed as being consistent with an anarchist reading of organisation: i.e. not coerced, undertaken for non-economic
rationales, altruism, reciprocity, and ethics of care and so on? Such an exercise, hopefully if nothing else, draws attention to the multiple ways in which
you (co)-organise with others to get work done, and the various rationales
for doing so. The complexity and richness of economic life, removed from a
capital-centric haunting will be aptly reinforced by the findings drawn from
the household work practice surveys shortly.

Recognising the diversity of work practices has necessitated ever more complex typologies being constructed to better capture and represent this. One of the
most nuanced examples of has been developed by Williams (2009: 405) through
advancing "a total social organisation of labour" approach (see Figure 12.1).

This representation is particularly important insofar as it emphasises the
blurring of lines between types of economic practices, and encourages recognition of the *spectrum* of differences according to the degree of formalisation (x-axis) and monetisation (y-axis) between these key forms of labour. For
Williams (2009: 412), "this conceptual lens therefore allows the limited reach
of the market to be identified as well as a fresh perspective on the nature of
work cultures and how they vary spatially."

Concerning the words 'most/ least anarchist praxis' in Figure 12.1, one
of the stated ambitions of this chapter is to read anarchism as "a description of human organisation rooted in the experience of everyday life"

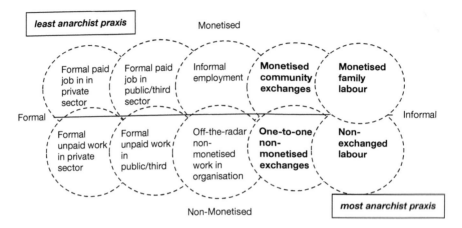

Figure 12.1 Beyond capitalo-centrism: reading anarchism praxis into a Total Social
Organisation of Labour framework.

(Marshall 2011: 17) and ask *where* is this present, and (conversely) where it is
absent across our economic work practices? Importantly, here, we must avoid
the temptation to essentialise. We may expect, for example, the household, to
be embedded within an anarchist sensibility – respect, mutuality, reciprocity,
co-operation etc. However, regrettably this is far from inevitable. Indeed, the
household has often been a space of coercion, repression, and domination
(most significantly perhaps through patriarchy, expressed in a highly gendered
division of labour). Similarly, it is important to continually interrogate, and
not romanticise, what 'the community' represents. As Ince (2011: 23) argues:

> We cannot assume a fixed understanding of what community or authen-
> ticity 'is' – either spatially or temporally – since they are both defined by
> those who constitute it every day. Authenticity thus becomes a locus for
> struggle rather than an a priori quality to be objectively imposed on a
> certain space, concept or phenomenon.

It is with this understanding in mind that a similar spectrum of difference
(more/ less) is applied vis-à-vis anarchist praxis.

Anarchy in action: evidencing community self-help in a "capitalist" society

The Household Work Practice Studies have been particularly influential in
revealing key geographies of community self-help practices (in particular the
extent, the social embeddedness, the rationales to participation and the barriers to participation) and how these vary between lower- and higher-income
localities. An early version of household work practice survey was developed

by Ray Pahl (1984) when investigating the divisions of labour within a local population on the Isle of Sheppey. Similar surveys were conducted during the late 1990s and 2000s to explore the geographies of household work practices, not least an English Localities Survey composed of 611 face-to-face interviews across both higher- and lower-income neighbourhoods in rural and urban areas (see Williams and Windebank 2002; White 2009; C.C. Williams 2010).

The household work practice survey examined organisation of labour used to undertake the everyday household tasks listed in Table 12.1. For each task, the respondent was asked whether the task had been undertaken. If it had been conducted, they were then asked to consider the last time that it had been conducted, who had conducted the work, why that particular individual had been chosen, whether they had been paid in anyway or given a gift in lieu of payment (and why). If formal labour had not been used, again the house-holder was questioned as to why this was the case. The participant was also asked about the extent to which they (or members of the household) engaged in community self-help with other households, again by asking whether they had conducted these tasks for other households, for whom they had con-ducted the work, whether they had received any form of payment or not, and why they had conducted this task.

Focusing on the results of the Household Work Practice Survey (see Table 12.2), noncapitalist forms of work practices and organisation to under-take the tasks investigated were central in coping strategies across both across deprived and affluent urban communities. Contrary to the widely held view that the market was permeating every nook and cranny of everyday life, few of

Table 12.1 Example of tasks explored through the household work practice survey

Nature of the task	Individual tasks
Property maintenance	Outdoor painting; indoor decorating (e.g. wallpapering; plastering) replacing a broken widow; maintenance of appliances; plumbing; electrical work
Property improvement	Putting in double glazing; house insulation; building an extension/ renovating; putting in central heating; DIY activities (carpentry/ putting up shelves etc.)
Routine housework	Routine housework (washing dishes/ clothes/ cooking meals) cleaning the windows; doing the shopping, moving heavy furniture
Gardening activities	Sweeping paths, planting seeds/ mowing lawn
Caring activities	Childminding; pet/animal care; educational activities (tutoring); giving car lifts; looking after property
Vehicle maintenance	Repairing and maintenance
Miscellaneous	Borrow tools or equipment; any other jobs

Table 12.2 Results from the Household Work Practices Survey: labour practices used to undertake 44 domestic tasks across 11 UK localities

% tasks last conducted using:	Deprived urban	Affluent urban	Deprived rural	Affluent rural	All areas
Non-monetised labour					
Non-exchanged labour	76	72	67	63	70
One-to-one non-monetised exchanges	4	2	8	7	6
Monetised labour					
Monetised family labour	1	<1	1	1	1
Monetised community exchange	3	1	4	1	3
Informal employment	**2**	**8**	**<1**	**4**	**2**
Formal paid job in private sector	12	15	18	22	16
Formal paid job in public and third sector	2	2	2	2	2
Total	100	100	100	100	100
χ^2	102.89	29.87	89.76	28.88	-

Source: adapted from White and Williams (2012a; 2012b: 1635)[2]

these households outsourced these tasks to the formal market economy; indeed, the overwhelming majority of these tasks were conducted on a self-provisioning basis. Similarly, nearly three times the number of tasks was carried out on an unpaid basis as mutual aid than by people working in the formal economy. The permeation of the formal market economy, in consequence, is shallow so far as everyday household life is concerned. The overwhelming source of work is self-provisioning and then mutual aid. In terms of the dominant rationales that underpin this form of work, the emphasis is very much on choice (including ease, enjoyment, pleasure) rather than an economic rationale (i.e., to save money). People prefer to use these non-market sources of labour (Burns et al. 2004; Williams and Windebank 2002). This reality poses a direct challenge to a capitalocentric imagination. Far from penetrating every nook and cranny of our lives, the spectre of capitalism would appear to cast an altogether smaller and less impressive shadow.

Addressing these findings, our argument is that this understanding how work is performed in contemporary 'capitalist' societies offers not only a refutation of the TINA perspective that capitalism is hegemonic, inevitable and immutable, but also contains an important framework of possibilities concerning the future world of work and organisation. It displays that there are many non-capitalist spaces that provide the seeds (or perhaps more accurately given their size they should be termed 'forests') of a "post-capitalist" world. More importantly for the purposes of this chapter, they represent examples of anarchy in action.

Promoting anarcho-geographies of community self-help at a time of austerity

Uncoupled from hegemonic representations of capitalism as the dominant form of work and organisation in society, and recognising the inherent crisis of capitalism, the need to harness anarcho-geographies of community self-help is an urgent one. At the time of writing, the winds of austerity are biting hard and disproportionality across in the UK, with the poorest people and most vulnerable communities bearing the brunt of the cuts to local government services (Hastings et al. 2015). Homelessness is rising, poverty is increasing. Given the overlapping and interlocking nature of the economic, of course this has direct consequences for community self-help strategies: the rolling back of the State and the Market places additional pressures communities to cope; in the home the cuts in services, reduction in employment opportunities and social welfare protection places more emphasis on unpaid domestic labour to fill the gaps. Given the gender division evidence here, this ultimately places more pressure on women to cope (Karamessini and Rubery 2013). Exploring the ways in which the geographies of community self-help have changed in response to the rolling back of the State and the Market, would be wonderful, particularly if some 'good practice' (of resistance/ resilience) could be identified, to encourage other communities to adopt similar practices.

Unfortunately, there is a real dearth of evidence, and the household work practice surveys identified here were undertaken prior to the imposition of austerity measures. That said, there is still much to be gained by drawing on the existing evidence base, and repeating the question asked by Ward (1982: 13): "What, in a phrase, will it be like to live in a world dominated more and more by household and hidden economies and less by the formal economy?!" A response to this question demonstrates how a radical re-appraisal of the importance of the 'spaces' focused on here (the local, the household), and a critical gaze over "alternative" ways to promote community self helps are necessary.

Valuing "noncapitalist" spaces

Resisting a myopic privileging of capitalist work spaces, and recognising the importance of the work that takes place in the household and the community, is to radically depart from liberal representations of the economic, which marginalise and trivialise the work that is undertaken in these spaces.

One only has to think about how the work that takes place through the labour of households is stripped of value and meaning through the oxymoronic use of the term the "unemployed" to describe the individual(s) who undertake work in this space (Leonard 2001). From a gendered reading of the division of labour, there is also disproportionally more work undertaken by women than by men, which also raises important questions, not least in terms of equity and reciprocity.

Recognising the power and importance of these spaces uncovers an emancipatory and liberatory intent, particularly when placed in the context of post-capitalist visions of work and organisation. As Byrne et al. (2001: 16) argue:

> Understanding the household as a site of economic activity, one in which people negotiate and change their relations of exploitation and distribution in response to a wide variety of influences, may help to free us from the gloom that descends when a vision of socialist innovation is consigned to the wholesale transformation of the 'capitalist' totality.

Focusing on the way in which work is undertaken in the household and community also encourages individuals to challenge and resist the propaganda that their lives and identities are defined in relation to a singular capitalist identity. The greater truth is that the "alternative" worlds of post-capitalism are found in the ordinary and everyday – be this in a rural or urban communities, in higher or lower income households. This is an important step to inspire individuals to think differently, more creatively, and reject neoliberal assertions about the contemporary nature of "the economic" and its (inevitable) capitalist trajectory. As Ward (1982: 5) observed:

> Many years of attempting to be an anarchist propagandist have convinced me that we win over our fellow citizen to anarchist ideas, precisely through drawing upon the common experience of the informal, transient, self-organising networks of relationships that in fact make human community possible, rather than through the rejection of existing society as a whole in favour of some future society where some different kind of humanity will live in perfect harmony.

Embracing an anarchist perspective is therefore *not* tantamount to taking a leap of faith into some 'new' unknown utopian future. Rather it necessitates recognising, celebrating, re-valuing and harnessing a web of existing economic practices – embedded in mutuality, reciprocity, co-operation, self-organisation and non-violence – that are already known and familiar to us. The reality is that there already exists a tremendous range of empowering economic and political forms of organisation in Western society; forms of organisation that in significant ways act as lived alternatives *beyond* the market and state. Indeed, the significant limits of the purchase of capitalism enables appreciation that we should acknowledge the continued, ongoing and resilience of an anarcho-libertarian[3] or anarcho-communist spirit that still burns brightly at the heart of society. As Graeber (2011: 199–200) argues,

> Everyday communism … can only be understood [by] examining everyday practice at every level of human life to see where the classic communistic principle of 'from each according to their abilities, to each according to their needs' is actually applied. As an expectation of mutual aid, communism in this sense can be seen as the foundation of all human sociality anywhere; as a principle of co-operation, it emerges spontaneously in times of crisis; as solidarity, it underlines almost all relations of social trust. Everyday communism then is not a larger regulatory body that co-ordinates all economic activity within a single 'society', but a principle that exists in and to some extent forms the necessary foundation of any society or human relations of any kind.

The resilience and pervasive nature of these spaces that lie beyond the private and public sector is striking, albeit not unexpected. As Scott (2012: xxi) argues,

> Forms of informal cooperation, coordination, and action that embody mutuality without hierarchy are the quotidian experiences of most people … Most villages and neighbourhoods function precisely because of the informal, transient networks of coordination that do not require formal organisation, let alone hierarchy. In other words, the experiences of anarchistic mutuality are ubiquitous.

It is these everyday forms of anarchy in action – particularly those which we are embedded in – that we need to value, recognise and harness to increase resilience in the face of a capitalist imaginary and rampant destruction of 'the social'.

Critically interrogating alterity: alternatives as a means to anarchist, or neoliberal ends?

Any 'alternative' strategies that promote anarcho-geographies of community self-help need to be aware of the danger of capitalist appropriation and recuperation. For example, Local Exchange and Trading Schemes and Time Banks have been enthusiastically promoted as a way of encouraging greater levels of community cohesion and informal support (see Seyfang 2003; 2004; Williams 2003). Yet in the present age of austerity and food banks, it is these same self-help strategies that are being promoted by the government and other elites (e.g. through 'Big Society' and resilience discourses and policy agendas) for neoliberal ends (see Gregory 2015). In the early noughties, for example, Time Banks were framed as a "radical manifesto for the UK" (Boyle 2001), yet these have been strongly promoted by the State as a means of complementing/ reinforcing, rather than to challenge neoliberal policies. Thus, for Gregory (2015: 144),

> There is a need to realign time bank theory and practice to promote resistance to neoliberalism. This should be pursued not in order to impose an alternative social order, but, rather, to create the social structure and definition of citizenship that allow people to engage the local community in action and debates about the lives they wish to lead.

Thus, here and elsewhere, there is an ongoing challenge to ensure that these alternatives maintain (or are redirected) toward their liberatory – and in the spirit of this chapter, *anarchist* – potential. The idea of freedom to decide how to engage emphasised by Gregory is certainly consistent with anarcho-geographies of community self-help. Promoting freedom and diversity across space in important strength: recognising the different challenges, and unique opportunities offered by social and spatial configuration in the everyday – rather than anticipating some predetermined revolution to happen – is vital here.

Paul Goodman (in Stoehr 2011: 34) argued, "A free society cannot be the substitution of a 'new order' for the old order; it is the extension of spheres of free action until they make up most of the social life." The hope is that there these emancipatory anarchic spheres of free action can transgress all socio-spatial geographies: in the home, the community, the city … and eventually the planet (see Lopez de Souza 2015). In many ways, much depends on embracing open and experimental discussion around what types of organisation are desirable and enactable. As Parker et al. (2007: x) note:

> Defining organisation as a verb rather than a noun brings to the fore the many decision and choices that have to be made in structuring and ordering human activities. Organisation is contingent upon choices relating to questions of means and ends. What is organisation for? What should its size be? How should activities be coordinated and controlled, and by whom? How should ownership be distributed? How should work be divided, regarded? and so on.

Resisting authoritative top-down solutions, or conservative appeals to the known and familiar, is fundamental. Indeed, as a general rule of thumb, and especially so at a time of austerity, the "more original voices that can be heard the better" (Kinna 2012: 9). In this way prefigurative praxis, which encourages individual and local people to recognise and experiment collectively with the power they have in making a difference in their everyday, local interactions (with people, with place) must be supported wherever possible. Furthermore, what must also be recognised is that accumulating freedom is never just about 'the economic'. A just and compassionate world, far removed from the forms of exploitation and abuse associated with a capitalism must seek to challenge *all* forms of domination and hierarchy in our everyday societal relations, many of which are not reducible to 'the economy' baseline. Certainly greater awareness of the intersectional natures of domination such as patriarchy, racism, heteorenormativity, and speciesism, and how these overlap with capitalism, for example, across time and space is needed (see Shannon et al. 2012).

Aiming to decentre capitalist representation of the economic, by constructing representations of 'the economic' from below, which explore the pervasive nature of community self-help and its associated mutual organisation of individual and social ties, is itself congruent with an anarchist sensibility. DeLeon and Love (2010: 160), for example, illustrate this well, arguing that "anarchist theory is informed by the autonomy of the individual, the importance of small and localised communities, the move toward more organic organisational structures, social justice and the freeing of our desires." Here, particularly when talking about anarchism in relation to mutual aid and self-help economies, we believe that the autonomy of the individual is actually augmented, rather than constrained, by association with others. As Bakunin argued: "[The] liberty of each man [sic] ... does not find another man's freedom a boundary but a confirmation and vast extension of his own".

Conclusions

Anarchist geographical praxis embodies and underpins many of the instinctive, natural, rational and *spatial* forms of economic, political and social organisation that symbolise everything that can be seen as good and positive in society. As this chapter has evidenced here, we continue to hold close and reconstitute such institutions in our communities. Mutual aid and self-help within our households and communities still run strong in our contemporary socio-spatial urban fabric, promising a valuable – and valued – means of support and solidarity at a time of a severe crisis of capitalism within the first world. Yet, interpreting these practices merely as means of support and solidarity woefully underplays their revolutionary potential as viable, enactable and desirable alternatives to the twin crisis of the State and Capitalism. It is toward these potential *anarchistic* lines of organisation in which we need to invest serious time and energy in developing further. This is a difficult task:

> It's one thing to say that we want a world where people manage our own lives, the environment isn't destroyed, and life (isn't) desolate and alienating – but it's another to start talking about what such (life) might actually look like. And starting to actually create forms of cooperative practice, to re-envision utopian thinking as lived reality, is another.
>
> (Shukaitis 2010: 303)

For those critical scholars and activists who reject the capitalo-centric representations of the economic, and narrations of 'economic crisis', the pressing question turns to one of how can these alternative spaces of mutuality and support be encouraged and harnessed, and new ones created? Here, as always, the contemporary specificities of people and place should be recognised and valued, in order to empower people and communities to take decisions and action that will make all the difference. If such a commitment could be coupled with embracing a prefigurative politics, and all the spontaneity, difference, diversity, experimentation, that comes with it that would a wonderful vision moving forward.

At every opportunity, taking back the locus of power and responsibility (in imaginary and in practice) from the state and the market, and reaffirming the power of the individual is an absolutely critical step moving forward. That said, it is also necessary and important to engage inclusively and constructive with those who contest such 'anarchist' readings. For example, the question of the role of the State is one which is keenly contested, particularly among other radical (Marxist) traditions, with some of the more robust challenges being found in the work of Cumbers (2012; 2015) in particular. Ultimately, if this chapter has encouraged greater critical reflection on the anarchist geographies that animate 'the economic', and has stimulated deeper thought and consideration about how to begin to understand the exciting possibilities that exist in the here and now as a means of both narrating, and confronting, our crisis and the limits of capitalism, then it will have served an important and timely purpose.

Notes

1 In this context it is important to ask: Who are the powers in question here? For the economic crisis in the Western world has also brought into focus the power relationships between state and private capital. As Mason (2015: xi) ruefully notes: "As the Greek experience demonstrates, any government that defies austerity will instantly clash with the global institutions that protect the 1%".
2 Note: $\chi^2 > 12.838$ in all cases, leading to a rejection of the H_0 within a 99.5 % confidence interval that there are no spatial variations in the sources of labour used to complete the 44 household services.
3 Anarchist communism "is a form of anarchism that advocates the abolition of the State and capitalism in favour of a horizontal network of voluntary associations through which everyone will be free to satisfy his or her needs" (Roux 2006: np).

References

Askimalopoulos, J. (2014) *Social Structures of Direct Democracy: On the Political Economy of Equality*. Brill: Boston.

Blyth, M. (2013) *Austerity: The History of a Dangerous Idea*. Oxford University Press: Oxford.

Boyle, D. (2001) *Time Banks: A Radical Manifesto for the UK*. New Economic Foundation: London.

Brietbart, M. (1981) 'Peter Kropotkin, the Anarchist Geographer' in Stoddart, d. [ed.] *Geography, Ideology and Social Concern*. Oxford: Basil Blackwell, 134–115.

Bruff, I. and Hown, L. (2012) 'Varieties of capitalism in crisis?' *Competition and Change*, 16(3): 161–168.

Buck, E. (2009) 'The flow of experiencing in anarchic economies' in Amster, R., DeLeon, A., Fernandez, L.A., Nocella, A. and Shannon, D. [eds.] *Contemporary Anarchist Studies: An Introductory Anthology of Anarchy in the Academy*. London: Routledge, 57–69.

Burns, D., Williams, C.C., and Windebank, J. (2004) *Community Self Help*. London: Palgrave.

Byrne, K., Forest, R., Gibson-Graham, J.K., Healy, S. and Horvath, G. (2001) *Imagining and Enacting Non-Capitalist Futures*, Rethinking Economy Project Working Paper no.1. Retrieved from: www.arts.monash.edu.au/projects/cep/knowledges/byrne.html

Clark J. and Martin, C. (2013) A*narchy, Geography, Modernity: Selected Writings of Elisée Reclus*. Oakland: PM Press.

Cumbers, A. (2012) *Reclaiming Public Ownership: Making Space for Economic Democracy*. London: Zed.

Cumbers, A. (2015) 'Constructing a global commons in, against and beyond the state', *Space and Polity*, 19(1): 62–75.

DeLeon, A. and Love, K. (2010) 'Anarchist theory as radical critique: Challenging hierarchies and domination in the social and 'hard' sciences' in Amster, R., DeLeon, A., Fernandez, L., Nocella II, A.J. and Shannon, D. [eds.] *Contemporary Anarchist Studies: An Introductory Anthology of Anarchy in the Academy*. London and New York: Routledge.

Duncombe, S. (1997) *Notes from the Underground: Zines and the Politics of Alternative Culture*. New York: Verso.

Gibson-Graham, J.K. (2006) *The End of Capitalism (As We Knew it): A Feminist Critique of Political Economy* with a new introduction. Minneapolis: University of Minnesota Press.

Graeber, D. (2011) 'Communism' in Hart, K., Laville, J-L., and Cattani, A.D. [eds.] *The Human Economy*. London: Polity, 119–210.

Gregory, C. (2015) *Trading Time: Can Exchange Lead to Social Change?* London: Policy Press.

Hall, S. Massey, D. and Rustin, M. (2013) 'After neoliberalism: analysing the present' *Soundings* 5: 8–22.

Hastings, A., Bailey, N. Glen Bramley, G., Gannon, M. and Watkins, D. (2015) *The Cost of the Cuts: The Impact on Local Government and Poorer Communities*. York: Joseph Rowntree Foundation.

Ince, A. (2011) 'Contesting the "authentic" community: Far-right spatial strategy and everyday responses in an era of crisis', *Ephemera* 11(1): 6–26.

Ince, A. (2012) 'In the shell of the old: anarchist geographies of territorialisation' *Antipode* 44(5): 1645–1666.

Ince A (2014) 'The shape of geography to come', *Dialogues in Human Geography* 4(3): 276–282.

Karamessini, M. and Rubery, J. [eds.] (2013) *Women and Austerity: The Economic Crisis and the Future for Gender Equality*. London: Routledge.

Kinna, R. (2012) *Anarchism: A Beginner's Guide*. London: Oneworld.

Kropotkin, P. (1998 [1912]) *Fields, Factories and Workshops Tomorrow*. London: Freedom Press.

Jun, N. (2012) *Anarchism and Political Modernity*. New York: Continuum.

Leonard, M. (2001) 'Old wine in new bottles? Woman working inside and outside the household', *Women's Studies International Forum*, 24(1): 67–78.

Lopes de Souza, M. (2015) 'From the 'right to the city' to the right to the planet', *City*, 19(4): 408–443.

Mason, P. (2015) *PostCapitalism: A Guide for Our Future*. London: Penguin Random House.

Marshall, P. (2011) 'Colin Ward: Sower of anarchist ideas', *Anarchist Studies*, 19(2): 16–21.

ONS (Office for National Statistics) (2006) *Time Use Survey 2005*. London: ONS.

Pahl, R.E. (1984) *Divisions of Labour*. Oxford: Blackwell.

Parker, M. Fournier, V. and Reedy, P. (2007) *The Dictionary of Alternatives*. London: Zed.

Polanyi, K. (2001 [1944]) *The Great Transformation. The Political and Economic Origins of Our Time*. Boston: Beacon Press.

Posey, J. (2011) 'The local economy movement: An alternative to neoliberalism?', *Forum for Social Economics*, 40(3): 299–312.

Roux, J. (2006) 'Anarchist communism – an introduction' Retrieved from: https://libcom.org/thought/anarchist-communism-an-introduction

Scott, J.C. (2012) *Two Cheers for Anarchism*. Princeton: Princeton University Press.

Seyfang, G. (2003) '"With a little help from my friends"': Evaluating time bank as a tool for community self-help', *Local Economy* 18(3): 257–264.

Seyfang, G. (2004) 'Time banks: Rewarding community self-help in the inner city' *Community Development Journal* 39(1): 62–71.

Shannon, D. Nocella, A.J. and Asimakopoulos, J. [eds.] (2012) *The Accumulation of Freedom: Writings on Anarchist Economics*. Edinburgh: AK Press.

Shannon, D. [ed.] (2014) *The End of the World as We Know It? Crisis, Resistance and the Age of Austerity*. Edinburgh: AK Press.

Shukaitis, S. (2009) 'Infrapolitics and the nomadic educational machine' in Amster, R., DeLeon, A., Fernandez, L., Nocella II, A.J. and Shannon, D. [eds.] *Contemporary Anarchist Studies: An Introductory Anthology of Anarchy in the Academy*. London and New York: Routledge.

Shukaitis, S. (2010) 'An ethnography of nowhere: Notes toward a re-envisioning of utopian thinking' Jun, N.J. and Wahl, S. [eds.] *New Perspectives on Anarchism*. Plymouth: Lexington Books, 303–311.

Springer, S. (2012) 'Neoliberalising violence: Of the exceptional and the exemplary in coalescing moments' *Area*, 44(2): 136–143.

Springer, S. (2013) 'Anarchism and geography: A brief genealogy of anarchist geographies' *Geography Compass* 7(1): 46–60.

Springer, S. (2014a) 'For anarcho-geography! Or, bare-knuckle boxing as the world burns' *Dialogues in Human Geography*. 4(3): 297–310.

Springer, S. (2014b) 'Why a radical geography must be anarchist' *Dialogues in Human Geography* 4(3): 249–270.

Stoehr, T. (2011) 'Introduction' in Stoehr, T. [ed.] *The Paul Goodman Reader*. Oakland: PM Press.

Ward, C. (1982) *Anarchy in Action*. London: Aldgate Press.

White, R.J. (2009) 'Explaining why the non-commodified sphere of mutual aid is so pervasive in the advance economies: Some case study evidence from an English city' *International Journal of Sociology and Social Policy*, 29(9/10): 457–472.

White, R.J. and Williams, C.C. (2014) 'Anarchist economic practices in a "capitalist" society: Some implications for organisation and the future of work' *Ephemera: Theory and Politics in Organisation*. 14(4): 951–975.

White, R.J. and Williams, C.C. (2012a) 'The pervasive nature of heterodox economic spaces at a time of neoliberal crisis: Towards a "postneoliberal" anarchist future' *Antipode* 44(5): 1625–1644.

White, R.J. and Williams, C.C. (2012b) 'Beyond capitalist hegemony: Exploring the persistence and growth of "alternative" economic practices' in Nocella, A.J. Asimakopoulos, J. and Shannon, D. [eds.] *The Accumulation of Freedom: Writings on Anarchist Economics*. Edinburgh: AK Press.

Williams, C.C. (2003) 'Harnessing social capital: Some lessons from rural England' *Local Government Studies*, 29(1): 75–90.

Williams, C.C. (2009) 'Beyond the market/ non-market divide: A total social organisation of labour perspective' *International Journal of Social Economics*, 37(6): 402–414.

Williams, C.C. (2010) 'Geographical variations in informal work in contemporary England' in Marcelli, E., Williams, C.C. and Joassart, P. [eds.] *Informal Work in Developed Nations*. Abingdon, Oxford: Routledge, 97–113.

Williams, C.C. and Windebank, J. (2002) 'The uneven geographies of informal economic activities: A case study of two British cities' *Work, Employment and Society*, 16(2): 231–250.

Williams, D.M. (2010) 'An anarchist-sociologist research program' in Jun, N.J. and Wahl, S. *New Perspectives on Anarchism*. Plymouth: Lexington Books, 243–266.

Index

For Product Safety Concerns and Information please contact our EU
representative GPSR@taylorandfrancis.com
Taylor & Francis Verlag GmbH, Kaufingerstraße 24, 80331 München, Germany

www.ingramcontent.com/pod-product-compliance
Ingram Content Group UK Ltd.
Pitfield, Milton Keynes, MK11 3LW, UK
UKHW020953180425
457613UK00019B/669